The Voices That Are Gone

The Voices That Are Gone

Themes in Nineteenth-Century American Popular Song

Jon W. Finson

New York   Oxford

OXFORD UNIVERSITY PRESS

1994

Oxford University Press

Oxford   New York   Toronto
Delhi   Bombay   Calcutta   Madras   Karachi
Kuala Lumpur   Singapore   Hong Kong   Tokyo
Nairobi   Dar es Salaam   Cape Town
Melbourne   Auckland   Madrid

and associated companies in
Berlin   Ibadan

Copyright © 1994 by Jon W. Finson

Published by Oxford University Press, Inc.
200 Madison Avenue, New York, New York 10016

Oxford is a registered trademark of Oxford University Press

Library of Congress Cataloging-in-Publication Data
Finson, Jon W.
The voices that are gone: themes in nineteenth-century
American popular song / Jon W. Finson.
p. cm.   Includes bibliographical references and indexes.
ISBN 0-19-505750-3
1. Popular music—United States—To 1901—History and criticism.
I. Title.   ML3477.F55   1994
782.42164'0973'09034—dc20
93-28889

Passages from *They All Sang: From Tony Pastor to Rudy Vallée*,
written by Edward B. Marks and Abbott J. Liebling,
used by permission of Edward B. Marks Music Company

Portions of ''The Romantic Savage: American Indians in the Parlor''
republished from *Journal of Musicological Research* 13 (1993)
by permission of Gordon and Breach Science Publishers S.A.

1 3 5 7 9 8 6 4 2

Printed in the United States of America
on acid-free paper

for Linda

Acknowledgments

Many friends and colleagues have helped to bring this repertory into focus for me. The roster begins with Dennis Moreen and continues with Barbara Kinsey Sable, Lawrence Gushee, Lenore Coral, Dena Epstein, Nan McMurray, Ellen Smith-Summers, Ingrid Arauco, Thomas Warburton, Charlotte Greenspan—in short all those with whom I have enjoyed discussing American popular song over the past twenty-five years. Some have lent their scholarly expertise directly to this project. They include Marjory Irvin, Robert Wiebe, Suzanne Gossett, Robert Allen, John Kasson, Joy Kasson, Townsend Ludington, Arthur Marks, Dan Patterson, Ralph Locke, Wayne Schneider, Mark Tucker, Carol Oja, and all the faculty involved in the American Studies Curriculum at Carolina.

A number of dedicated librarians and archivists have helped me collect the material for this book. The largest measure of gratitude must go to the Newberry Library in Chicago; its Driscoll Collection has been an invaluable aid, with particularly rich, varied, and well-organized holdings. The whole staff has been uniformly and immensely helpful, but I should single out Paul Gehl, Mary Wyly, Ruth Hamilton, and Richard Brown for their special attention. Leslie Troutman at the University of Illinois (Urbana), Marie Lamoureux of the American Antiquarian Society, Richard Ryan at the William L. Clements Library (Ann Arbor), Ida Reed, and Ruthann McTyre at the University of North Carolina (Chapel Hill) all provided documents for this study. Initial research at the Newberry was supported by a Pogue grant from the University of North Carolina at Chapel Hill.

Graduate assistants at the University of North Carolina have helped gather material for this study, including Steve Shearon and Mark Snow. Above all I am grateful to Brad Maiani for setting the musical examples.

ACKNOWLEDGMENTS

Finally, two people have lent support, encouragement, and a keen editorial eye to this endeavor. Richard Crawford has been a source of ideas and helpful comment. And Sheldon Meyer at Oxford University Press has provided the main impetus and much enthusiasm for completing the study.

Chapel Hill, N.C.   J.F.
March 1994

Contents

Introduction

When I first thought of this book on American popular song in the nineteenth century, I knew that I did not want to write a standard survey. Surveys in musicology usually take the form of chronological narratives that trace the history of style in conjunction with the lives of composers. And for the genre of American popular song, Charles Hamm has produced a perfectly good account along these lines:[1] anybody working on a large collection of sheet music in an American library will typically find the kinds of the music and the composers represented in Hamm. The best part of Hamm's book comes in his assessments of popular style, most of which I have adopted here with some important modifications and additions. Though I may differ with him on this or that point, I am deeply indebted to his history.

Instead of surveying the whole field, I have chosen to present a guided tour of selected songs. I have tried to glimpse the most important landmarks, I have mentioned some of the lesser sights that provide color and context, and I have occasionally pointed out obscure but treasurable parts of the scenery that have been overlooked. But I have not felt compelled to view every spot of interest along the way. Writers understandably rate the importance of a given popular song by the number of copies sold, but there is little apart from anecdotal evidence about sales of songs in the nineteenth century. Multiple editions provide an indirect idea of circulation, and groups of songs on the same subject also give some notion of distribution. Composers of popular music tend to imitate one another, and the discovery of many pieces running in the same vein suggests general interest, even when each member of a particular group appeared in relatively few copies. The reception history of nineteenth-century

---

[1] *Yesterdays: Popular Song in America* (New York, 1979).

xi

popular song has many perils: we cannot assume, for instance, that the wide circulation of a song reflects general agreement with its lyrics. The public may have enjoyed a song mostly for its music. I have adopted the rather more guarded stance, therefore, that lyrics written during a given period are tokens of the songwriter's views and of his or her belief that such a sentiment will be well received by the prospective audience.

My approach to ordering examples has been topical; I have chosen subjects that emerged from twelve years of teaching courses on American popular song. Within each topic I have proceeded in a roughly chronological fashion to follow changing mores. The first two chapters cover courtship as it appears in popular song, and they also discuss how entrepreneurs pursued the business of publishing popular songs. The third and fourth chapters discuss respectively the views of death and technology found in songs. The second half of this study deals with various issues of race and ethnicity, with two chapters on blackface, one on the American Indian, and one on Western European ethnicity. Under no circumstances should this approach be construed as an attempt to establish some sort of *catalogue raisonné*. Most songs touch a variety of different subjects, and it would be impossible to classify lyrics strictly on the basis of their content. I have discussed them under various topical headings simply to illustrate songwriters' views in a way that strikes me as most illuminating. Biographies of composers, per se, play a lesser role in this book than they would in a survey. But I have tried to encapsulate a bit of information about each composer when one of his or her songs is first discussed at length, especially when something in the biography bears on the content of the song at hand.

Though it may appear at first glance that a topical book on popular song must ignore questions of music in favor of concentration on lyrics, I have tried to show how various musical features assume connotations that play with or against sentiments expressed by the texts. The Italianate gentility that marks some songs early in the century serves as a foil for the folkish Anglo-Celtic attributes of early minstrelsy. And the ensuing ebb and flow of various styles formed from the conjunction of musical attributes interlock with the meaning of lyrics in ways that contemporary writers will sometimes reveal or that we can infer. The interplay of musical style runs as a thread from the beginning to the end of the book, rendering it more than just a discrete set of essays. Though chapters can be read in isolation, they will not make as much sense without a sequential reading of the whole argument. I have tried to hold technical terms about musical style to a minimum, glossing them briefly when they first appear, in order to make the narrative accessible to a more general readership. Those interested in a more analytical approach can consult books like Hamm's or Nicholas Tawa's *The Way to Tin Pan Alley.*[2]

Both the lyrics and music of popular song are documents of a broader American history. I have ventured interpretations of these songs in a wider context,

[2] *The Way to Tin Pan Alley: American Popular Song, 1866–1910* (New York, 1990).

drawing much help from various writers outside of musicology. Because I have included so much material, the reading assigned to any given song may seem to hang on a rather slender and capricious wire. Patterns emerge, nonetheless. It is more important to offer general historians the insight these songs yield about America's past than to establish an authoritative interpretation of any one example. I will feel rewarded if the book sparks debate about the significance of lyrics or stylistic trends.

Finally, I have observed two major constraints in defining "American" "popular" song. I have limited my discussion to pieces written by composers who dwelled in this country for a substantial period of time. Most songs published in America during the first part of the nineteenth century came from the pens of British authors, but I have concentrated on those composers who extended their tours. This may seem a rather pharisiacal distinction, but on the whole I think it fair to include British-born composers like Charles Edward Horn and Henry Russell, while excluding Henry Bishop (to give just a few examples). As for what constitutes "popular music," I have followed the general rule that a song must be non-esoteric in its content, composed for commercial profit, and distributed as sheet music. At certain points in the nineteenth-century history of music publishing, this last distinction may seem artificial. But there is something about an individual consumer picking out a single item (rather than a collection that happens to contain the song) that suggests a process of specific interest. My reasons for this restriction were also practical: I simply had to find a way to limit the immense repertory still extant.

PART I

It is easy to write correctly a simple song, but so to use the material of which such a song must be made that it will be received and live in the hearts of the people is quite another matter.

George Frederick Root, *The Story of a Musical Life*

1

The Distant Beloved

Genteel Romance Before
the Civil War

"The wine of Love is music," the nineteenth-century British poet James Thomson avers in *The Vine,* "And the feast of Love is song . . . ," a sentiment that seems commonplace when viewed in the context of twentieth-century popular songs that devote themselves overwhelmingly to matters of courtship. Thomson's conviction applies less clearly to the American practice of his own time, when song was the feast of humor, of economic ambition, of nostalgia, of racial fear, and of mourning, among many other things. Yet it seems appropriate to begin reflection on nineteenth-century American popular song by seeing how composers and lyricists conceived the activity surrounding one of our most elemental and persistent concerns. And if we allow for earlier lyrics' wider attention to matters beyond initial attraction and passion, then songs about romance can reasonably form the backdrop against which we understand the whole field. Because in a real sense, compositions about all other topics, even in this period, play against the musical style and poetic content found in songs of love and courtship.

What are normally considered genteel songs provide the best starting point for discussion. By "genteel" I simply mean songs with polite rather than vulgar lyrics (though they may sometimes be genteel, songs involving ethnicity appear later). I do not use this term to create a rigid category, but rather to provide a loose rule of thumb. Nineteenth-century genteel lyrics about love are rooted in the changing attitudes of the late eighteenth century. Composers gradually associated a catalogue of musical features with polite lyrics in the ensuing decades, and this linkage proved crucial to the course of American popular song in the first half of the century.

Changing Images of Courtship:
From Husbands and Shepherds to Knights Errant

The last part of the eighteenth century saw a transition in attitudes about the proper conduct of love, courtship, and marriage. Colonial America dealt with these issues in a strongly communal fashion, leaving the regulation of behavior to the church and to localities.[1] Marriage was often arranged by the elders of a family for economic benefit, and courtship occurred under community surveillance. But toward the end of the eighteenth century and continuing into the nineteenth these customs changed, partly under pressure of increased mobility engendered by better transportation, growing commerce, and westward expansion. As the strictures of local sacred and secular communities waned somewhat in influence, individuals became self-regulated and internalized standards of behavior. In this atmosphere courting couples

> . . . began to employ the language of romantic love, expressing passion in their correspondence and exploring intimate emotions, rather than mere property arrangements, when they planned for marriage. Open expression of sentiment replaced the religious language of earlier couples. . . . By the late eighteenth century, many American women viewed affection as a precondition for engagement.[2]

The selection of a mate became a matter of choice ruled by feeling, a concept supported by the Enlightenment's view of an individual's right "to pursue happiness." Self-determination developed not only a political but also a personal aspect which "infected individuals everywhere with a heady feeling of command over their destinies, a sense of marvelous potential in their own lives that they came to project onto the nation as a whole."[3]

American popular song during the late eighteenth and early nineteenth centuries reflected to some extent the way in which the new standards of courtship and marriage became internal. American songs around the turn of the century emphasized pragmatism of the kind found in the anonymous composition "The Day of Marriage" (1803), which Richard J. Wolfe records in thirteen printings before 1825.[4] The text of this song, narrated by a female speaker, records the events leading up to matrimony. They include a proposal in the first verse—

> 'Twas on the twenty first of June
> In charming summer weather,

1. For a brief summary of colonial practice, see John D'Emilio and Estelle B. Freedman's *Intimate Matters: A History of Sexuality in America* (New York, 1989), 3–52.
2. Ibid., 42.
3. Robert H. Wiebe, *The Opening of American Society, from the Adoption of the Constitution to the Eve of Disunion* (New York, 1984), 143.
4. *Secular Music in America, 1801–1825* (New York, 1964), no. 2354.

> When Harry told his tender boon,
> That we might live together.

—the answer to which is bandied about for almost twelve months. The second
verse relates rejected attempts at communal interference,

> 'Tho oft our friends have frowning said,
> And call'd it sense and reason
> Twas time enough as yet to wed
> At any future season,
> But Harry vow'd it shou'd be Soon,
> And own'd too long we'd tarried,

while the third gives the moral:

> Three years have pass'd in mutual bliss,
> So maidens do not tarry,
> As single life is sure amiss,
> So I advise to marry.
> For was the time to come again,
> To Church I wou'd be carried,
> And truly bless the happy day,
> The day that we were married.

Courtship revolves around private resolve in this song, and the lyrics speak
mainly to individual happiness, but taken as a whole they have a practical
rather than idealistic ring to them. The lesson of the song would seem to be:
courtship is not a mere romantic indulgence but should end in a proper religious
wedding. And the lyrics use plain, everyday language to communicate the
message.

The music accompanying this advice bolsters its common sense (Ex. 1.1).
The texture is very simple (though we may assume that more accomplished
musicians would fill out the two-voice framework using chords commensurate
with their technical proficiency), and the melody generally sets the text syllabi-
cally (one note of melody per syllable of verse, the exception coming at the
beginning of each phrase). Moreover, the song assumes a folklike, Scottish
tone that early nineteenth-century Americans would have recognized easily
from imported examples by composers like James Hook.[5] The anonymous author of "The Day" begins over a single repeated bass note, or "pedal," that
carries the connotations of a drone, one of the standard allusions to folkish

5. Hook (1746–1827), a church organist and director of music at Vauxhall Gardens in London,
may have been the most widely published writer of songs in America during the late eighteenth
and early nineteenth century. See Charles Hamm, *Yesterdays: Popular Song in America* (New
York, 1979), 12–17.

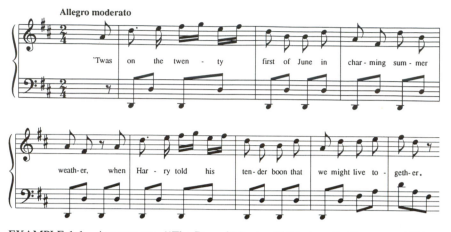

EXAMPLE 1.1   Anonymous, ''The Day of Marriage'' (Boston: G. Graupner, 1803)

style. And the melody begins in both prelude and vocal line by avoiding the leading tone (the seventh degree of the scale), thus hinting at some exotic mode or perhaps at pentatonicism (the pentatonic or ''gapped'' scale consists of five pitches, usually the first, second, fourth, fifth, and sixth notes of a normal seven-note ''diatonic'' scale. A pentatonic scale can also be produced by playing just the black keys on the piano). Of course the melody is not truly pentatonic, nor is the uneven rhythm of the ''Scottish snap'' present. The tune indulges, rather, a hint of folkish seasoning, as if to indicate that this text provides down-to-earth counsel for the genteel.

The early nineteenth century also retained from previous times a somewhat more cultivated approach to the subject of courtship in songs like ''Claudine'' (ca. 1802) by Benjamin Carr.[6] Carr selected his central conceit from the pastoral tradition imported throughout much of the eighteenth century from the British pleasure garden (peopled by composers like Hook and Thomas Arne).[7] In the first verse we learn that Claudine is a despondent shepherdess:

> The sun had sunk behind a hill
> Claudine went forth, went forth from home
> To seek her sheep at yonder rill,
> Too wont, alas, too wont to roam,
> Her sheep she may restore again,
> But will she e'er her peace regain?
>   Ah! never, never, never.

6. This song is reprinted in Nicholas E. Tawa's anthology, *American Solo Songs Through 1865*, vol. 1 of *Three Centuries of American Sacred and Secular Music*, Martha Furman Schleifer and Sam Dennison, eds. ([Boston], 1989), 288–89.

7. For a discussion of songs in pleasure gardens, see Hamm, *Yesterdays*, 1–17.

The second verse speaks of her plight in a metaphor about nature, asking whether her smile might return again like spring following winter. And the third verse gives the grounds for her complaint:

> Sad luckless maid then wander forth,
> And bare thy bosom to the rain,
> Heed not the pelting of the north
> That sweeps along the trackless plain.
> But he who caus'd the maiden's woe,
> Can she not hate the traitor—no.
> Ah! never, never, never.

The pastoral element in Carr's text is, nonetheless, relatively informal: he does not mention the classical figures—Phyllis, Chloe, Damon, Mirtilla, Aminta, and the rest—who populate English pastoral songs. Though he had written a successful opera, *Philander and Silvia, or Love Crowned at Last*, for the London stage,[8] the composer takes a more practical tack for his American audience with the fairly direct message that "when innocence is lost" it might never "awake from mis'ry's chilling frost." He simply chooses a more stylized manner to communicate his moral than "The Day of Marriage" does.

Carr's music for "Claudine" takes a higher road accordingly. Its harmonic vocabulary and accompanimental texture present a simplified version of the common practice used by Classic composers like Mozart and Haydn. The vocal line is rather square, and filled with constant leaps and unequal rhythms, almost as if it had been conceived for an instrument. It also features many more melismas (single syllables of text set to a succession of several pitches) than we see in "The Day," and even includes a modest cadenza where the singer pauses to add a few embellishments, "ad lib." All these features of lyrics and music raise the tone of the song.

Carr (1768–1831) had a background and career typical for a composer during this period, and his life reveals much about the American musical scene around the turn of the nineteenth century. Born and educated in London, he received his training in music from Samuel Arnold and Charles Wesley. He came to the United States in 1793 with his father Joseph and brother Thomas; together they established a network of "musical repositories" (music stores) in New York, Philadelphia, and Baltimore. Benjamin led a polyglot existence as organist, music teacher, music dealer, and publisher, just as his "musical repository" served to distribute music, sell instruments, and coordinate lessons for patrons.[9] Not only did Carr occupy a middling social status as entrepreneur,

8. A good account of Carr's career in London appears in Benjamin Carr, *Selected Secular and Sacred Songs*, Eve R. Meyer, ed., vol. 15 of Recent Researches in American Music (Madison, WI, 1986), vii.

9. For an account of the family, see Virginia Larkin Redway, "The Carrs, American Music Publishers," *Musical Quarterly* 18 (1932), 150–77.

his music engaged this same social milieu. Printed songs with simple accompaniment aimed during this period to please an urban, middle-class public. Sheet music was a relatively expensive indulgence, and the price of "25 ct." for a folio or two, if not luxurious, required more disposable income than the working classes could muster.[10] Performance of the music demanded an instrument (either a keyboard or guitar, for which Carr provides an alternate accompaniment), an investment in itself, along with the means to pay for the lessons that would initiate its owner into the skills of reading and playing.

The business of publishing songs remained essentially unchanged from the beginning of the century until the changes wrought by Tin Pan Alley at its end. Almost all music publishers were, like the Carrs, wholesalers and retailers. Either they wrote their own songs, they bought them from local composer-performers, or (most frequently until the 1840s) they reprinted music imported from London and the continent. They ran presses in their own shops, where they sold the resulting sheet music to customers off the street. They also maintained a limited number of "corresponding" relationships with wholesale-retail publishers across town or in other cities (for instance, "The Day of Marriage," published by G. Graupner in Boston, also lists J. Hewitt's Musical Repository in New York as a place to obtain the music). In its early stages the industry did a limited business, serving those who could afford the increasingly popular piano. Many publishers sold pianos (and other instruments) in their shops and offered lessons on the new instrument, as well. Arthur Loesser relates, for instance, that the wife of Peter Albrecht van Hagen, a Boston publisher and music retailer, offered piano lessons in 1799 for "six dollars every eight lessons" in her home (or a dollar per lesson for house calls).[11] And some publishers even became involved in the manufacture of pianos (Dubois & Stodart made pianos in New York during the 1830s, printed music, and sold both). Popular songs followed the piano into the parlor, and as the number of instruments grew, so did the size of wholesale-retail houses and, later, their capacity to print more copies of music on steam presses. But the firms retained very much the character of musical general stores, often run by men who performed, composed, published, sold, and taught music.

James Hewitt (1770–1827) had just such a career, similar to Carr's, writing songs in much the same vein. Hewitt was also born in London and trained there. He immigrated in 1792 as part of a group of theater people recruited by the Old American Company, becoming the music director of the Park Theater soon after arriving. He taught music lessons (violin, viola, 'cello, and keyboard), managed and played in concert series, and in 1797 purchased the New York branch of Carr's Musical Repository. There Hewitt sold music and instru-

10. For an extensive discussion of the audience for popular song before the Civil War, see Nicholas E. Tawa, *Sweet Songs for Gentle Americans: The Parlor Song in America, 1790–1860* (Bowling Green, OH, 1980), 15–43.
11. *Men, Women and Pianos* (New York, 1954), 455.

ments, published music, and offered an assortment of silver plate on the side.[12] Like Carr, Hewitt brought the style of pastoral pleasure-garden songs in his immigrant baggage, fitting it to American tastes. His lyrics for "Advice to the Ladies," first published in 1794 and reprinted around 1800 and 1803, begin with the mildly pastoral imagery of "Claudine" in the first verse:

> No more along the daisy mead
> I meet my fickle swain,
> Whose charms and falsehood far exceed
> The shepherds of our plain.
> He sighing followed where I roved
> Till pity touched my heart,
> Then laughing boasted how I loved
> And played a traitor's part.

Hewitt combines these sentiments, however, with something more like the kind of cautionary moral provided in "The Day of Marriage" in the third verse:

> Ladies, ladies, while you fly
> The men will still pursue.
> But if you pity when they sigh
> Alas they'll fly from you.
> They practice and they must approve
> An innocent deceit.
> Affect indifference where you love
> Or you'll indifference meet.

If we find the recommended strategy coy and passive (unastonishingly in this period, women must not pursue men), Hewitt nonetheless states his case plainly, without affected language. And his melodic style is equally straightforward: he indulges few ornaments, and his setting remains almost entirely syllabic (see Ex. 1.2). His accompaniment is simple, both in its limited selection of chords and in its texture. An amateur player of modest abilities could easily do this piano part justice.

The mildly pastoral conceit embodied in "Advice to the Ladies" represented the persistence of an older style into the nineteenth century, but Hewitt would soon begin to explore a newer trend in lyrics and music, with a grander tone. A good example appears in his "Remember Me" (1804), with text "Taken from the Romance of Don Raphael written by Walker," according to the title

12. Information on Hewitt's life comes from John W. Wagner, "James Hewitt, 1770–1827," *Musical Quarterly* 58 (1972), 259–76; and from Vera Brodsky Lawrence, "Mr. Hewitt Lays It on the Line," *19th Century Music* 5 (1981–82), 3–15.

EXAMPLE 1.2   James Hewitt, ''Advice to the Ladies'' (1794; Wolfe no. 3676)

page. This song no longer takes place in the world of artificial simplicity occupied by ''Claudine'' and ''Advice,'' but moves instead into an aristocratic realm of parting lovers who express themselves using appropriately heightened images:

> Remember me when far away
> I journey thro' the world's wide waste,
> Remember me at early day
> Or when the ev'ning shadows haste,
> When high the pensive moon appears
> And night in all her starry train
> Gives rest to human hopes and fears,
> Remember I alone complain.

The more elevated tone derives not only from the poetic invocation of night but also from what I will call the high speech, especially archaic forms like ''thy'':

> Remember me, when e'er you sigh,
> Be it at midnight's silent hour;
> Remember me, and think that I
> Return thy sigh, and feel its power,
> When e'er you think on those away,
> Or when you bend the pious knee,
> Or when your thoughts to pleasure stray,
> O then, dear Maid, remember me.

The exoticism of a ''Romance'' elicits from Hewitt a more elaborate setting. He uses a slightly fuller texture for his instrumental prelude and postlude (often called ''symphonies'' in the first part of the nineteenth century). And his vocal line includes more ornaments, even a bit of expressive chromaticism for the words ''starry train'' (see Ex. 1.3). Hewitt has created something distinctly more fanciful here than we see in the very direct ''Day of Marriage'' or the unpretentious ''Advice.''

This loftier tone became increasingly prevalent in popular song as the first

and night in all her star - ry train gives

rest to hu- man hopes and fears

EXAMPLE 1.3 James Hewitt, "Remember Me" (New York: J. Hewitt, [1804]; Wolfe no. 3772)

decade of the nineteenth century progressed. We find it again in Samuel Priestly Taylor's "Adieu Sweet Girl" (ca. 1806) with lyrics from Maria Regina Roche's *Romance of the Children of the Abbey.* Taylor (1779–1875), cut from a mold by now familiar, received his musical education in Britain and immigrated around 1806 to become a church organist in New York, later doing a brief stint with the Handel and Haydn Society in Boston.[13] The lyrics from Roche's *Romance* have many things in common with the text of Hewitt's "Remember Me" taken from Walker's *Don Raphael.* The title and first verse confirm that this is also a song of parting, its sentiments expressed in relatively formal tones:

> If fortune had propitious smil'd
> My love had made me bless'd,
> But she like me was sorrow's child
> With sadness dire oppress'd

We learn in the third verse that the speaker is a soldier journeying to "India's sultry climes," and his high speech continues in the fourth verse:

> No kindred spirit there shall weep
> Or pensive musing stray;
> My image thou alone wilt keep
> And love's soft tribute pay.

13. Wolfe, *Secular Music,* II, 903.

11

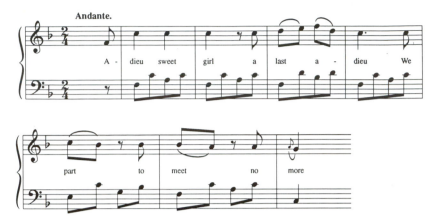

EXAMPLE 1.4 Samuel Priestly Taylor, "Adieu Sweet Girl" (New York: J. Hewitt, [ca. 1806]; Wolfe no. 9297a)

In this style of courting song, separation between lovers becomes increasingly fashionable. But the musical style changes little: Taylor's piano accompaniment retains a common two-voice texture, with an Alberti pattern for the left hand that recalls eighteenth-century music for amateurs of very elementary abilities (see Ex. 1.4). Taylor composes more gracefully for the voice than either Carr or Hewitt, and he includes a certain quotient of melismatic writing (on words like "last") with a number of appoggiaturas (accented dissonant notes resolving downward) on words like "part," "meet," and "more." Other songs invoking this loftier style include Mrs. Robinson's and Joseph Willson's "Let Others Wreaths of Roses Twine" (1804),[14] Hewitt's "In Vain the Tears of Anguish Flow" (ca. 1805), Charles Gilfert's "Thy Song Has Taught My Heart to Feel" (ca. 1807), Victor Pelissier's "Soft Ringlets of Auburn" (ca. 1810), and even the native-born Oliver Shaw's "The Hussar's Adieu" (ca. 1811).

The increasing penchant for a more cultivated style in American popular song followed a fashion set in Great Britain. Most of the very few composers active in the United States during the first decades of the nineteenth century—men like Carr, Hewitt, and Taylor—had received their training in London and naturally hearkened to British taste. Even more important, at least 90 percent (possibly more) of the sheet music published in America originated in England, a state of affairs that persisted throughout the first four decades of the nineteenth century. The prominent American music printers established themselves in port cities—Boston, Providence, New York, Philadelphia, Baltimore, and Charleston—where they could quickly receive the British music they reprinted.

14. Unless specified otherwise, the lyricist's name will appear before the composer's in joint efforts throughout this book. Readers may assume that the composer wrote the words where I indicate no collaboration.

Whether firms obtained their material through trade agreements in England or whether they simply stole the music in the absence of international copyright laws, most of it reflects the British vogue.

When the British began to draw courting imagery from increasingly distant regions of romantic fantasy in the second decade of the nineteenth century, American composers naturally followed suit. The trend had been some time in developing, as the various references above to the genre of the romance suggest. But it came into full bloom under the influence of Sir Walter Scott, who in turn drew his initial inspiration from the German romantics: his first published book (1799) was a translation of Goethe's *Goetz von Berlichingen,* and he even tried his hand at "Der Erlkönig." [15] Scott had immense influence on music and drama through his epic poems and novels. The continental operas based on his stories include Rossini's *La Donna del Lago,* Bellini's *I Puritani,* Donizetti's *Lucia di Lammermoor,* Boieldieu's *La Dame blanche,* Flotow's *Rob Roy,* Marschner's *Der Templer und die Jüdin,* and many others continuing into the later nineteenth century. Berlioz wrote concert overtures on *Waverley* and *Rob Roy.* And countless composers set individual songs from Scott's poems and novels, among them, to take just one prominent instance, Schubert in his "Ave Maria! Jungfrau mild!"—a translation of "Hymn to the Virgin" from the third canto in *The Lady of the Lake.* In the United States Scott's works appeared frequently in dramatized versions. Odell lists New York productions of *Marmion* (1808) and *Lady of the Lake* (1810) in 1812, while *Guy Mannering* (1815) and and *Rob Roy* (1817) appear in adaptation barely a year after they were first published. [16]

American composers addressed Scott's poetry either through the vehicle of dramatic adaptations or in its original form. In 1812, for instance, the French Caribbean immigrant Victor Pelissier (ca. 1745–ca. 1820) provided incidental music and songs for Edmund John Eyre's Philadelphia dramatization of *The Lady of the Lake,* [17] though none of these concerned courtship. Direct settings of *Lady,* which Scott published in May of 1810, appear even earlier in Benjamin Carr's *Six Ballads from the Poem of the Lady of the Lake,* copyrighted October 6, 1810. [18] Carr's elaborate setting of "Hymn to the Virgin" hardly qualifies as popular music, even during a time when the distinction between classical and popular seems small. But Carr's later music for portions of *Rokeby* is somewhat more accessible, especially his "Allen-a-Dale" (ca. 1813), taken from canto three. While Scott places *Rokeby* in 1644, its songs

15. See *The Complete Poetical Works of Sir Walter Scott,* Horace E. Scudder, ed. (Boston and New York, 1900), 7–8.

16. George C. D. Odell, *Annals of the New York Stage* (New York, 1927), II, 383–84, 464, 504.

17. See Victor Pelissier, *Pelissier's Columbian Melodies: Music for the New York and Philadelphia Theaters,* Karl Kroeger, ed., vols. 13–14 of Recent Researches in American Music (Madison, WI, 1984), xxi, 48–52.

18. For the dating of Scott, see *Complete Poetical Works,* 153; for Carr his *Selected Songs,* xvii.

EXAMPLE 1.5   Benjamin Carr, "Allen-a-Dale" (Baltimore: J. Carr, [ca. 1813])

often refer to a medieval England peopled by minstrels, knights errant, and fair maidens. Allen is a traveling bard usually associated with Robin Hood, and Scott sings the exploits of his courtship in appropriately elevated language:

> Allen-a-Dale to his wooing is come;
> The mother, she asked of his household and home;
> "Though the castle of Richmond stand fair on the hill,
> My hall," quoth bold Allen, "shows gallanter still;
> 'T is the blue vault of heaven, with its crescent so pale
> And with all its bright spangles!" said Allen-a-Dale.

Carr retains his earlier two-voice texture for this song and casts its meter in rollicking compound time (see Ex. 1.5). The simplicity of the texture aside, "Allen" enters a world much more fantastic than the mildly pastoral realm of "Claudine," and the selection of meter commonly found in the *romanza* (the operatic genre in which tales of olden times often unfold) may reflect the change.

Scott's chivalrous world also attracted Charles Gilfert (1787–1829), who set some of the same poems from *Rokeby* chosen by Carr, including "Allen-a-Dale" and "A Weary Lot Is Thine, Fair Maid." Gilfert, possibly born in Prague, was yet another immigrant whose musical career followed a typical course. He began in New York as a pianist and music teacher, but turned to directing theater orchestras, later moving to South Carolina where he managed the Charleston Theater. He briefly ran a music shop and publishing house there, before returning to New York at the end of his life.[19] "A Weary Lot Is Thine, Fair Maid" (1813) features, in addition to its mock-archaic language, the conceit of parting which becomes increasingly frequent in this style. Love from a distance and the separation of lover and beloved are common:

> "This morn is merry June, I trow,
>   The rose is budding fain;
> But she shall bloom in winter snow
>   Ere we two meet again."
> He turned his charger as he spake
>   Upon the river shore,
> He gave his bridle-reins a shake,
>   Said, "Adieu for evermore,
>   My Love!
> And adieu for evermore."

Gilfert, one of the more talented popular composers of his generation, gives a good account in this music. He tends toward a chromaticism not found in Hewitt or Carr, which grows to excess and deforms the melody of "The Cypress Wreath" in this same series from *Rokeby*. In "A Weary Lot," however, it intensifies expression for words such as "rue" (see Ex. 1.6) in this well-balanced and clearly formed melody. The style remains that of the late eighteenth and early nineteenth century's common practice, with its propensity for rather disjunct vocal writing accompanied by a piano playing lightly.

Even when composers did not borrow texts directly from Scott, they often chose poets who emulated the same chivalric themes. The American-born Thomas Van Dyke Wiesenthal (1790–1831), a naval surgeon by profession, set at least one poem from *Rokeby* in 1818, "Oh! Lady Twine No Wreath for Me" ("The Cypress Wreath"), and in this same series he included "The Minstrel's Song" (1818) with lyrics from James Hogg's poem, *The Queen's Wake*. The distance between lover and beloved translates here into fundamental differences in the nature of man and woman:

> "O! Lady dear, fair is thy noon,
> But man is like the inconstant moon:
> Last night she smiled o'er lawn and lea;
> That moon will change, and so will he."

19. The best biographical sketch on Gilfert appears in John Joseph Hindman, "Concert Life in Ante Bellum Charleston" (Ph.D. dissertation, University of North Carolina at Chapel Hill, 1971), 165–67.

EXAMPLE 1.6   Charles Gilfert, "A Weary Lot Is Thine, Fair Maid" (New York: J. Appel, [1813]; Wolfe no. 3084)

If women were coy in earlier songs, in this tradition they become almost entirely passive objects of affection. Their function consists in being admired, and they must sit helplessly as they lose their attractiveness:

> "Thy time, dear Lady's a passing shower;
> Thy beauty's but a fading flower:
> Watch thy young bosom, and maiden eye,
> For the shower must fall, and the flowret die."

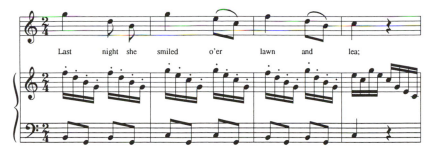

EXAMPLE 1.7 Thomas Van Dyke Wiesenthal "The Minstrel's Song" (Philadelphia: Bacon & Co., [1818]; Wolfe no. 9909)

Wiesenthal is not a talented composer of popular songs by anybody's standards, but he tries, nonetheless, to reproduce the style more practiced musicians apply to these faux-medieval situations. Minstrels in the Romantic tradition generally play harps, and the arpeggiations in the upper voice of Wiesenthal's accompaniment (see Ex. 1.7) mean to intimate this instrument.

Benjamin Carr actually specifies harp to accompany "The Minstrel Knight" (1824) from his *Six Canzonetts (sic),* Op. 14. The fantasy of medieval courtliness has become even more pronounced in this song than it was in the composer's settings of Scott's *Rokeby:*

> A Maid within this Castle dwelt
> More fair than any that grac'd the hall,
> Tho' many a Knight to her had knelt,
> She lov'd the Minstrel best of all.
> In bard's disguise to her he sung,
> But his name was of ancient noble pride,
> And his Harp so sweetly to love was strung,
> That she now is his blooming bride.

Such high rhetoric requires an elaborate accompaniment, and Carr rises to the occasion with many flourishes for the harp. But he has not changed his basic style, with its disjunct vocal lines retained from around the turn of the century (see Ex. 1.8). This same approach marks contemporary songs like "The Gallant Troubadour" (ca. 1825), an anonymous composition with lyrics by "S. of New Jersey."

Enthusiasm for the figure of the minstrel knight carried over into the next generation of composers. John Hill Hewitt appropriated it for "The Minstrel's Return'd from the War," written in 1825[20] though it appeared some years later, published in New York by E. S. Mesier (ca. 1833). Hewitt (1801–90),

20. See Hamm, *Yesterdays,* 103.

EXAMPLE 1.8   Benjamin Carr, "The Minstrel Knight" (Philadelphia: T. Carr, 1824; Wolfe no. 1585)

the son of New York publisher James Hewitt, is most familiar today for his Civil War song "All Quiet Along the Potomac To-night" (words by Ethel Lynn Beers, 1863). He began his career as a music teacher, though he eventually abandoned it for the study of law and later for journalism.[21] The lyrics for "The Minstrel's Return'd from the War" might pass for a simplified variation on "The Crusader's Return" from Chapter 17 of Scott's *Ivanhoe* (1819), which begins:

> High deeds achieved of knightly fame,
> From Palestine the champion came;
> The cross upon his shoulders borne,
> Battle and blast had dimmed and torn.
> Each dint upon his battered shield
> Was token of a foughten field;
> And thus beneath his lady's bower,
> he sung, as fell the twilight hour:

21. He gives a rambling account of this life in *Shadows on the Wall, or Glimpses of the Past* (Baltimore, 1877 (photofacsimile, New York, 1971)).

"Joy to the fair! —thy knight behold,
Returned from yonder land of gold. . . ."

While Hill omits actual mention of the crusades, he begins:

The minstrel's returned from the war,
With spirits as buoyant as air;
And thus on his tuneful guitar,
He sings in the bower of his fair.
The noise of the battle is over,
The bugle no more calls to arms,
A soldier no more but a lover,
I kneel to the power of thy charms!

Hewitt's setting for this perennial favorite (it would appear in multiple editions throughout the follow decades) falls, as Hamm observes, in an older musical style. The melodic line is so plain as to be almost declamatory, and the accompaniment suggests a kind of Federal-era march. This is rather unaffected musical language for so lofty and distant a tale.

The fantastic ennoblement of such lyrics, however, ultimately sought a more elegant musical style, that lay conveniently at hand. Like Scott's writing, the latest fashion in music came speedily from Britain with the newly regularized packet service[22] in the form of Rossinian opera adapted by composers like Henry Rowland Bishop (1786–1855). His English version of *Barber of Seville*, for instance, appeared at Covent Garden in October of 1818 and opened at the Park Theater, New York in May 1819, playing frequently until 1834.[23] And Bishop, among many others, established precedent for incorporating self-consciously Italianate style into popular songs like his "Home! Sweet Home!" from *Clari, or the Maid of Milan* (1823), billed in its early American editions as "Composed & partly founded on a Sicilian Air."[24] The gracefulness and overall shape of the vocal line distinguished the new fashion in writing. Italianate melody generally begins in the lower range of the voice and rises gradually by conjunct (stepwise) motion to the upper range, before falling gently back to the point of origin at the end. This arched shape and relatively gradual ascent and descent facilitates an evenness of vocal production which has become known as *bel canto* (literally: beautiful singing). The style is also marked at times by elaborate ornamentation (though cadenzas, trills, and turns appear abundantly in American songs from the very beginning of the century). Among the British composers using Italianate music in songs with chivalric themes

22. It began in 1818 between Liverpool and New York, soon spreading to all major ports in the United States; see Wiebe, *American Society*, 191.

23. Hamm, *Yesterdays*, 70.

24. For an American edition of "Home! Sweet Home!" see Richard Jackson, ed., *Popular Songs of Nineteenth-Century America* (New York, 1976), 80–82.

were men like Augustus Meves in "The Crusader" (words by Fred. F. Cooper, 1829) and Thomas Haynes Bayly in "Gaily the Troubadour Touch'd His Guitar" (ca. 1830).

The combination of archaic imagery and Anglo-Italian style spread widely in American songs of courtship during the 1830s. Instances include Charles H. Purday's "Lay of the Minstrel Knight" (ca. 1832) and Daniel Johnson's "The Carrier Dove" (1836), which depicts an imprisoned crusader on Gothic battlements sending messages to his distant beloved. But one of the most telling examples appears in John Hill Hewitt's "The Bridesmaid," advertised on its cover as "A Romantic Ballad" (1836).[25] In this song Hewitt shows how chivalric references intrude into modern fantasy, and at the same time he embraces the newer Italianate influence by writing a miniature operatic drama. As the scene unfolds, the anxious bridesmaid voices her thoughts:

> The last, the last faint sound I hear,
> Of groom and bride departing,
> With lady bright and cavalier,
> And helms in sunlight darting.

Hewitt has cast the present day in medieval terms, as the bridesmaid's own "knight" delays, having "bowed to honor's call." Tension mounts in the second verse as she watches the wedding carriage disappear from view, but the day is saved in the third verse:

> Be still—be still, my throbbing breast,
> I hear the bugle sounding;
> I see a warrior's snowy crest—
> A war steed proudly bounding.
> He comes—I know his gallant mien,
> His helmet, sword and spear;
> I know him by his doublet green
> My own brave cavalier!
> True to his word at eventide,
> He's come to claim me as his bride.

Hewitt's accompaniment for this dramatized narrative is far more elaborate and varied than anything his father would have provided. Rather than simple two- or three-part chords, the younger composer supplies a much heavier texture, and for the third verse he uses the compound meter to support a musical figure often applied to riding. Many of these patterns appear in transcriptions for voice and piano of Italian operatic favorites of the day by Rossini, Bellini, or Donizetti. On occasion Hewitt's melody approaches the graceful lines of *bel*

---

25. Facsimile in Tawa, *Solo Songs,* I, 283–87.

EXAMPLE 1.9 John Hill Hewitt, "The Bridesmaid" (Philadelphia: John F. Nunns, 1836)

canto melody, with their conjunct motion and gradually arched shape (see Ex. 1.9).

Hewitt's perfected his command of this style in "The Knight of the Raven Black Plume" (1844),[26] which, like "The Bridesmaid," emulates the operatic genre of the *romanza* (again, the title given to arias that speak of olden times). Hill uses the standard compound meter generally employed for telling such tales, 6/8, and he refines his melodic style, using *bel canto* throughout the song. The engraved cover on the sheet music bills this song as written by the "author of the Minstrels return from the War" *(sic),* and the words "Black Plume" may allude to *Ivanhoe's* Black Knight who sings "The Crusader's Song" printed above. He could chant this one as well:

> A lady sat mute in her bow'r,
> While her page from the turret on high,
> Look'd out at the lone midnight hour,
> To see if her lover was nigh.
> "Ho! Ho!" said the page as he toss'd
> His scarf 'mid the moon's mellow light,

26. Ibid., 332–37.

"A horseman the meadow has cross'd,
And his corslet and helmet are bright."

[Refrain:]
"Lady fair! Lady fair! banish thy gloom,
For here is the Knight of the raven black plume."

The serenade produces the desired effect in the second verse, as the lady appears at the "lattice." And as the warden opens the gate to him in the third verse, the knight asks her hand in marriage. But we do not learn the result of his suit; the polite separation between lover and beloved is not bridged in the listener's presence. At times this separation grows even more severe in Hewitt's output, as in "When Thou Wert True" (1843) with lyrics by F. W. Thomas. Set in Elizabethan times to judge from the archaic language and the costumes in the engraving on the cover, this song shows the suitor abandoning his damsel after she fails the test of perfect fidelity.

Hewitt was not alone by any means in carrying this tradition of anachronism into the forties. James G. Maeder provides a similar combination of theme and style in his "Answer to The Carrier Dove" (1841) with "words by a lady"; it comes in reply to Daniel Johnson's song mentioned above. Husband of the famous actress Clara Fisher, Maeder (1809–76) was born in Dublin, educated in London, and served as pianist and vocal coach for opera singers in numerous American cities.[27] His operatic training serves him well in "The Carrier Dove," which much resembles Hewitt's "Knight" in its 6/8 meter and full accompaniment. The lyrics do not specifically mention a medieval setting, but the elevated language of the second verse uses some stock phrases from songs in the anachronistic tradition:

You may tell him I seek my bower of light
But his footsteps I do not hear,
And I wander forth again at night,
For perchance he may then be near.
But no, he is chained in a distant clime,
He weeps where no sympathies come;
Oh had I thy wings, sweet dove, for a time,
I'd fly to his desolate home.

The engraving on the cover (Illus. 1.1) confirms the reference, for it depicts the lady standing on the balcony of a crenelated turret, looking out over walls of her castle. Dressed in nineteenth-century costume, she represents a modern-day figure enveloped in fantasies of chivalry, just as Hewitt's "Bridesmaid" was. These fantasies persist in songs like Alfred Wheeler and Francis H.

27. Some details of his life appear in his wife's *Autobiography of Clara Fisher Maeder* (New York, 1897).

Brown's "Will You Come to My Mountain Home?" (1845) and Frances Irene Burges and Brown's "Yes I'll Come to Thy Mountain Home" (1852), another question-and-answer pair featuring feudal references.[28]

We must wonder what appeal the fantastic world of errant knights and distressed damsels held for the urban, middle-class purchasers of sheet music in a republican society that had pointedly rejected feudal aristocracy. The answer must be more than a simple yearning for exoticism or a fashionably Romantic "spirit of the times." In part these songs promoted an ideal that coincided with the increasingly pronounced separation of roles for men and women of the urban middle class. In agrarian surroundings men and women shared work and would often perform some of the same tasks. And lower-class people of both sexes worked in factories during the nineteenth century. But in middle-class households amidst the turmoil of rapidly growing nineteenth-century American cities, men became crusaders dealing with a wicked outside world. They protected women, who governed the home by setting examples of goodness and purity.[29] Songs fashioned by middling urban composers primarily for middling urban audiences might invoke the courtly romance's division of gender by role to great advantage in matters of love, while lending themselves at the same time to the listeners' pretensions. For the other element in the popularity of these lyrics seems to have involved social ennoblement. The American middle class realized some of its new power during the early nineteenth century, and it was not initially averse to cultivating an art which invested its rituals of courtship with aristocratic overtones. This strange penchant mirrored the growing popularity of books on etiquette which first arose in the 1830s; they also appropriated what their readers supposed were the manners and customs of the gentry.[30]

Translating Courtly Love

It would be an exaggeration to suggest that all songs from the teens through the forties appropriated mock-medieval conceits from the writings of authors like Sir Walter Scott. But it is fair to say that chivalric themes influenced many popular songs about serious courtship beginning in the 1820s and continuing

28. Stephen Foster includes "Will You Come" in *The Social Orchestra for Flute or Violin: A Collection of Popular Melodies Arranged as Solos, Duets, Trios, and Quartets,* Early American Music, 13 (New York, 1973), 5.

29. Barbara Leslie Epstein provides a good outline of this process in *The Politics of Domesticity: Women, Evangelism, and Temperance in Nineteenth-Century America* (Middletown, CT, 1981), 2. Its effects on courtship and sexual relations appear in D'Emilio and Freedman, *Intimate Matters,* 55–84.

30. See John F. Kasson, *Rudeness & Civility: Manners in Nineteenth-Century Urban America* (New York, 1990), 34–69.

until the Civil War.[31] Where lyricists did not invoke explicitly medieval, aristocratic images, they borrowed some superficial features traditionally associated with them, especially high language, both verbal and musical. And they also reflected the deeper implications of an idealized romance almost devoid of erotic contact. These included distinct, strictly defined roles for men and woman which resulted in an immense remove between lover and beloved. By the end of this period songwriters had sublimated the mores of courtliness beneath a more mundane surface, though occasional features, both linguistic and musical, reveal their continuing presence.

The process of translation runs just behind the craze for medieval anachronism in songs like "Her Smiling Eyes" (1818) by Peter K. Moran. Moran (d. 1831) brought his skills as organist, violinist, and cellist from Ireland to New York, where he played in pit orchestras and eventually owned a store selling instruments and music. One of the immediate references to the tradition of the romance comes in his selection of harp for accompaniment: this is the instrument of medieval bards in the parlance of the day. Its idiomatic figurations would mark the instrumental part, even if they were played on piano. Moran's lyrics speak of an undisclosed love that implies a substantial distance, even if it does not qualify precisely as love from afar:

> Her language charm'd, Her smiles alarm'd,
> My heart I felt emotions new;
> I blest the sound yet still the wound
> Came from her Eyes of lovely blue.
> But when I speak, how short my breath!
> Perhaps she'll favor when I woo;
> If not, in faith, I'll lay my death,
> To those dear Eyes of lovely blue.

This last line sounds more drastic than it is in context. The first verse explains that the suitor has caught cold strolling through the damp on the evening when he first beholds his lady fair. Moran's other songs translating courtly love into modern circumstances exaggerate the separation between lover and beloved even more. "The Carrier Pigeon" (1822), with lyrics by the American James Gates Percival, uses the conceit of a woman sending messages to her distant suitor. Percival's lyrics contain no explicitly archaic references, but its vocabulary is high enough for any damsel:

> Come hither thou beautiful rover,
> Thou wand'rer of earth and of air;
> Who bearest the sighs of a lover,

---

31. Blackface minstrelsy, a countercultural movement, arises in the 1830s as a direct challenge to this style, providing more earthy, comic images of courtship; see Chapter 5.

EXAMPLE 1.10   Peter K. Moran, "The Carrier Pigeon" (New York: Dubois & Stodart, [1822]; Wolfe no. 6087b)

> And bringest him news of his fair:
> Bend hither thy light waving pinion,
> And show me the gloss of thy neck;
> O perch on my hand dearest minion,
> And turn up thy bright eye and peck.

In this case Moran's melody employs the appropriate and fashionable vocabulary of *bel canto,* the musical counterpart to poetic elevation (Ex. 1.10). Unlike James Maeder's "Answer to The Carrier Dove" discussed earlier, Moran and Percival's "Carrier Pigeon" does not invoke specifically medieval scenes, even on its cover. But chivalry lurks just below the surface.

One of the most common sublimations of courtliness in nineteenth-century song appears in the serenade. In pseudo-medieval scenes from the period, knights errant often sing of love beneath the towers of fair maidens, an image that not only separates the sexes but also positions them symbolically. The passive woman remains inside, where her elevated purity and goodness are protected. The active man takes time from his combat with the harsh outside world to assert his admiration and seek her attention (but rarely demands admittance). The lyrics of "The Serenade" (1825) by "a Lady," music by Francis Delochair Mallet, allow occasional glimpses of sublimated archaism:

> Rise lovely Maid, shake off thy balmy slumbers,
> Haste to thy casement, list the tuneful strain,
> Fondly he loves who breathes in warbling numbers,
> Ne'er wilt thou meet a heart so true again.

The suitor even uses one of the archetypal instruments of the minstrel:

> Hark! tis the lute whose gentle murmurs stealing
> Wraps the charm'd sense and fills the list'ning ear,
> List! to that voice each tender hope revealing
> In pity drop one sympathetic tear.

Mallet (1750–1834), a Boston actor, organist, and music teacher of French origins, elevates his accompaniment with word painting. He responds to "warbling" in the first verse with a piano cadenza, and his vocal melody is more than unusually ornate, suggesting a conscious invocation of high musical style.

This climate of chivalrous distance gives renewed vitality to songs of parting during the next decade, including numbers like "Leave Me Not Yet" (1834), with words by Felicia Hemans and music by Christopher Meineke.[32] Hemans was an English writer popular on the American scene, who contributed titles on medieval themes like "The Captive Knight." Meineke, a Baltimore church organist of German birth, must have chosen her lyrics for their ennobled appeal. She uses very delicate images in her first stanza:

> Leave me not! through rosy skies from far
> But now the songbird to their nests return;
> The trembling image of the first pale star,
> On the dim lake but now begins to burn.
> Leave me not yet! Leave me not yet!

The second stanza describes the sounds at close of day, while the last verse leaves a sense of romantic solitude:

> My thoughts are like those gentle tones dear love,
> By day shut up in their own sweet recess;
> They wait for dews on earth, for stars above;
> Then to breathe out their voice of tenderness.

The metaphors employed to characterize the speaker's feelings seem devoted to indirection. Separation is not just a painful necessity but an occasion for

---

32. Facsimile in Tawa, *Solo Songs*, I, 297–302. Information on Meineke (spelled Meinecke) appears in Grace D. Yerbury's *Song in America from Early Times to About 1850* (Metuchen, NJ, 1971), 163–4.

EXAMPLE 1.11   John Hill Hewitt, "I'll Think of Thee, Love" (Baltimore: John Cole [ca. 1836])

lofty thoughts. We need no knights or maidens here to understand the language of courtliness; as the contemporary writer Almira Phelps puts it, ". . . everything that comes from [Hemans's] pen is pure, and bears the image and superscription of the elevated and chastened mind."[33] Meineke knows well the musical style appropriate to such lyrics: he composes a fairly elaborate accompaniment with restless sixteenth notes and an equally elaborate melody which means to imitate Italian tones. If the frequent melismas are not a sufficient hint, the composer adds markings like "con amore," "dolce," "lentando," and "retenute," using constant dramatic changes of mood to make his point about musical "superscription."

John Hill Hewitt provides his own version of parting in "I'll Think of Thee, Love" (ca. 1836), which does not require the explicitly aristocratic setting of his father's "Remember Me" ("from the Romance of Don Raphael," see above, Ex. 1.3) to make a point about courtly fidelity. The gentle curve of the Italianate vocal line emerges clearly in the excerpt (Ex. 1.11), and a brief cadenza toward the end of each stanza (not shown) ennobles the scene. The text of the second two strophes is particularly plummy:

> I'll think of thee, love, when the first sound of day,
> Scares the bright pinion'd bird from his covert away;
> For the world's busy voice has no music for me—
> I'll think of thee, dearest— and only of thee!
>
> I'll think of thee, love, when the dark shadows sleep
> On the billows that roll o'er the emerald deep:
> Like the swift speeding gale, every thought then shall be—
> I'll think of thee, dearest— and only of thee!

33. Quoted in Judith Tick, *American Women Composers Before 1870* (Ann Arbor, MI, 1983), 28.

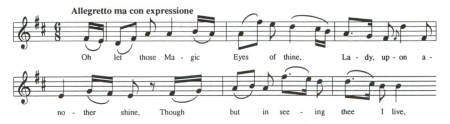

Allegretto ma con expressione

Oh let those Ma - gic Eyes of thine, La - dy, up - on a -
no - ther shine, Though but in see - ing thee I live,

EXAMPLE 1.12   A. F. Winnemore, "Those Magic Eyes" (Philadelphia: Geo. Willig, 1836)

The imagery here is not at all pseudo-medieval, but the vocabulary comes straight out of the high speech, with its "pinioned birds" in "coverts" and "billows" on the "emerald deep." Implicit courtliness pervades the lyrics, and this undercurrent affects the choice of musical style.

Love is more chivalrous, of course, when the lover not only admires from afar but disguises his affections as in "Those Magic Eyes" by A. F. Winnemore with accompaniment by John Conrad Viereck (1836). Winnemore—about whom we know nothing, save that he composed and engraved this song— addresses his complaint to the usual "Lady," and the title page claims that this song comes from a larger collection, "The Magic Lute." Invocation of this instrument sets the tone for the first verse in which the speaker confesses the power of his beloved's glance. So intimidating is her purity that he cannot bear even to return her gaze, and he concludes disconsolately in the second verse:

> 'Tis thus that love and fate ordain,
> That which is guerdon for my pain,
> Should but add fuel to my grief,
> And to my woes bring no relief.
> From those dear eyes I light receive,
> 'Tis only in their light I live,
> Yet when they do but glance at me,
> Vainly I strive to gaze on thee.

Winnemore selects a very special melodic language, of a type we have not encountered before, for this secret love (see Ex. 1.12). His tendency to use continual, large, upward leaps on words like "Eye's," "upon," and "seeing," followed by gradual descent to the point of origin, recalls a vocal type Charles Hamm associates with Thomas Moore's *Irish Melodies*.[34] Its adoption here would appear at first to be a turn away from the Italianate toward the folkish. But we should remember that Moore elevates his basic melodic

34. *Yesterdays*, 54–59

material by adding all sorts of ornaments and encasing them in refined settings by Sir John Stevenson. This raised style of ethnic music is particularly associated with nostalgia and longing for unattainable objects (the departed, the old country, and so forth). Used to this end it shares some polite connotations with *bel canto*. And in fact, we see here some of the melismatic vocal writing associated with Italianate style as well as Viereck's artful, if not overly elaborate "symphonies." Viereck, obviously of German birth or descent, must have been active in Philadelphia around this time, since his arrangements and compositions appeared frequently from the publishers of that city. He works with familiar themes in songs like "Farewell! Farewell!, Yes, I Must Leave Thee!" and "The Maiden from Afar" (both issued by A. Fiot in 1836 and 1843, respectively).

The last stage in separation between lovers was achieved through death, and partly for this reason it played a prominent role in antebellum songs of courtship. (I am concerned here with instances where death serves mainly to create distance. I will deal with pieces that explicitly outline funereal customs in Chapter 3.) Perhaps the most famous song engaging this theme in the thirties was "On the Lake Where Droop'd the Willow" (1837).[35] It later appeared under the title "Near the Lake Where Drooped the Willow" (1839), and its history is worth exploring at length. The 1839 edition, published in New York by Hewitt and Jacques, attributes the lyrics to George Pope Morris, editor of the New York *Home Journal* and occasional contributor to the *Visitor*. John H. Hewitt writes of him in 1877, "we had been associated in earlier days and were considered *the* ballad-writers of the times. . . ."[36] Indeed, Morris's most famous text, "Woodman! Spare That Tree!" (1837), is still known today in Henry Russell's setting. "On the Lake," like almost all songs of this type, features a man mourning his dead beloved:

> On the lake where droop'd the willow,
>   Long time ago!
> Where the rock threw back the billow,
>   Brighter than snow;
> Dwelt a maid, beloved and cherish'd,
>   By high and low;
> But, with autumn's leaf, she perish'd,
>   Long time ago!

The second verse describes loving hours spent together and refers very obliquely to erotic content with the phrase, "Bird, and bee, and blossom taught her, Love's spell to know." The last verse, however, is the most revealing:

35. This version appears in Tawa, *Solo Songs*, I, 371–75.
36. John Hewitt, *Shadows*, 29.

Mingled were our hearts forever!
   Long time ago!
Can I now forget her? Never!
   No, lost one, no!
To her grave these tears are given,
   Ever to flow!
She's the star I miss'd from heaven,
   Long time ago!

The beloved is idealized as a remote and unapproachable object, floating high above and beyond her mortal lover. From the vantage point of a later, more realistic time Hewitt renders a sharp verdict on this text:

> There are several of [Morris's] ballads which have been highly lauded, though they possess but very common merit. I instance, in defense of the position I have taken, the songs of "Near the lake where droops [sic] the willow" and "Meeta." The former was adapted to a negro refrain and beautifully harmonized by Charles E. Horn. The simplicity of the melody tallied with the words, and hence its popularity.[37]

While his jealousy of Morris's success might be discounted, Hewitt has a point about Charles Edward Horn's accompaniment. The cover of "On the Lake" calls this tune "a popular southern refrain," and though we cannot be sure of its folkloric authenticity, we know that Horn took it from a well-known blackface tune, "Long Time Ago." (The earliest edition I can find has words attributed to Thomas Dartmouth Rice, Baltimore: John Cole, 1833. "Blackface," incidentally, involved white singers darkening their complexions with burnt cork so as to assume the exaggerated appearance of African-Americans.) Horn (1786–1849) was one of the composers in the mold of British actor, singer, music director, and sometime publisher. He arrived on these shores late, in 1827, and returned to England from time to time, but his activity betrayed a sincere interest in the culture of the United States. True to his "scientific" musical education, he smoothes the deliberately disjunct melody of his blackface model into slightly less jagged contours, endowing the refrain ("Long time ago") with cadenza-like ornaments. He accompanies this reshaped and embellished vocal line with a part of utmost simplicity for the piano. This song would eventually gain a lasting place in American culture through Aaron Copland's arrangement in his *Old American Songs.*[38]

"On the Lake" represents another important step in the translation of chivalric courtship from the exotic and foreign into the familiar and native. For just as Scott would not continue to serve as a direct source of language for Ameri-

---

37. Ibid.
38. ((New York), 1950), 13–15.

can song, Italian opera would fade as the predominant style (though it lingered on as an compositional option for some time). After the success of "On the Lake," Morris wrote a series of lyrics for blackface tunes adapted by George Loder, including a serenade on the water, "Oh! Boatman, Haste!" (1843) to the tune of "The Boatman's Dance," and "The Pastor's Daughter" (1844) to "Old Dan Tucker." This last number graphically displays the absorption of courtly themes into an American context: a preacher's daughter resists all suitors until the arrival of a "bard" who strikes "his harp," wins her heart, and takes her to the altar. In the last verse Morris provides the moral that the "worldly gay" cannot court the pure. The undefiled damsel in her crenelated tower and the minstrel knight linger here immediately below the surface, but even more important are the differences the stereotypes suggest between men and women, the distance between courting couples, and the persistence of fantasy. At the same time, it appears that the more earthy tradition of blackface minstrelsy was beginning to exert some pull on songs of courtship.

We might be tempted to think that the idealization of romance projected male fantasy only, given the heavy predominance of men in the profession of music during the nineteenth century. But female lyricists and composers adopted the same images in their songs of courtship. We have already seen Felicia Hemans's lyrics from the 1830s and any number of songs with lyrics by anonymous "ladies." A female composer like Jane Sloman takes much the same approach as her predecessors. Sloman, an English pianist, singer, music teacher, and composer, was born in 1824 and arrived in America in 1839. She had a distinguished career as a concert pianist playing repertory by composers like Herz, with a debut at Niblo's Gardens in New York (1841) and appearances in Philadelphia and Boston as well (her last known concert took place On February 18, 1850).[39] As we might expect from a classically trained pianist of some accomplishment, Sloman's accompaniments are quite artful in songs like "Forget Thee?" (1843),[40] though less so than those of her fellow expatriate, Henry Russell. Nonetheless, her songs fit well into the popular scene. The cover of "Forget Thee?" depicts a man with lute serenading a passively admiring woman. And Sloman casts his promise of fidelity in tones familiar by now:

> Forget thee!
> If to dream by night and muse on thee by day,
> If all the worship wild and deep, a true one's heart can pay.
> If pray'rs in absence said for thee to Heav'ns protecting pow'r,
> If winged thoughts that flit to thee, a thousand in an hour,
> If busy fancy blending thee, with all my future lot.
> If that thou call'st forgetting, thou indeed shall be forgot.

39. See Tick, *Women Composers*, 188–91.
40. The music appears in Tawa, *Solo Songs*, I, 290–94.

EXAMPLE 1.13   Jane Sloman, "Forget Thee?" (Boston: Wm. H. Oakes, 1843)

The language is elevated in this song of parting, and the woman even more so, worshiped at a distance by her admirer. The second verse describes this admiration in terms of nature. The vocal line decorates the whole scene with profuse melismas, turns, trills, and cadenzas, joined to the conjunct melodic shape of true *bel canto* (see Ex. 1.13). Sloman uses an unusual amount of chromatic movement in both the vocal line and accompaniment, perhaps influenced by contemporary operatic idiom.

Sloman's most popular song, "Roll On Silver Moon" (1848),[41] adopts a distinctly simpler piano part (arranged by N. Barker) than we find in "Forget Thee?" and a catchy melody to take up the theme of separation through death from a woman's point of view. Sloman simply reverses the stereotype. We begin with a verse from the narrator:

> As I stray'd from my cot at the close of the day,
> 'Mid the ravishing beauties of June,
> 'Neath a jessamine shade I espied a fair maid,
> And she plaintively sigh'd to the moon.

41. The sheet music appears in Tick, *Woman Composers,* 196–99.

A four-part chorus follows, of the kind that blackface troupes had recently popularized as a possible format for American song (for more about the four-part chorus, see Chapter 5):

> Roll on silver moon, point the trav'ler his way,
> While the nightingale's song is in tune,
> I never, never more with my true love will stray
> By thy soft silver beams, gentle moon.

The second verse describes "Edwin" as "brave, noble, manly, and clever" rather than "pure," as a woman would be. He departs beyond recall, all the same:

> But alas he is dead and gone to death's bed,
> Cut down like a rose in full bloom;
> All alone doth he sleep while I thus sadly weep
> 'Neath thy soft silver light, gentle moon.

The remaining stanzas portray the usual devoted mourning at the grave and pledges of eternal love similar to those in "On the Lake." The themes of fidelity and palpable remove permeate these lyrics in precisely the same way they do Morris's, while the musical style is as accessible as Horn's. Sloman composes a series of short, angular, reciprocating phrases that show the influence of the blackface tradition. Stephen Foster includes the tune in his anthology of arrangements, *The Social Orchestra*,[42] an indication of Sloman's success in striking a popular note.

The Acme of Tradition

Stephen Foster's own marvelous assortment of songs provides both a summation of sublimated chivalry and its nineteenth-century apogee. His unique talent for drawing together the various threads running through popular song in America has often been noted, and his greatest biographer, John Tasker Howard, maintains that Foster's geographic origins had an important influence on his wide stylistic acquaintance.[43] Born in Pittsburgh on July 4, 1826, Foster absorbed the genteel tradition in his upper middle-class home and at school, but he also encountered a tradition of blackface that had roots in the Ohio River valley. Instruction in music came from Henry Kleber, a German immigrant who plied the usual combination of trades: performer, teacher, shopkeeper, and

42. *Social Orchestra*, 11.
43. *Stephen Foster, America's Troubadour* (New York, 1953), 1–3.

music publisher.[44] Though Foster began his adult career as a bookkeeper in a family business, his royalty agreement with Firth, Pond and Company of New York in 1849—unprecedented in the annals of popular song to that time—allowed him to pursue the life of a professional composer.[45] In the financial context of his own day he made a moderate living from his compositions, averaging about $1300 per year. He unfortunately mismanaged these revenues, dying in straitened circumstances. Nonetheless, it is a mark of his aptitude for distilling the essence of various popular traditions in his songs that he could even consider devoting himself solely to composition.

Foster's first published song, "Open Thy Lattice Love" (1844),[46] takes its lyrics signally from a poem by George P. Morris, published in his *New Mirror* (1843). In the courtly genre of the serenade, the song uses language familiar from other texts by Morris:

> Open thy lattice, love listen to me!
> The cool balmy breeze is abroad on the sea!
> The moon like a queen, roams her realms of blue,
> And the stars keep their vigils in heaven for you.
> Ere morn's gushing light tips the hills with its ray,
> Away o'er the waters away and away!
> Then open thy lattice, love listen to me!
> While the moon's in the sky and the breeze on the sea!

Morris does not directly elevate the beloved here, but he connects her obliquely to the heavens (the stars shine for her) and likens the moon to a queen.

Foster's music compares with that of other composers in Morris's orbit such as Charles Edward Horn, as Hamm suggests.[47] An accompaniment of very simple texture gently reinforces the lilting 6/8 meter and supports a vocal line with roots in the British translation of operatic writing (see Ex. 1.14). Even though no ornamentation intrudes, the lines generally rise and fall in graceful arches with little rhythmic syncopation, producing the simplified *bel canto* found earlier in songs like Horn's "All Things Love Thee, So Do I" (1838). Many other American composers from around this time contributed songs in the style, from Reynell Coates and William R. Dempster in "Oh! Show Me Some Blue Distant Isle" (1841) to W. V. Wallace in "The Star of Love" (1851), another serenade with a text by Morris. But none of these composers possessed Foster's particular knack of combining simplicity with elegance. The

44. Ibid., 107.
45. Ibid., 152–54.
46. The most accessible reprinting of this and other Foster songs is found in the *Stephen Foster Song Book* (New York, 1974), 108–9; unless specified otherwise, all the texts quoted below appear in this collection. The composer's collected works appear in *The Music of Stephen Foster*, Steven Saunders and Deane L. Root, eds., 2 vols. (Washington and London, 1990).
47. *Yesterdays*, 204.

EXAMPLE 1.14   Stephen Foster, "Open Thy Lattice Love" (Philadelphia: George Willig, 1844)

composer repeated this accomplishment in "Wilt Thou Be Gone, Love?" (a duet-nocturne with words taken from Shakespeare's *Romeo and Juliet,* 1851), and in his "serenade, per voci soli," "Come Where My Love Lies Dreaming" (1855). References to the earlier tradition of chivalric love surface just briefly in this last number as part of the refrain: "Come with a lute, Come with a lay—My own love is sweetly dreaming, Her beauty beaming."

"Sweetly She Sleeps, My Alice Fair" and "Linger in Blissful Repose" also fall in the genre of the serenade, but in both of them the distinction between active lover and passive beloved is intensified because the man silently admires the woman while she sleeps. An English maiden from medieval fantasy peeks around the edges of Charles G. Eastman's lyrics for "Sweetly She Sleeps" (1851):[48]

> Sweetly she sleeps, my Alice fair,
> Her cheek on the pillow pressed,
> Sweetly she sleeps, while her Saxon hair,
> Like sunlight, streams o'er her breast.

48. A copy of the sheet music appears in Stephen Foster, *Household Songs,* vol. 12, of Earlier American Music (New York, 1973), 18–21.

EXAMPLE 1.15 Stephen Foster, "Linger in Blissful Repose" (New York: Firth, Pond & Co., 1858)

For this song Foster completely masters the Anglo-Italian style of melody, again in 6/8 time. He uses almost exclusively conjunct motion for "Linger" in 9/8 time (marked as 3/4 but with constant triplets, see Ex. 1.15).[49] It is enough for the beloved in "Linger" (1858) merely to sleep and absorb her suitor's admiration unconsciously:

> Linger in blissful repose,
> Free from all sorrowing care, love,
> While round thee melody flows,
> Wafted on pinions of air love.
> Let not thy visions depart,
> Lured by the stars that are beaming,
> Music will flow from my heart
> While thy sweet spirit is dreaming.

"Pinions of air" carry expressions of the lover's thoughts much as did the "pinions" of the dove or pigeon in earlier songs, and the distance between the couple is no less pronounced.

49. Reprinted in *Music of Foster*, II, 27–31.

Like composers before him, Foster created the greatest courtly distance between lover and beloved by means of death. He raised the delicate remembrance of departed beauties to a fine art, usually conveying nostalgia through the ennobled folkishness of "Irish" melodic shapes. Hamm links "Ah! May the Red Rose Live Alway" (1850) specifically to Moore's "The Last Rose of Summer," and this conceit of fading nature transfers easily and directly to courtship in "Jeanie with the Light Brown Hair" (1854). In his first verse Foster uses daisies, birds, "bright streams," and the breezes of summer as metaphors for Jeanie's loveliness, then gives the reasons for his wistful mood in a darker second verse:

> I long for Jeanie with the day-dawn smile,
> Radiant in gladness, warm with winning guile;
> I hear her melodies, like joys gone by,
> Sighing round my heart o'er the fond hopes that die:
> Sighing like the night wind and sobbing like the rain,
> Wailing for the lost one that comes not again:
> I long for Jeanie, and my heart bows low,
> Never more to find her where the bright waters flow.

The influence of the *Irish Melodies* reveals itself not only in the extraordinary, isolated melodic leaps approaching "*glad*ness" and "never *more*," but also in the cadenzas prefacing the penultimate line of each stanza. This is the same style seen earlier in Winnemore's "Those Magic Eyes," but in "Jeanie" it accompanies not just love from afar but permanent remove.

"Gentle Annie" (1856) arrives even more quickly at the same conceit joining nature, nostalgia, and separation through death:

> Thou wilt come no more, gentle Annie,
> Like a flower thy spirit did depart;
> Thou art gone, alas! like the many
> That have bloomed in the summer of my heart.
>
> [*Chorus:*]
> Shall we never more behold thee;
> Never hear thy winning voice again—
> When the Springtime comes, gentle Annie,
> When the wild flowers are scattered o'er the plain?

In this song Foster displays his particularly strong aptitude for wedding words to music. His vocal line follows the "Irish Melody" type, and its isolated leaps emphasize the key words—"Annie" and "many" in the verse, both occurrences of "never" in the chorus (Ex. 1.16). The first three instances employ

EXAMPLE 1.16   Stephen Foster, "Gentle Annie" (New York: Firth, Pond & Co., 1856)

strong syncopation to accentuate the leap, and the composer sets the remaining text with great care for the declamation of the syllables in natural speech. As a result the elevated terms in which the male speaker addresses his beloved seem somewhat more familiar. She is remote and pure, but not entirely alien, and her lover can still contemplate her from afar, even across the ultimate barrier:

> Ah! the hours grow sad while I ponder
> Near the silent spot where thou art laid,

> And my heart bows down when I wander
> By the streams and the meadows where we strayed.

All this takes place over a minimal piano texture in which simple arpeggiated and block chords alternate, rendering the song accessible to the widest possible audience of middle-class consumers. Foster could translate chivalric distance almost perfectly into everyday terms and yet retain its ennobled air, something he does repeatedly throughout his career in "Where Is Thy Spirit Mary?" (1847), "Lily Ray" (1850), "Annie My Own Love" (1853), "Lula Is Gone" (1858), "Linda Has Departed" (1859), and "Cora Dean" (1860).

Even when Foster's beloved is alive, she is often held beyond reach, as in the case of "Gentle Lena Clare" (1862). The composer selects a dance-like rhythm and extremely short phrases for this brief song with a verse of only eight measures and a chorus of equal length. He abandons the more pretentious melos of Italianate writing here, partly because it does not tally with the figure described in the chorus—"Her heart is light, her eyes are bright, My gentle Lena Clare"—and partly because the story has no tragedy to suggest affective writing. But despite the cheerful tone, courtliness does intrude, superficially in the selection of language for the second verse ("I love her wild and birdlike *lays*") and also in the quest the narrator must undertake to find her in the third:

> Her home is in the shady glen
> When summer comes I'll seek again
> On mountain height and lowland plain;
> My gentle Lena Clare.

Innocence and purity joined to distance attract the desire of suitors in many other songs by Foster, including "The Spirit of My Song" (1850), "Laura Lee" (1851), "Fairy-Belle" (1859), "Sweet Little Maid of the Mountain" (1861), and "Little Jenny Dow" (1862),[50] a woman so pure that she becomes unattainable in Foster's second verse:

> Many are the hearts that have sigh'd for her,
> And many that have sigh'd in pain,
> Many that I know would have died for her,
> And alas they would have died in vain—
> Little Jenny Dow never clouds her brow
> In sorrow o'er a lovelorn swain;
> With spirits full of glee none so gay as she,
> As she rambles o'er the hill and plain.

50. Ibid., 175–79.

"Thou Art the Queen of My Song" (1859) indicates that the man will be more ardent yet in pursuit of a beloved both pure, absent, and ennobled:

> I long for thee; must I long and long in vain?
> I sigh for thee; wilt thou come not back again?
> Though cold forms surround us,
> To sever all that bound us,
> Gentle queen of my song.
> The fields and the fair flowers shall welcome thee,
> And all to thy pleasures shall belong;
> Pride of my early years,
> Thou art the queen of my song.

Foster attempts an elevated musical style for this text, but the irregular verse already reveals some of his difficulties. The conceit is clear, nonetheless: this impassive woman is not just aristocratic, she is royal, and her courtier must plead for the renewal of her lost affections.

"Beautiful Dreamer" (1864) presents the composer's most successful interweaving of the themes surrounding the distant beloved. The cover of the sheet music advertises it as "the last song ever written. . . composed but a few days before his death," though Steven Saunders and Deane Root cast doubt on this claim, dating its composition 1862.[51] Even if it does not represent Foster's last word, "Dreamer" epitomizes courtliness in genteel popular song before the Civil War. The sheet music bears the appropriate subtitle of "Serenade":

> Beautiful dreamer, wake unto me,
> Starlight and dewdrops are waiting for thee;
> Sounds of the rude world heard in the day,
> Lull'd by the moonlight have all pass'd away!
> Beautiful dreamer, queen of my song,
> List while I woo thee with soft melody;
> Gone are the cares of life's busy throng,
> Beautiful dreamer, awake unto me!

Not only is the maiden royal, she is undefiled and may not be exposed to the "rude" and crowded outside world. The singer, on the other hand, lives amidst "life's busy throng," and stands so far beneath his beloved that he must beseech her to glance down:

> Beautiful dreamer, out on the sea
> Mermaids are chaunting the wild lorelie;
> Over the streamlet vapors are borne,

51. Ibid., 437.

Waiting to fade at the bright coming morn.
Beautiful dreamer, beam on my heart,
E'en as the morn on the streamlet and sea;
Then will all clouds of sorrow depart,
Beautiful dreamer, awake unto me!

These elevated sentiments call forth Foster's most limpid version of Anglo-Italian style, with fluid rhythms in 9/8 meter and graceful arpeggiations ("Beautiful dreamer . . ."), answered by scales ("Starlight and dew drops . . .") with multiple appoggiaturas. The phrases move regularly, feature motivic economy, and fit the text with graceful fidelity. "Beautiful Dreamer" represents the ultimate in middle-class sublimation of chivalry.

Popular songs about courtship (or about any other subject, for that matter) do not record precisely the customs of their day, nor do they prescribe. They do offer, however, lyricists' and composers' conceptions of how men might interact with women, ideas which the general public encounters. We should be careful about assuming that the wide reputation of a given number stems from complete acceptance of the precepts in its text: an attractive tune may play an equal or even more important role in the fame of a given song. But we should not refrain from probing the possible meanings of both the words and music in popular song, even if we must be wary of drawing simple conclusions.

The picture of courting created by American popular song in the first half of the nineteenth century seems to have served its public, both male and female, in a variety of ways. The lyrics seem designed to elevate the urban middle class by presenting a mock-aristocratic approach to courtship, at first explicitly through the images of knights and maidens, and then implicitly through constant allusions to selected vocabulary from the earlier tradition. This imagery was reinforced by an ennobled musical style that used as its touchstone the fashion of Italian opera as adapted by British composers. Even the "lower" style of music with folkish origins (*Irish Melodies*, "On the Lake," and so forth) rose to genteel status by passing through the filter of Italianate graces and accompaniment. The concept of ennobled courtship invoked by lyrics and music tended to intensify the different position of the sexes, showing active men in a sordid and violent outside world, while passive women occupied a secluded and untainted domestic realm. Though popular songs progressively suggested greater limitations on the influence and freedom of women to act in the outside world, they also endowed women with an innate superiority (expressed literally in serenades) and moral authority.

In the end, though, some dissatisfaction leaked around the edges of this idyllic and innocent courtship. Both male and female writers subscribed to standard forms and mores, but the figures in their songs seem perpetually unhappy beneath their fantastic disguises, partly because of the distance between knight and maiden, partly because of the discomfort elicited by feigned nobility.

41

American popular song would pose various answers to this dissatisfaction, one beginning contemporaneously during the 1830s in the form of blackface minstrelsy. The other emerged from the course taken by non-ethnic songs over the remainder of the century, many of which also sought to bridge the chasm between separated lovers, even when they could not alter stereotypical roles.

2

Realism and National Industry

Courtship in the Gilded Age

The intensified sectional division that ended eventually in the Civil War provides more than a convenient point of division in the cultural history of the United States. By resolving the important moral and economic issues surrounding slavery, this conflict also settled certain basic matters of federal authority, and in so doing caused a reassessment in all other spheres of life. Americans increasingly came to regard themselves as constituents of a larger nation rather than residents of localities. The new national identity did not emerge without travail, and some writers view the period following the war as tragic.[1] At the very least, extraordinary turbulence marked these decades, but out of what Robert Wiebe calls "the search for order"[2] came the institutions and customs of twentieth-century America. The process was as influential on the industry of popular song as it was on heavy manufacturing, transportation, communication, and government.

At the same time, genteel popular songs about courtship began to develop the new, more realistic voice that later songwriters would use with great success at the end of the century. This new realism was studied: it invested familiar situations with heightened drama in order to arrest public attention. But these songs were realistic all the same, despite their intensifying surface of sentimentality and nostalgia carried over from the first half of the century. Realism caused suitors who had already abandoned their chargers and armor to surrender their harps and lutes, their Italian musical accents, and their high speech as well. Men (not knights) began to deal with women (not damsels) directly. And as fair maidens descended from their balconies, they too engaged actively in romance and began to participate in the affairs of the outside world.

---

1. Charles Hamm choses the title "The Old Home Ain't What It Used to Be" to represent this period (*Yesterdays: Popular Song in America* (New York, 1979), 253–54).
2. I quote the title of his book, *The Search for Order, 1877–1920* (New York, 1967).

Change engendered unrest and unhappiness, but also occasioned the energy and excitement lying just below the surface of this music. It has a vitality often lacking in the predominant mode of genteel song before the Civil War.

The Immediate Beloved

Even as sublimated courtliness reached its ripest form in songs like "Jeannie with the Light Brown Hair" (1854), "Linger in Blissful Repose" (1858), and "Thou Art the Queen of My Song" (1859), a new style of courtship pressed increasingly into genteel songs, one in which the couple enjoy close proximity and physical contact in recognizable surroundings. Silas Steel and Fred Buckley's "Kiss Me Quick and Go" (1856)[3] provides a classic example:

> The other night while I was sparking
>   Sweet Turlina Spray,
> The more we whispered our love talking,
>   The more we had to say;
> The old folks and the little folks,
>   We thought were fast in bed,
> We heard a footstep on the stairs,
>   And what d'ye think she said?
>
> *[Chorus:]*
> Kiss me quick and go my honey,
>   Kiss me quick and go!
> To cheat surprise and prying eyes,
>   Why kiss me quick and go!

The couple appears in a family parlor here (not isolated in the romantic fantasy of a medieval setting), they enjoy some intimacy rather than suffering separation, and most remarkable of all, the woman plays an active role in this ritual. She continues to play this part during a moonlit walk through the garden in the second stanza, and she retains it for the punchline in the third:

> My heart with love was nigh to split
>   To ask her for to wed,
> Said I: Shall I go for the priest,
>   And what d'ye think she said?
>   O kiss me quick and go, &c.

3. For a reproduction of the sheet music see Nicholas E. Tawa, ed., *American Solo Songs Through 1865*, vol. 1 of *Three Centuries of American Sacred and Secular Music*, Martha Furman Schleifer and Sam Dennison, eds. ([Boston], 1989), 48–50.

EXAMPLE 2.1   Fred Buckley, "Kiss Me Quick and Go" (New York: Firth, Pond & Co., 1856)

Turlina not only controls the situation, she does not even desire undying fidelity from her beau, an irony that the lyricist uses to great effect. With the disappearance of active knight and passive maiden from this song, archaic language also vanishes.

Close proximity of lover and beloved had a precedent in American popular song, particularly in the tradition of blackface, which specialized in earthy courtship and occasionally bawdy innuendo. The authors of "Kiss Me Quick" wrote originally for the minstrel stage: Fred Buckley (1833–64) toured with his family "Serenaders" after they immigrated to American from England in 1839,[4] and Silas Steel wrote many lyrics for minstrel tunes. Though this song politely rises above the lustier smirking of blackface, Buckley's music takes its cue from minstrel style (see Ex. 2.1). The phrases are short (usually two measures long), the melody tends to begin high and end in the middle of the range (avoiding the gently arched shapes of Italianate writing), the melody lacks ornamental frills, and the song ends with a four-part chorus.[5]

4. Edward Le Roy Rice, *Monarchs of Minstrelsy, from "Daddy" Rice to Date* (New York, 1911), 18.

5. Blackface style insinuated itself into more genteel realms by appropriating some aspects of more "scientific" writing. An extensive discussion of melodic style in early blackface appears in Chapter 5.

"Kiss Me Quick" participated in a vogue for songs about "sparking" that extended from the fifties into the sixties and included numbers like the anonymous "Sparking Sunday Night" (1855), "Kissing thro' the Bars" (1856) by Joseph Wood, Jr., "I Never Kiss and Tell" (1861) by C. Chauncy Burr and J. Maurice Hubbard, "If You Want a Kiss, Why, Take It" (1866) by S. H. M. Boyers and H. M. Higgins, and "Kiss Me Before You Go" (1866) by J. A. Signaigo and Alfred Langley. Stephen Foster himself tried his hand at this modern approach under the influence of the lyricist George Cooper, with "Kissing in the Dark" (1863) and "Somebody's Coming to See Me To Night" (1864). And songs continued in this vein until the craze died in the eighties with numbers like "Kiss, but Never Tell" (1873) by Frank Howard, "There Is No Harm in Kissing" (1874) by George Cooper and W. H. Brockway, "Kissing in the Moonlight" (1875) by Frank Lavarnie, "Keep on Kissing Me" (1875) by Howard Rollin, "One Sweet Kiss Before We Part" (1878) by S. Turney, and "Is There No Kiss for Me Tonight?" (1879) by Thomas P. Westendorf.

Even when realistic songs do not mention explicit contact, they offer the possibility in clearly familiar settings. James Pierpont's "Jingle Bells" (1859; originally published under the title "The One Horse Open Sleigh" in 1857)[6] devotes two of four verses to the joys of riding in the winter with young ladies:

> A day or two ago
> I thought I'd take a ride,
> And soon Miss Fannie Bright
> Was seated by my side;
> The horse was lean and lank,
> Misfortune seemed his lot,
> He got into a drifted bank,
> And we, we got upsot.

This young man engages in a common pastime and clearly relishes huddling with his sweetheart for warmth. Thus his closing recommendation about courting "in a one horse open sleigh":

> Now the ground is white
> Go it while you're young,
> Take the girls to night
> And sing this sleighing song;
> Just get a bob tailed bay
> Two forty as his speed,

6. The 1859 version appears in Richard Jackson's *Popular Songs of Nineteenth-Century America* (New York, 1976), 93–96.

> Hitch him to an open sleigh
> And crack, you'll take the lead.

Pierpont (1822–93), son of a Unitarian minister and uncle of J. Pierpont Morgan,[7] backs these words with a clipped, economic style that is the antithesis of sweet Italianate blandishments. The short phrases (reflected by the brief lines in the lyrics), narrow melodic range, and repeated-note chorus ("Jingle bells, Jingle bells, Jingle all the way . . . ") all arise from minstrel style, and they render this song so accessible and memorable that it has remained a perennial favorite. More than this, the musical style swiftly imparts a sense of immediacy to courtship: the man in this song will not languish beneath the window of his queen. Instead, he addresses courtship directly, as does the narrator in Bobby Newcomb's "Dark and Roguish Eye" (1867), who tries to pick up a woman already attached, or the equally unsuccessful suitor in Frank Howard's "My Landlady's Pretty Little Daughter" (1869).

Given the direct approach to courtship, it stands to reason that songs about the new style of love end not in death but in marriage. The ever popular "Aura Lea" (1861)[8] by William Whiteman Fosdick (1825–62) and George R. Poulton (1828–67) shows the transition between the ennobled tradition and the new directness. The lyrics spend most of their energy in praise of the beloved, and invoke high speech accordingly, for example, in the second verse:

> In thy blush the rose was born,
> Music, when you spake,
> Through thine azure eye the morn,
> Sparkling seemed to break.

The chorus continues this artificial politeness:

> Aura Lea, Aura Lea,
> Maid of golden hair;
> Sunshine came along with thee,
> Swallows in the air.

Unlike "Jeannie," or "Gentle Annie," however, Aura Lea remains both alive and proximate: in the fourth verse the enraptured suitor actually proposes after alluding to a polite intimacy:

> When the mistletoe was green,
> Midst the winter's snows,
> Sunshine in thy face was seen,

7. Ibid., 272.
8. Ibid., 14–17.

47

Kissing lips of rose.
Aura Lea, Aura Lea,
Take my golden ring;
Love and light return with thee,
And swallows in the spring.

The short phrases of this song, dedicated to S. C. Campbell of Hooley and Campbell's Minstrels, reflect the popular American idiom mastered by the English-born Poulton. The tune (Ex. 2.2), with its repeated-note refrain foreign to a more cultivated style of melody, proved so accessible that it endured long beyond the Civil War, first as "Army Blue" at West Point and later as "Love Me Tender" with words by Elvis Presley and Vera Matson. Direct confrontation between lover and beloved go hand in hand with easily comprehensible melody in unembellished style, even where the high speech persists.

Suitors in growing numbers prefer to marry living women rather than mourn dead ones in songs from around this time, and they propose with increasing alacrity. The narrator in George F. Root's "Kitty Ryder" (1861) sees "Kate" mirrored in the water and asks straightaway for her hand. The man in Frank Howard's "Minnie Munroe" (1869) spends two verses describing his beloved but declares his intentions immediately in the third, while in Harry Hunter and C. D. Fox's "Over the Garden Wall" (1870?) the couple simply elopes against the wishes of a disapproving father. Frank Dumont and John S. Cox's "The Afternoon We Met" (1870) tells the story of a whirlwind courtship in which a man uses the pretext of a dropped glove to obtain a woman's address; after one night on the town they marry. Gus Williams's "Pull Down the Blind" (1875) moves immediately from kissing in the parlor to matrimony, while the lovers in "Don't Tell Papa!" (1879) forgo the protracted arrangements of a formal wedding. Romance carried on at this pace has its pitfalls: a mother warns the young woman in "I Am Too Young to Marry" (1862) by W. H. Bourne not to accept quickly but to wait for a "man of wealth." And in "Breach of Promise" (1874) by Paul Howard, "Matilda Minking" uses love letters to

EXAMPLE 2.2   George R. Poulton, "Aura Lea" (Cincinnati: John Church, 1861)

prosecute a broken engagement, then marries another man on the day of settlement. All these songs depict real people in believable situations talking in everyday language and acting with a rapidity that would have taken the distant beloved's breath away (if she did not die first).

Realism does not exclude sentimentality, which appears in songs about marriage and fidelity with some frequency during the war and later. The most common theme concerns love that endures into old age, and such lyrics usually proceed from a retrospective point of view. A song like "When I Saw Sweet Nelly Home" (1859)[9] by John Fletcher sets the scene of initial courtship in its first stanza, and relates the proposal in the second:

> When the autumn tinged the greenwood,
> Turning all its leave to gold,
> In the lawn by elders shaded
> I my love to Nelly told.

In the last verse the husband addresses his wife:

> White hairs mingled with my tresses,
> Furrows steal upon my brow,
> But a love smile cheers and blesses
> Life's declining moments now.
> Matron in the snowy kerchief
> Closer to my bosom come,
> Tell me do'st thou still remember
> When I saw sweet Nelly home?

Just as the text mixes elevated language with plainer speech, the music also retains elements of Anglo-Italian writing amidst the more terse American style. We can find melismatic setting of text for isolated words in the verse as well as an ornamental turn (on "moments"), but the brief phrases do not allow expansive melodic lines. And Fletcher uses a four-part chorus (Ex. 2.3) with syncopations from the minstrel tradition on "glittered," "party," and "Nelly."

Other well-known members of the "fidelity" genre include George W. Johnson and James A. Butterfield's "When You and I Were Young" (1866), as well as George Cooper and Henry Tucker's "Sweet Genevieve" (1869),[10] which still sports the high speech:

> Fair Genevieve, my early love,
> The years but make thee dearer far!

9. Ibid., 229–31; also reproduced in Tawa *Solo Songs,* I, 346–49.
10. Both of these numbers appear in Jackson, *Popular Songs,* 237–40 and 202–5, respectively.

EXAMPLE 2.3   John Fletcher, "When I Saw Sweet Nelly Home" (New York: Wm. A. Pond, 1859)

My heart shall never, never rove:
Thou art my only guiding star.
For me the past has no regret,
Whate'er the years may bring to me;
I bless the hour when first we met,—
The hour that gave me love and thee!

However elevated Cooper's beloved may be, she does not dwell beyond the reach of her suitor, and the same holds true for the couple in J. Ford's "Will You Love Me When I'm Old?" (1872), and H. Strachauer's "Kiss at the Door" (1872), in which the husband's morning kiss is a sign of continuing love.

By the time of "Silver Threads Among the Gold" (1873)[11] ennoblement has disappeared completely from "fidelity" songs, leaving the sentimentality intact. The lyrics by Eben Rexford (1848–1916) present a touching story that is not at all tragic, despite its nostalgia:

When your hair is silver white,
And your cheeks no longer bright,
With the roses of the May;
I will kiss your lips and say
Oh! my darling, mine alone,
You have never older grown.

This is not a song of despondency about fading days, but a song of comfort:

Cheeks may fade and hollow grow,
But the hearts that love will know
Never, never winter's frost and chill:
Summer's warmth is in them still.

The characters in "Silver Threads" express affection plainly, without maudlin overstatement. By way of comparison with the earlier approach we might view Stephen Foster's version of the same thought in "I'll Be True to Thee" (1862):

I will be true to thee;
    I will pray for thee night and day;
Wilt thou be true to me,
    As in years that have rolled away?
When all thy childhood's dearest hopes have fled
And gloomy visions linger round thy head,

11. Ibid., 194–97.

51

When all thy dear and early friends are dead,
Then I will be true to thee.

Foster's lyrics are more melancholy by far than Rexford's.

Hart Pease Danks (1834–1903), composer of "Silver Threads," was an old hand at providing appropriate music for popular songs. Raised in Connecticut and New York, Danks spent some time in Chicago, where he became involved in church choirs as a singer and conductor. His success with a hymn tune called "Lake Street" in William B. Bradbury's *Jubilee* convinced Danks to become a composer. He soon turned to popular songs in the prewar style, with titles like "The Old Lane" (1856), "Anna Lee" (1856), and a classic serenade, "Come to the Window Love" (1865), written after he had moved to New York.[12] But he abandons genteel operatic frills in "Silver Threads" for the distinctively American popular style that emerged in the late sixties and early seventies. This style includes terse melodic periods, an intermixture of lyrical and declamatory vocal writing, a relatively narrow range, and frequent syncopation imitating the natural rhythms of speech. Danks achieves the sentimental tone in "Silver Threads" by beginning on the third note of the scale and moving upward by half-step. He also makes expressive use of large melodic leaps (Ex. 2.4). But none of his phrases lasts longer than two measures, and he sets the poetry with perfect regularity and faultlessly syllabic declamation. This is a touching ballad about a real situation painted in a manner so accessible that it generated "You Are Life and Light to Me" (1875) by Samuel Mitchell and Danks. They billed it as a "companion song to 'Silver Threads Among the Gold' " in hopes of generating another run of 300,000 copies.[13] The tradition continues in "Darling Do You Love Me Yet" (1878) by Arthur W. French and Edwin Christie and survives into the twentieth century with "Will You Love Me in December as You Do in May" (1905) by J. J. Walker and Ernest R. Ball.

Angelic Women, Demonic Men

Songs about fidelity suggest that even when women play an active part in courtship, their roles afterward remain strictly defined: they must marry and stay in the home where men still adore them as shining examples of purity. All women, in fact, marry to secure a domestic realm according to Josephine Pollard and Henry Tucker's "Girls, Get a Home of Your Own" (1866). In the first two verses Pollard discourages a woman from living with her parents,

12. A contemporary biography appears in George Birdseye, "America's Song Composers. V. H. P. Danks," *Potter's American Monthly* 12 (1879), 333–35.
13. Ibid.

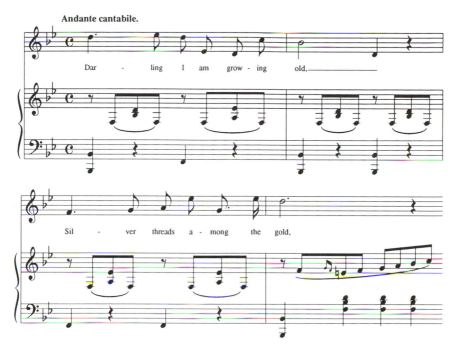

EXAMPLE 2.4 Hart P. Danks, "Silver Threads Among the Gold" (New York: Charles W. Harris, 1873)

because they inevitably expect her to act as a maid. A woman would much prefer to engage her own domestics and run her own household. Pollard advises in her third verse:

> Don't listen to those who suggest,
> A patient submission to fate,
> But try, if you can, to secure
> A partner, before it's too late.
> Though life is a lottery, girls,
> The chances we shouldn't despise;
> For we may have luck, where so many draw blank,
> To win from all others the prize!
>
> [Chorus:]
> Oh, girls, get a home of your own,
> 'Tis surely an excellent plan,
> And get, if you can, a "nice little man,"
> For who would "keep house" all alone.

There's ma-ny a maid like my-self,   With no in-cli-na-tion to   roam,

EXAMPLE 2.5   Henry Tucker, "Girls, Get a Home of Your Own" (New York: Henry Tucker, 1866)

Pollard's wife is neither passive in courtship nor subordinate in domestic matters. Tucker (1826–82), a Brooklyn music teacher and composer, sets Pollard's text to a patter song in 6/8 (see Ex. 2.5), repeating short motives in catchy patterns. His piano accompaniment is typical of the later sixties and the decade of the seventies: block chords prevail, punctuating various rhythms. But these do not take the simple shape they do in Foster: Tucker often doubles the bass at the octave or doubles the fifth and the root in the right hand, creating a more substantial sound and calling for a slightly more accomplished technique. This is still music for the middle classes, though, and it reflects their musical abilities and moral values.

Once in the home, women continued in popular song to be the acme of purity and goodness. "Every Household Has Its Angel," declares John Summers Cox in the title of his 1862 song. She is "loving in affliction, constant in her sorest trials," and also a splendid parent. The stereotype became so pronounced that Nellie Parker was moved to write a song at the end of the century entitled "There Are No Angel Men" (1890), which projected a lack of company for women in paradise, since they alone were beatified in popular lyrics. The sexual divisions of role established at such great length by the chivalric tradition of prewar songs remained in the background, even when outward custom changed.

Realism in popular song after the war brings an ironic twist to the legacy of distinct male and female realms, however. Because men no longer play the knight errant, their contact with the sordid outside world simply makes them mean, even habitually evil. The female narrator in "You Naughty, Naughty Men" (1866)[14] by T. Kennick and G. Bicknell sketches males as slightly ignoble suitors:

14. Reprinted in Stanley Appelbaum's *Show Songs from "The Black Crook" to "The Red Mill"* (New York, 1974), 1–6; Appelbaum suggests that the song may be British in origin, but its first appearance in print seems to be American (xix).

When you want a kiss or favour
You put on your best behaviour,
And your looks of kindness savour,
Oh! you naughty, naughty men,
Of love you set us dreaming,
And when with hope we're teeming,
We find you are but scheming,
You naughty, naughty men.

Although Kennick intends these lyrics playfully, their banter takes a sinister turn. Men pursue women for money,

And when married how you treat us,
And of each fine wish defeat us,
And some will even beat us,
Oh! you naughty, naughty men,
You take us from our mothers,
From our sisters, and our brothers,
When you get us, flirt with others,
Oh! you cruel, wicked men.

Because women are still morally superior, they can castigate men in this hit song from *The Black Crook*,[15] even when they are temporarily liberated from a domestic setting and actively express their attraction to the opposite sex. The narrator in "Naughty Men" spins out a patter of condemnation, even as she flirts and eventually forgives male shortcomings in the last verse.

Limited to their undefiled private world, women exert power over the squalid public domain of men by projecting domestic values into it. This process manifests itself most clearly in popular songs about temperance. The temperance movement in American history was heavily dominated by women and served them as a model for organizing the kind of political action that would eventually secure their civil rights.[16] Popular song had seen a scattering of early temperance songs like the Hutchinsons' "King Alchohol" (1843), a parody on the folk song "King Andrew." Testimony to the efficacy of the movement also appears in the form of anti-temperance songs, common before the war in minstrelsy (see "Pop Goes the Weasel" in Chapter 5) and also in more genteel songs like Henry Russell's "The Total S'iety" (1840).[17] Adopting the spirit of the movement later, Stephen Foster would contribute a standard plot for many other temperance songs in "The Wife" (1860):

15. For an account of the production see Deane L. Root, *American Popular Stage Music, 1860–1880* (Ann Arbor, 1981), 79–96.

16. See Barbara Leslie Epstein, *The Politics of Domesticity: Women, Evangelism, and Temperance in Nineteenth-Century America* (Middletown, CT, 1981).

17. See Tawa, *Solo Songs,* I, 65–68.

He'll come home, he'll not forget me,
For his word is always true.
He's gone to sup the deadly cup,
And while the long night through
He's gone to quaff, and talk and laugh
To while the drear night through:
He'll come home, he'll not forget me,
For his word is always true.

The master of the temperance song, however, was Henry Clay Work (1832–84), the ultimate composer of quintessentially realistic popular song during the sixties and seventies. According to the short biography included in a collection of his songs by nephew Bertram, Work was the son of the abolitionist Alanson Work, who was briefly imprisoned for his efforts with the Underground Railroad.[18] Henry grew up in Connecticut, but eventually moved to Chicago, and George Frederick Root, the musical director of the publishing house Root and Cady, recalls:

> One day early in the [Civil War] a quiet and rather solemn-looking young man, poorly clad, was sent up to my room from the store with a song for me to examine. I looked at it and then at him in astonishment. It was "Kingdom Coming,"—elegant in manuscript, full of bright, good sense and comical situations in its "darkey" dialect—the words fitting the melody almost as aptly and neatly as Gilbert fits Sullivan—the melody decidedly good and taking, and the whole exactly suited to the times. "Did you write this—words and music?" I asked. A gentle "Yes" was the answer. "What is your business, if I may inquire?" "I am a printer." "Would you rather write music than set type?" "Yes." "Well, if this is a specimen of what you can do, I think you may give up the printing business." He liked that idea very much, and an arrangement with us was soon made. He needed some musical help that I could give him, and we needed just such songs as he could write. The connection, which continued some years, proved very profitable both to him and to us. This was Henry C. Work, whose principal songs while he was with us were "Kingdom Coming," "Babylon Is Fallen," "Wake, Nicodemus," "Ring the Bell, Watchman," "Song of a Thousand Years," "Marching thro' Georgia" and "Come Home, Father."[19]

Work's family background led him to endow most of his songs with a pronounced moralistic zeal, and none bears these marks more clearly than the last song on Root's list. The Women's Christian Temperance Union, with headquarters in the Chicago suburb of Evanston, would adopt "Come Home, Fa-

18. Henry Clay Work, *Songs,* Bertram G. Work, ed., vol. 19 of Earlier American Music (New York, 1974); Richard S. Hill corrects some of Bertram's biography in "The Mysterious Chord of Henry Clay Work," *Notes* 10 (1953), 211–25, 367–90.
19. George Frederick Root, *The Story of a Musical Life* (Cincinnati, 1891), 137–38.

ther!'' (1864)[20] as its theme, and the dedicatory verse on the first page leaves no doubt as to its tone:

> 'Tis the Song of Little Mary
> Standing at the bar-room door
> While the shameful midnight revel
> Rages wildly as before.

The miscreant husband in this veristic account is a ''mechanic'' (the generic term for a worker) squandering his pay:

> Father, dear father, come home with me now!
> The clock in the steeple strikes one;
> You said you were coming right home from the shop,
> As soon as your day's work was done.
> Our fire has gone out, our house is all dark
> And mother's been watching since tea,
> With poor brother Benny so sick in her arms,
> And no one to help her but me.

As the bell tolls progressively later hours, the child grows weaker and dies. True, Work uses heightened sentimentality to punctuate his moral, but the overstatement does not exclude realism. The characters inhabiting the story are meant to be common folk brought into mean circumstances by an all-too-prevalent human failing. Here we see the moral purity of the home projected into the hard outside world in the form of innocent Mary, as the chorus suggests (Ex. 2.6). The composer's melodic writing exemplifies the ease and fluidity attained in the best popular songs from this period, which often feature an increasingly chromatic palette. Work had a peculiar talent for close part-writing in his choruses, and as Root reminds us, ''[He] was a slow, painstaking writer, being from one to three weeks upon a song; but when the work was done it was like a piece of fine mosaic, especially in the fitting of words to music.''[21]

Work did not recapture the musical charm of ''Come Home, Father!'' in ''Lillie of the Snow-Storm or 'Please, Father, Let Us In!' '' (1866),[22] though he clearly meant its lyrics to capitalize on his earlier success. But the text tells us much about the changed status of men, who sometimes bring the cruelty of the outside world into the domestic scene:

20. Work, *Songs*, 53–56.
21. Ibid.
22. Ibid., 75–78.

EXAMPLE 2.6   Henry Clay Work, "Come Home, Father!" (Chicago: Root & Cady, 1864)

To his home, his once-loved cottage,
Late at night a poor inebriate came;
To his wife, the waiting wife and daughter
Who for him had fann'd the midnight flame.
Rudely met, they answer'd him with kindness,
Gave him all their own untasted store;
'Twas but small, and he with awful curses,
Spurn'd the gift, and drove them from his door.

In the midst of a "wild, wintry tempest" the mother and child make their way to an abandoned shack on the prairie, where the mother dies, and

> Morning dawns, the husband and the father,
> Sober'd now, to seek his flock has come,
> Lillie dear is living, but her mother
> Hours ago, an angel bore her home.
> Ah, poor man! how bitter is his anguish,
> As he now repents his punish'd sin,
> Bending o'er the child, who, half unconscious,
> Sadly cries, "Please father let us in!"

This song is no less moving than "Come Home, Father!," but lacking Work's usual gift of tunefulness, it failed to make the lasting impression of the earlier hit. One contemporary biographer claimed in 1879 that "Come Home, Father!" "was the pioneer and pattern for all the many temperance pieces now in the market, not a few of which are very palpable imitations."[23] As testimony we have Mrs. E. A. [Susan] Parkhurst's "Father's a Drunkard and Mother Is Dead" ("Dark is the night, and the storm rages wild, / God pity Bessie, the drunkard's lone child," 1868), her "Don't Marry a Man If He Drinks" (ca. 1868), and Frank Howard's "Little Bother" (published by Root and Cady in 1869), who asks at the door of the saloon, "Tell me have you seen my father?" Later Work himself would continue with "King Bibler's Army" (1877).

The separation between the domains of the two genders intensified by the fantasy of early nineteenth-century song thus worked to the detriment of both men and women. Men became demons whose public behavior injured those around them. Women remained in confinement (though the purity used as an excuse to segregate them from the outside world also endowed them with the means to challenge male domination). The image of the demonic man remained so vivid throughout the century that Isidore Witmark would write many decades later:

"Mother has been praised in all sorts of songs for centuries," said the late lamented J. W. Kelly. "No one seems to think it worth while to bother with sentimental songs about the old man." . . . To be sure, there were a few daddy songs: *Father, Dear Father, Come Home with Me Now,* and *The Old Man's Drunk Again.* "But why," asked Kelly, "don't somebody reach into the soup pot and place Papa on the pinnacle of fame by writing a

23. Work practiced what he preached as a dedicated teetotaler. See George Birdseye, "America's Song Composers. IV. Henry C. Work," *Potter's American Monthly* 12 (1879), 285.

dacent song about him?'' . . . Years and years later, what was the song that that same civilized world would be singing? *Everybody Works But Father*. . . .[24]

To paraphrase Witmark, after Henry Clay Work it was difficult to rehabilitate the "stronger sex."

Work not only produced some of the most vivid art during the sixties and seventies, his career reveals a good deal about the business of popular music in these decades. Though he had no notion he would become a professional composer when he moved to Chicago, he earned a tidy sum from the songs he published exclusively with Root and Cady during the sixties (enough to invest in a family truck farm outside New York City, which unfortunately went bankrupt). He returned to typesetting in the seventies, taught music sporadically, and signed yet another exclusive contract with Chauncey M. Cady, now relocated in New York after the Chicago fire of 1871. Here Work composed his most famous song, "Grandfather's Clock," published in 1876. But his reward for this one number, $4000 (a tidy sum at that time), could not support him through fallow periods.[25] If we guess that Work received two or three cents in royalties for each copy of his songs, a hit over a period of several years would sell between 100,000 and 300,000 copies, just a fraction of the potential, national market.

Music publishers had yet to organize on a national scale. They persisted in the same basic wholesale-retail approach they had taken since the beginning of the century in concerns run by men like Graupner, Carr, Hewitt, Atwill, and Fiot. Root and Cady—Henry Clay Work's publisher—presented a typical picture of such a business at mid-century in George F. Root's description:

> In 1863, having outgrown our quarters on Clark street, we moved into the Crosby Opera-house building, then just erected on Washington street, near State. This store and basement were one hundred and eighty feet long by thirty in width, to which was eventually added a building just across the alley in the rear, which aggregated a still larger floor area. The basement in this rear building was occupied by our printing-office and steam presses, and the main floor by pianos and organs. The second story had rooms for band and orchestra instruments and "small goods," and one fitted up for my use. Here I made my books and songs, and looked after the publishing interests of the house. This large amount of room was necessitated by the buying out of various small musical establishments, culminating in the purchase of the ex-

24. Isidore Witmark and Isaac Goldberg, *From Ragtime to Swingtime* (New York, 1939), 177–78.

25. The details of Work's career come from Hill, "The Mysterious Chord," and Birdseye, "Henry C. Work."

tensive catalogue, with all its music plates, of the entire stock of Henry Tolman & Co., of Boston—two or three car loads.[26]

The only way such local establishments extended their reach was to expand their corresponding relationships with similar publishers in other cities (a tactic that dated from the beginning of the century). The cover of sheet music like that for "Sweet Genevieve" (Illus. 2.1) will often list corresponding firms. Others in this network included Balmer and Weber in St. Louis, Werlein in New Orleans, S. Brainard and Sons in Cleveland, John Church in Cincinnati, Oliver Ditson in Boston, Lee and Walker in Philadelphia, and Lyon and Healy in Chicago. Advertising and distribution remained decentralized, and diversified wholesale-retail enterprises could not focus their energies on publishing alone. Under these conditions, even a composer fortunate enough to have an agreement for royalties (instead of receiving a lump sum for a song) could earn only a limited return on his labor.

This conduct of business also affected the style of popular music during the period. We can speak of a loose dialect in songs from the decades immediately after the war: the short phrases, four-part choruses, and syncopated declamation developed by minstrelsy became generic in pieces from the late sixties to the early eighties. Composers also added a certain amount of chromatic motion in both harmony and melody as well as slightly fuller writing for the piano (see any of the examples cited above). But aside from these general traits, we do not see a succession of narrowly focused styles dominating the national scene for brief, defined periods. The localized industry of music publishing was not, in the end, sufficiently coherent to enforce such uniformity.

Entertainment and Specialty Publishing: The Creation of Tin Pan Alley

The development of popular song as a national industry resulted from a convergence of several factors, including a centralization of the entertainment business facilitated by more rapid communication and travel, the rise of wholesale publishing houses, and a standardization of musical technique in songs coupled with more alluring lyrics. Edward Marks, one of the most successful songwriter-publishers in this new system, identifies the first of its components:

Tony Pastor's new Fourteenth Street house was an institution, and always packed to the roof from the opening night, October 24, 1881. Tony was the first manager to tour the country with variety in 1878. In the Christmas number of the *Dramatic Mirror* for 1881 he advertised that his theater "has become a great success; its clientele are the best families of the metropolis,

26. Root, *The Story,* 141.

61

its endorsers the entire press of the city.'' He boasted that it was ''the first specialty and vaudeville theater of America, catering to polite tastes, aiming to amuse, and fully up to current times and topics.'' This is the first professional use of the word ''vaudeville'' that I have seen.[27]

The institution of vaudeville would begin officially in 1894 with the opening of Benjamin Franklin Keith's house in Boston,[28] but ''variety'' (an entertainment combining many different acts on one bill) had taken over many theaters from minstrelsy long before the nineties. It was considered a ''family'' entertainment because it did not involve the rude jokes and risque costumes of burlesque nor the drinking and carousing of the dance hall.

Technological advance in the service of national mobility was the essential factor in spreading the craze for variety. Linking the far-flung, newly solidified union by a system of rails had been one of the most important postwar enterprises, accomplished so quickly and with such explosive vigor that railroading became the goal of many ambitious capitalists and the downfall of almost as many more. Though the excesses of the railroads would ultimately demand redress, the Vanderbilts, Goulds, and Harrimans did succeed within the span of a few decades in speeding travel by several orders of magnitude for all Americans, including entertainers. The combination of rapid transit by rail and instant communication by telegraph enabled variety to expand across the country. The benefit to individual theater owners was manifest. Individual acts traveled from city to city, accepting engagements for short runs as part of composite bills. Each theater would feature famous performers (known as Head-liners) along with lesser known acts on the side, and at least some part of the show would appeal to every member of the audience:

> No act or ''turn'' consumes much over thirty minutes. Everyone's taste is consulted, and if one objects to the perilous feats of the acrobats or jugglers he can read his program or shut his eyes for a few moments and he will be compensated by some sweet bell-ringing or a sentimental or comic song, graceful or grotesque dancing, a one-act farce, trained animals, legerdemain, impersonations, clay modelling, or the stories of the comic monologist.[29]

If a particular player failed to make hit, the rest of the show carried the house along.

At the same time theater owners limited their risk and drew two or three houses a day, performers capitalized on the market:

> At first the [famous] actor, who is sentimental rather than practical, was inclined to the belief that it was beneath his dignity to appear on the stage

---

27. Edward B. Marks and Abbott J. Liebling, *They All Sang, from Tony Pastor to Rudy Vallée* (New York, 1934), 12.

28. See Charles W. Stein's ''Preface'' to *American Vaudeville as Seen by Its Contemporaries* (New York, 1984), xi.

29. Edwin Milton Royal, ''The Vaudeville Theatre,'' ibid., 26.

with "a lot of freaks," but he was tempted by salaries no one else could afford to pay (sometimes as high as $500 to $1000 per week) and by the amount of attention afforded to the innovation by the newspapers.[30]

Because a run would last no longer than a few weeks, acts were free to seek better offers on a regular basis. Entertainers relied on agencies to negotiate bookings by wire, and the most important of these conducted their business from New York, partly because institutionalized variety made its start there, partly because the city had a large pool of talent, including access to foreign acts.[31]

It did not take long for a few clever publishers in New York to realize the implications of this newly centralized, national system of entertainment for the merchandising of popular songs. Isidore Witmark, an enterprising teenager, opened a printing shop in the mid-eighties with his brothers, backed by their father's financing. Coincidentally, one of the family was also a stage performer:

> Julius Witmark was a natural-born "plugger." For him to sing a song was to start the song on the road to possible fortune. In 1885 there were no phonographs, no gramophones, no radios, to duplicate simultaneously the singing of a piece. For that matter, long after the invention and the commercialization of the phonograph, the singer would remain the great vehicle of publicity for composer and publishing firm.[32]

The notion of having famous singers present songs in public and endorse them by attaching their name was not new; from the beginning of the century popular sheet music had listed performers, and minstrels had often promoted songs. But the variety circuit on which a single performer could present a composition several times a day in several cities over a period of weeks raised the level of exposure exponentially. Edward Marks sketches the process from beginning to end:

> People in the business have a saying that "a plug's a plug," meaning that any is better than none. Today, the most esteemed plugs are those given by the radio stars. Forty years ago, however, with its initial break in the beer hall, a song might work up to the smaller variety houses, and finally to Tony Pastor's, on Fourteenth Street, or Koster and Bial's, whence some British singer might carry it home to London. If it scored there, it might come back here as a society sensation. And the whole process, from bottom to top, might take several years, during which the gross sales mounted steadily.[33]

30. Ibid., 27; a lengthy discussion of theater finances by Hartley Davis appears in this same volume, "The Business Side of Vaudeville," 114–23.
31. See Alfred L. Bernheim, "The Facts of Vaudeville," ibid., 124–30.
32. Witmark, *From Ragtime*, 60.
33. *They All Sang*, 3.

At the same time variety offered new opportunities in promotion and advertising, publishers with foresight founded wholesale firms which offered a limited catalogue of recent popular hits. They ran their enterprises out of offices, owned no retail outlets, and sometimes contracted for outside printing of their songs. Among the early firms to employ the new method were T. B. Harms, M. Witmark & Sons, Willis Woodward, and Spaulding & Gray. In the 1890s these and other wholesalers congregated in a district on West 28th Street, which composer Monroe H. Rosenfeld dubbed "Tin Pan Alley."[34] Here singers could audition songs in the small piano studios of various publishers, who often provided them with incentives to include pieces as part of their vaudeville acts.[35]

At first the new system offered by variety affected the style more than the content of songs about courtship by lending them a more polished and professional air. "Kissing in the Rain" (1884) by Monroe Rosenfeld presents a good instance of a transitional song from the eighties. The theme of the lyrics continues a subject popular in songs from the fifties through the seventies. As in many of those songs, the suitor here does not dally beneath the window of his beloved:

> Upon one stormy evening
> I met a lassie fair,
> Her eyes were full of sunshine,
> Her locks of flaxen hair,
> I watched her gaily tripping,
> With graceful flowing train,
> And stooping tho' I know 'twas wrong,
> I kissed her in the rain.

The woman puts up token resistance in the second verse (indicating she really likes him), and in the third verse he concludes the story:

> May e'vry cloud grow darker,
> My heart is ever light,
> With me 'tis always summer,
> With flowers blooming bright;
> And I'm as proud as any
> All honors to disdain,
> She says I am her *rain beau*
> Since I kissed her in the rain.

34. Ibid., 74
35. Marks discusses this early "payola" and its later currency in radio in ibid., 133–35.

EXAMPLE 2.7   Monroe H. Rosenfeld, "Kissing in the Rain" (New York: Hitch-cock's Music Store, 1884)

Though the sentiment is nothing new, punning in the lyrics—that cleverness which moves us to smile—provides one of the song's "hooks" (the feature that catches attention). This arresting quality extends to the music as well, especially the chorus which has now grown longer than it was in the preceding decades and omits four-part writing in favor of a solo voice for a one-man act (Ex. 2.7). To render the chorus memorable, Rosenfeld tends to repeat short melodic phrases, either in modified sequence (the two initial settings of "Kissing in the rain") or at pitch ("One sweet kiss" is a variation on "Kissing in the rain," and so forth). In addition, the accompaniment has become more elaborate when compared with those by earlier composers, with an active right hand (whose ornaments significantly are not reproduced by the voice) and full chords in the left. The musical language has become even more chromatic, featuring many more flats and sharps inserted in music. Both of these developments reflect the practice of the professional singers and composers populating variety, and significantly, Rosenfeld dedicated this song to "Mr. Tony Pastor." Marks writes:

> . . . [Rosenfeld] had the knack of producing hit tunes—his own or others—
> and he could get them sung. He would nurse young singers along as he did
> song writers. Emma Carus was one of his finds. (She was working in a hotel

when he first detected a valuable timbre in her speaking voice.) Then he was ever ready to put a performer's name on the covers as author. That flattered them.[36]

The sheet music for "Kissing in the Rain" still aimed at the middle-class consumer and its publisher (Hitchcock's Music Store) was still an old-fashioned wholesale-retail house. But this song imported into the parlor just a bit of the glamour and calculated luster that attached to variety acts.

In the same year that Monroe Rosenfeld published "Kissing in the Rain," Edward Haley applied a similar formula to "The Fountain in the Park" (1884)[37] with more spectacular results. Haley tells yet another story of impulsive romance:

> While strolling in the park one day,
> All in the merry month of May,
> A roguish pair of eyes they took me by surprise,
> In a moment my poor heart they stole away!
> Oh a sunny smile was all she gave to me
> And of course we were as happy as could be.

The man proposes marriage the same day and is accepted, of course: there is nothing in this story to render it more memorable or appealing than Rosenfeld's or many others. But the tune (Ex. 2.8) is unforgettable, because it incessantly repeats the same material in different transpositions, first for the beginning of each line, then within one line (the music for "they took me by surprise" is just a variation on the music for "A roguish pair of eyes") and extends the pattern into the chorus as well. Willis Woodward, one of the earliest wholesalers specializing in the publication of popular music, used the hook provided by this "sequential" treatment of melody to much more commercial advantage than Hitchcock had for "Kissing in the Rain." As a result "The Fountain in the Park" would later become a perennial favorite when the heyday of Tin Pan Alley finally arrived, and the song would remain popular into the twentieth century.

By the end of the eighties, then, all but one of the basic preconditions for a national industry of popular song had been fulfilled. Variety offered an extended and coherent system for promotion, Tin Pan Alley publishing houses specializing in popular music stood ready, and composers had a standardized musical technique at their service. But songwriters had not yet discovered a conceit sufficiently arresting to guarantee commercial success, and this they would find in the music and situations associated with the waltz.

36. Ibid., 75.
37. A facsimile of this sheet music appears in Robert A. Fremont's *Favorite Songs of the Nineties* (New York, 1973), 86–89.

EXAMPLE 2.8   Edward Haley, "The Fountain in the Park" (New York: Willis Woodward, 1884)

The Lascivious Waltz

Waltz songs were not at all new to America in the eighties and nineties. Most of the early ones originated in Great Britain, including "The Flying Trapeze" (American copyright, 1868) by George Leybourne, "Love's Old Sweet Song" (American copyright, 1884) by G. Clifton Bingham and J. L. Molloy, and "Daisy Bell" (or "A Bicycle Made for Two," 1892) by Harry Dacre, which initiated a craze in 1890 according to Marks.[38] With this history of importation and with roots in German ethnicity, the waltz seems an unlikely candidate for the honor of generating the first Tin Pan Alley hits. But somehow the foreign, ethnic origins of the waltz were forgotten. Instead, listeners concentrated on its properties as a dance and on the associations with that activity. We should remember that before the Civil War society preferred contra dances where men and women were separated by distance and touched minimally for discrete intervals. Even the polka was performed most often as a square dance according to Albert Smith's and John Parry's "The Polka Explained" (1842). However much the waltz in its early history may have been related to a folkish contra dance, the *Ländler,* in nineteenth-century Britain and American partners held

38. *They All Sang,* 34.

each other closely and often whirled vigorously (the fact would provide a subject for "Waltz Me Around Again Willie" (1906), which amuses itself over two hapless clerks devoured by a dance maven after long hours at the store).

The physical contact and energy demanded by the waltz ultimately led to a covert association with the more titillating aspects of courtship, as the cover engraving from "After the Ball" (Illus. 2.2) suggests. This opulent vision of the dance floor shows some couples whirling madly, others in close embraces, while on the edge of the dance floor some gossip and others (in the foreground) flirt. As beholders of the scene, we stand just on the edge of a libidinal maelstrom. This kind of dancing held the potential for very intimate dealings, indeed. As Isaac Goldberg recalls vividly regarding this very waltz song at the 1893 Columbian Exposition:

> What the dance itself may have been, with its abdominal rotations and its slithering insinuations, was left to the day-dreams of the millions who could not hope to visit the Midway Plaisance. The music of it, however, with its insistent tom-tom and lascivious twists, worked its spell wherever it could penetrate, and the parodies left no doubt that the Nineties, if they ever got the chance, could be most orientally naughty.[39]

Waltz songs about courtship (the generalization does not apply to waltz songs on other subjects) contain an element of sexuality which they sublimate for presentation in the primary venue of sheet music, the family parlor. Marks observed of this polite subterfuge, "Only ladies played the piano, and ladies never admitted that they were not innocent."[40] Because waltz songs disguised desire, they were often associated with frustrated romance, though of a kind very different from the chivalric fantasy dominating the first half of the nineteenth century. Disappointment in courtship at the end of the century stemmed not from distance but from proximity: the waltz held the promise of an intimacy that sometimes went unfulfilled. This connotation became so strong that it persisted far into the twentieth century as a poignant symbol. In *Show Boat* Kern and Hammerstein used it to denote the ill-fated courtship of Magnolia and Gaylord in "You Are Love." Rodgers and Hammerstein selected a waltz as the very emblem of the failed relationship in *Carousel*, as a reminiscence of a dead spouse in "Hello Young Lovers" *(The King and I)*, as a plaint about lost love in "This Nearly Was Mine" *(South Pacific)*, and as a reminder of a lost innocence and rural beauty in "Edelweiss" *(The Sound of Music)*. As late as Meredith Willson's *Music Man* frustrated courtship sounded to the strains of the waltz in "Good Night My Someone."

Waltz songs began to multiply at an astonishing rate in the 1880s, and they generally portray lovers arranging meetings. "When the Dew Begins to Fall"

39. Isaac Goldberg, *Tin Pan Alley: A Chronicle of the American Popular Music Racket* (New York, 1930), 103.
40. *They All Sang*, 38.

(1882) by J. W. Turner tells the story of an evening tryst; "I'm Just Going Down to the Gate" (1882) by Gus Williams and Joseph P. Skelly relates how a woman escapes her parents to meet and later elope with her suitor; "Chicadee" (1882) by the same pair features a comic story of a meeting foiled by the family dog; and "When Nelly Was Raking the Hay" (1885) by Charles A. Davies places the meeting "by the millstream." The waltz also attaches to the intimacy of established couples in "Alone at Last" (1882) by Harry B. Smith and George Schleiffarth, in "My Shy and Timid Way" (1886) by Sidney Rosenfeld and Henry Widmer, and in "Beneath the Mistletoe" (1886) by J. E. T. Dowe and Frank H. Brackett.

Composers did not fully realize the potential of the waltz song until the nineties, though. The classic was Charles K. Harris's "After the Ball" (1892),[41] which sold more than 400,000 copies in the first months of publication at the rate of over 5000 a day. Harris (1867–1930), a self-taught banjoist and pianist, assimilated the clearly defined style of Tin Pan Alley by ear and dictated his tunes to arrangers (Joseph Clauder in the case of "After the Ball"), who also provided the accompaniment.[42] He realized right away that the first hook set by a hit song came from its tune, "the music or the harmony is the thing . . . first, last, and all the time."[43] And because of its origins in the abstract motivic repetition of instrumental practice, Harris also knew that the waltz provided the perfect vehicle for the melodic economy established earlier by composers like Rosenfeld as the basis of Tin Pan Alley songs. Harris's verse for "After the Ball" features the same opening motive for five of eight phrases (most of which are sequential variations of one another; see Ex. 2.9), while the remaining three use an alternate. The chorus utilizes the device, with a head motive taken from the verse and repeated exactly or in sequence for the first three appearances of the word "after" (Ex. 2.10) and later for the phrase "many a heart." This constant reiteration makes the tune memorable.

Harris also understood that the text could provide a second hook to reinforce the musical one:

> Of course, if the lyrics are particularly good or out of the ordinary, as is sometimes the case with a comic or jazz song having a catch line, such as *Yes, We Have No Bananas*, which appeals to the sense of humor of the average person, so much the better for the song and its ultimate success.[44]

In "After the Ball" this "catch line" is the constantly repeated phrase used for the title (the line would become so famous that the publishing firm founded by Harris would put a boy chasing a ball on its covers as a logo). The content of the lyrics was the third factor in creating a hit: all early Tin Pan Alley songs

41. Reprinted in Fremont, *Favorite Songs,* 1–5.
42. For an account of the song's genesis, see Charles K. Harris, *After the Ball: Forty Years of Melody* (New York, 1926), 62–63.
43. Ibid., 19.
44. Ibid.

EXAMPLE 2.9 Charles K. Harris, "After the Ball," verse (Milwaukee and New York: Chas. K. Harris, 1892)

have narrative verses that progressively unfold a miniature drama, preparing a chorus that supplies a moral, commentary, or sentiment. "After the Ball" presents a story of failed courtship with an undercurrent of frustrated sexuality:

> A little maiden climbed an old man's knee,
> Begged for a story— "Do Uncle please."
> Why are you single; why live alone?
> Have you no babies; have you no home?
> "I had a sweetheart, years, years ago;

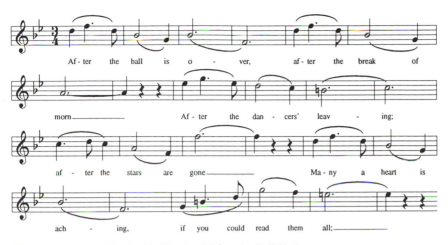

EXAMPLE 2.10   Charles K. Harris, "After the Ball," chorus

> Where she is now pet, you will soon know.
> List to the story, I'll tell it all,
> I believed her faithless after the ball."

The old man then relates how he catches his beloved talking to another man at the dance and abandons her, only to discover after her death (of a broken heart) that the interloper is no suitor but her brother. The promise of romance goes unfulfilled:

> After the ball is over, after the break of morn—
> After the dancers' leaving; after the stars are gone;
> Many a heart is aching, if you could read them all;
> Many the hopes that have vanished after the ball.

However exaggerated the story, it portrays essentially middle-class people in a familiar ritual of courtship. In fact, Harris drew the scene from a personal encounter he witnessed at a dance in Chicago.[45] This is realism heightened by a sentimental dramatization in the service of commerce, as Harris freely admits:

> Of course, I capitalized on the sentiment in the last four lines of the chorus, and out of its fabric were spun the three verses contained in that ballad. . . .
> In all my ballads I have purposely injected goodly doses of sentiment, and invariably the whole country paused.[46]

45. Ibid., 54–56.
46. Ibid., 57–62.

Not only did the country pause, it purchased nearly two million copies of sheet music for this song in about two years, sales an order of magnitude larger than publishers in the sixties or seventies enjoyed over the period of many years. This commerce owed much to the ingredients used to create the song but just as much to Harris's enlistment of a famous singer, J. Aldrich Libby; he sang the number as part of his act in variety theaters across the country. By the time of the Columbian Exposition in Chicago, Harris was famous as the man who wrote "After the Ball."

After Harris set the style, many successful waltz songs capitalized on the sexual undercurrent surrounding the dance, the most obvious being "The Band Played On" (1895)[47] by John F. Palmer and Charles B. Ward (who brought it to the stage).[48] Palmer's protagonist, "Matt Casey," forms a social club, hires a hall, and holds a gathering on Saturday night:

> Such kissing in the corner and such whisp'ring in the hall,
> And telling tales of love behind the stairs.
> As Casey was the favorite and he that ran the ball,
> Of kissing and lovemaking did his share.
> At twelve o'clock exactly they all would fall in line,
> Then march down to the dining hall and eat.
> But Casey would not join them although ev'ry thing was fine,
> But he stayed upstairs to exercise his feet.

Ward sets this and the other verses to a march, while he reserves the waltz for the chorus:

> Casey would waltz with a strawberry blonde,
> And the Band played on,
> He'd glide cross the floor with the girl he ador'd,
> and the Band played on,
> But his brain was so loaded it nearly exploded,
> The poor girl would shake with alarm.
> He'd ne'er leave the girl with the strawberry curls,
> And the Band played on.

To satisfy propriety, he chastely marries his partner in the third verse, but not before Palmer has engaged in some racier innuendo. Palmer and Ward, like Harris before them, have indulged double realism here by combining their tale about ordinary characters and events with musical description: Casey's dancing takes place to appropriate dance rhythms in the chorus. Ward has developed

---

47. Reprinted in Fremont, *Favorite Songs,* 15–19.
48. Marks prints an appendix of famous songs, their publishers, and the artists that introduced them in *They All Sang.*

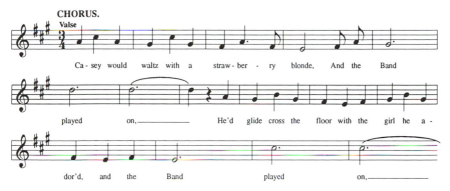

CHORUS.

Ca - sey would waltz with a straw - ber - ry blonde, And the Band played on,——— He'd glide cross the floor with the girl he a - dor'd, and the Band played on,———

EXAMPLE 2.11   Charles B. Ward, ''The Band Played On'' (New York: The New York Music Company, 1895)

his musical hook intensively here: the head motive of each phrase descends sequentially in one measure units (with some variation; see Ex. 2.11). And the second phrase presents a variation on the first. Both phrases end with the poetic ''catch line'' that becomes the title of the song.

The chorus increasingly became the focus of Tin Pan Alley composers, to the point where Edward Marks wrote of a trip to the Atlantic Gardens dance hall:

> . . . Louis [the Whistler] had been circulating among the tables, distributing sheets of the refrain from ''Elsie from Chelsea.'' . . . Having polished off a second bottle of Bass, Jennie [Lindsey] ascended the platform. . . . The verse doesn't matter. Nobody ever remembered it anyway. When she sang the second refrain, Louis picked it up and whistled. A fair number of the men in the crowd whistled with him. It was a cinch that some of the women would want it for their pianos tomorrow.[49]

Though the ''refrain'' set the hook, Marks underemphasized the importance of the verse: it created the situation that gave the chorus meaning, even if the music for the verse was less memorable. And the meaning had to be something relevant to a crowd at the Atlantic Gardens.

Even when a waltz song features characters from the upper class, its message must have a wider appeal. ''The Moth and the Flame'' (1899) by George Taggart and Max S. Witt sounds an egalitarian note by telling the story of a woman about to marry a wealthy bigamist. Her ''honest love'' of former years warns of her peril in the first verse, and she is saved at the end of the second verse, while the waltzing chorus proclaims the moral. The classic variation on this theme, ''A Bird in a Gilded Cage'' (1900)[50] by Arthur J. Lamb and Harry Von Tilzer, also combines lofty setting and egalitarian sentiments:

49. Ibid., 7–8.
50. Reprinted in Fremont, *Favorite Songs*, 34–37.

73

The ballroom was filled with fashion's throng,
It shone with a thousand lights,
And there was a woman who passed along,
The fairest of all the sights,
A girl to her lover then softly sighed,
There's riches at her command;
But she married for wealth, not for love, he cried,
Though she lives in a mansion grand.

The chorus focuses on frustrated sexuality:

She's only a bird in a gilded cage,
A beautiful sight to see,
You may think she's happy and free from care,
She's not, though she seems to be,
'Tis sad when you think of her wasted life,
For youth cannot mate with age,
And her beauty was sold,
For an old man's gold,
She's a bird in a gilded cage.

In the second verse this beauty dies, leaving her "happier" than she was in a loveless marriage. The whole song has an ironic quality to its melodrama, as if the authors' manipulation of sentiment were meant to be obvious. Von Tilzer (1872–1946) overdoes the chromatic interludes between phrases (see Ex. 2.12), making a caricature of a period cliché in which important cadences sported harmonies descending by half-step (for instance, the end of the chorus in "On the Banks of the Wabash Far Away"). He highlights the artificiality of the grand scene he envisions to lend more weight to the obviously middle-class narrator and his moral about wealth. The composer had extra motivation for creating songs that would arrest public attention through their combination of innuendo, drama, and musical accessibility, for he owned a share in the company that published his songs. This highly self-conscious art served commerce in a national system that offered huge rewards in its expanded and quickly changing market. The waltz song would continue to provide a recipe for success in songs of fulfilled and unfulfilled courtship like Andrew B. Sterling and Von Tilzer's "On a Sunday Afternoon" (1902), "In the Good Old Summertime" (1902) by Ren Shields and George Evans, "Take Me Out to the Ball Game" (about the courtship of Katie Casey who was "baseball mad," 1908) by Jack Norworth and Albert Von Tilzer, and "Down by the Old Mill Stream" (1910) by Tell Taylor.

'Tis sad when you think of her wast - ed life, For youth can - not mate with age,

EXAMPLE 2.12   Harry Von Tilzer ''A Bird in a Gilded Cage'' (New York: Shapiro, Bernstein & Von Tilzer, 1900)

The Confused Double Standard

The entry of the suggestive waltz into the parlor during what Goldberg calls the ''Gay, Naughty, Roisterous, Electric, Romantic, Moulting, and . . . thomasbeery Mauve'' nineties[51] marked an encroachment on domestic purity that tended to confuse the facile distinction between corrupt men and pristine women. Most songs proceeded from a male point of view, because men had traditionally dominated business when popular song became industry on a national scale: ''Maude Nugent, Anita Owen ('Sweet Bunch of Daisies,' 'Sweet Marie'). The women—an armful of them—were in at the beginning of Tin Pan Alley. Why were there not more?''[52] If women were not captains of industry, however, they increasingly formed part of the *corps de bataille* as factory workers in light industry, as secretaries in offices, and as clerks in the newly popularized department stores, where they became powerful consumers as they made ever bolder forays into the city.[53] The fabric of everyday life for both married and unmarried women changed drastically in urban centers ''with

51. Goldberg, *Tin Pan Alley,* 101.
52. Ibid., 98.
53. See Linda L. Tyler, '' 'Commerce and Poetry Hand in Hand': Music in American Department Stores, 1880–1930,'' *Journal of the American Musicological Society* 45 (1992), 75–120.

the result,'' as John D'Emilio and Estelle Freedman explain, ''that the sex-segregated world of the nineteenth century became less descriptive of [women's] existence.''[54]

Male songwriters could not avoid reflecting the changing role of women in an art that held realism as a central tenet. During the nineties women are not only aggressive in initiating courtship, they even adopt risqué stances. ''Ta-Ra-Ra Boom-De-Ay'' (1891), usually credited to the Henry J. Sayers, manager of the Thatcher, Primrose and West Minstrels,[55] features a female narrator who calls herself ''a smart and stylish girl'' of ''good society—not too strict, but rather free'' who unabashedly pursues what she wants:

> I'm not extravagantly shy,
> And when a nice young man is nigh,
> For his heart I have a try,
> And faint away with tearful cry!
> When the good young man, in haste,
> Will support me round the waist;
> I don't come to, while thus embraced,
> Till of my lips he steals a taste!

The devious means used by this young lady cannot obscure her command of the action and subsequent situation. And she uses the famous nonsense chorus that lends the song its title to imply something beyond romance:

> Sometimes Pa says, with a frown,
> ''Soon you'll have to settle down—
> Have to wear your wedding gown—
> Be the strictest wife in town!''
> Well, it must come by and by—
> When wed, to keep quiet I'll try;
> But till then I shall not sigh,
> I shall still go in for my—
> Ta-ra-ra Boom-De-Ay . . .

Sayers accompanies this last line with a progression of sequences, setting the musical hook. But the syllables have no meaning without the verse, and can take on a juicy one with it. Contemporaries clearly saw the song as risqué according to Marks's anecdote about a dispute over its copyright:

> [Theodore] Metz testified that the tune originated in ''Babe Conners' '' place
> in St. Louis, a notorious resort, with colored female inmates, which was

54. John D'Emilio and Estelle B. Freedman, *Intimate Matters: A History of Sexuality in America* (New York, 1988), 189.
55. Witmark, *From Ragtime,* 61; a reprint appears in Fremont, *Favorite Songs,* 299–301.

frequented by traveling minstrels in search of material—songs and otherwise. . . . When asked by the Judge what kind of a place "Babe Conners" ran, Metz answered, "Let's be polite and call it a cabaret!"[56]

"Ta-Ra-Ra Boom-De-Ay" clearly reflects a conflict between what the narrator does and propriety demands.

At the same time men seem to greet aggressive women with relish, they praise more traditional roles and behavior. The heroine exhibits all the typical virtues in "The Sunshine of Paradise Alley" (1895),[57] "introduced with great success by Julius P. Witmark" and written by Walter H. Ford and John W. Bratton:

> There's a little side street such as often you meet,
> Where the boys of a Sunday night rally,
> Tho' it's not very wide, and it's dismal beside,
> Yet they call the place Paradise Alley,
> But a maiden so sweet, lives in that little street,
> She's the daughter of widow MacNally,
> She has bright golden hair, and the boys all declare
> She's the sunshine of Paradise Alley.

Ford positions his ideal firmly within the domestic realm in the chorus:

> Ev'ry Sunday down to her home we go,
> All the boys and all the girls they love her so. . . .

And from this position she projects an angelic aura into the outside world. She braves the contagion of a sick child in the second verse, bringing it comfort and cheer and saving it from certain death to the rejoicing of her neighbors. And she appropriately marries "Tommy Killeen" in the last verse of this waltz song which received its most important plug (the cover of the sheet music notwithstanding) from Lottie Gilson at the New York Casino with the help of a "utility" man in the audience, Johnny "Woozy" Leffler.[58] Women with a secure domestic base seem to do well, and in retrospect we can see that even the narrator of "Ta-Ra-Ra" requires the domestic protection of her father in the end.

As women ventured forth into the outside world, warnings occurred with some regularity about the dangers of the urban environment where the narratives of popular songs increasingly took place. A version of this theme sounds in "Mother Was a Lady" (1896)[59] by none other than Edward Marks and

---

56. *They All Sang*, 72.
57. Reprinted in Fremont, *Favorite Songs*, 282–85.
58. Witmark, *From Ragtime*, 143.
59. Reprinted in Fremont, *Favorite Songs*, 208–11.

Joseph Stern. In this song we again behold the propensity for realism that moved Marks to take the tale from experience:

> It was a German restaurant on Twentieth Street, and some of the male customers were joshing a new waitress. ("Joshing" was a popular word then.) The girl, a comely, simple sort with a great bun of taffy-colored hair, burst into tears. "No one would dare insult me," she said, "if my brother Jack was only here." And she added, "My mother was a lady." Meyer Cohen, known as "the California tenor," a favorite ballad singer, was at our table and suggested the possibilities of this line as a song title. Stern and I wrote it that afternoon, and Meyer introduced it at Pastor's the next day.[60]

Marks sets up the story in the first verse, while the waitress's protestations come in Stern's waltz chorus. The second verse provides the obvious solution to the plight of a woman who has "come to this great city":

> It's true one touch of nature,
> It makes the whole world kin,
> And every word she uttered
> Seemed to touch their hearts within,
> they sat there stunned and silent,
> Until one cried in shame,
> "Forgive me Miss! I meant no harm,
> Pray tell me what's your name?"
> She told him and he cried again,
> "I know your brother too,
> Why we've been friends for many years
> And he often speaks of you,
> He'll be so glad to see you,
> And if you'll only wed,
> I'll take you to him as my wife,
> For I love you since you said."

In 1934 Marks admits about this piece and his "Little Lost Child":

> The two songs have been kidded a lot since, but they have the indefinable essence of popularity, and three years ago, when Victor made a record of "Mother," using the title "If Jack Were Only Here," it sold 200,000 records. We didn't take them seriously, except as merchandise. But if I should say that we wrote them as travesties, it wouldn't be the truth.[61]

The maudlin qualities Marks observes only provided the mechanism that caught the audience's attention. The popularity of the song played on nothing less than

---

60. Marks amd Liebling, *They All Sang,* 33–34.
61. Ibid.

confusion about the role of women outside the home. Marks's waitress defends herself aggressively but is ultimately encouraged to return to the domestic fold, where a man might protect her.

Women who do not return to the domestic scene, but remain in the outside world, succumb to the evil influence of men. There is a hint of the sordid estate to which they might sink in James Thornton's "She May Have Seen Better Days" (1894), where a "poor creature" has fallen "by the wayside," abandoned by her husband to an unspecified fate that sounds a great deal like prostitution. "She Is More to Be Pitied, Than Censured" (1898)[62] by William B. Gray attacks the subject directly (and may have been inspired by Thornton's piece). The cover of this song bills it as "a story of life's 'other side' taken from an actual occurrence," adding, "the theme of this song is indeed a delicate one to handle, and is offered in sympathy, and not defense, for the unfortunate erring creatures, the life of one of whom suggested its construction." Set in a wicked Bowery saloon where young men "carouse,"

> At the very next table was seated
> A girl who had fallen to shame,
> All the young fellows jeered at her weakness,
> 'Till they heard an old woman exclaim;
>
> [Chorus:]
> She is more to be pitied than censured
> She is more to be helped than despised,
> She is only a lassie who ventured,
> On life's stormy path, ill advised;
> Do not scorn her with words fierce and bitter,
> Do not laugh at her shame and downfall,
> For a moment just stop and consider,
> That a man was the cause of it all.

Gray (d. 1932), who had begun his career as a professional boxer,[63] naturally chooses the waltz for both verse and chorus, partly because of its sensuality, partly because of the music-hall setting. He uses the same signature motive, a chromatic inflection (see Ex. 2.13), throughout the song as the hook that compels the listener to consider his story and its moral. Both reflect the legacy of the divided spheres and natures established in the preceding nine decades. Men may be evil by nature but never "fallen"; women, angelic by nature, become prey to men and corruption if they leave the domestic sphere. Thus the dual standard for men and women in the urban setting, where a woman may redeem herself only by rejecting material gain, as a "kept woman" does in Louis W. Pritzkow's and Monroe Rosenfeld's "Take Back Your Gold" (1897).

62. Reprinted in Fremont, *Favorite Songs*, 247–50.
63. Marks and Liebling, *They All Sang*, 73.

EXAMPLE 2.13   William B. Gray, "She Is More to Be Pitied Than Censured" (New York: Wm. B. Gray, 1898)

Songwriters gradually began to recognize the double standard, admitting women reluctantly to a kind of equality. Sweethearts began to abandon men with increasingly regularity in songs like "Good Bye, My Lady Love" (1904), a ragtime song by Joseph E. Howard, or in "Meet Me in St. Louis, Louis" (1904) by Andrew B. Sterling and Kerry [F. A.] Mills. This famous waltz song has a comic tone, but features a remarkable story about a man who comes home to find his wife has departed:

> A note on the table he spied,
> He read just once, then he cried,
> It ran, "Louis dear,
> It's too slow for me here,
> So I think I will go for a ride."

The chorus offers the return of connubial bliss ("I will be your tootsie-wootsie"), if only the husband will follow. In one sense the woman as ruler in the domestic realm has a right to take such action, but her decision to leave the home (taking all of the household goods with her) indicates a new independence as well as her newfound confidence in surviving by herself amid an urban setting.

Will Hough and Frank Adams address the new bent toward a single standard more directly in "I Wonder Who's Kissing Her Now" (1909):

> You have loved lots of girls in the sweet long ago,
> And each one has meant Heaven to you,
> You have vowed your affection to each one in turn,
> And have sworn to them all you'd be true;
> You have kissed 'neath the moon while the world seemed in tune,
> Then you've left her to hunt a new game,

Chorus.

I won-der who's kiss-ing her now,———— Won-der who's

teach-ing her now,———— Won-der who's look-ing in-

to her eyes Breath-ing sighs, tell-ing lies;

EXAMPLE 2.14   Joseph Howard [and Harold Orleb]: "I Wonder Who's Kissing Her Now" (New York and Chicago: Chas. K. Harris, 1909)

> Does it ever occur to you later my boy,
> That she's probably doing the same?

The vaudeville singer, Joseph Howard (1867–1961), took the idea for this song from a group of college boys he overheard while staying at a Chicago hotel. Though Howard's name appears on the sheet music as composer, Harold Orleb would later claim authorship of the melody setting the realistic situation.[64] He uses the waltz ironically, almost as if to mock the values of the nineties and their trade in sublimated sexuality. The song captures the overstatement of the previous era perfectly in the chorus (see Ex. 2.14) by setting the suggestive initial lines to limpid descending sequences,

> I wonder who's kissing her now,
> Wonder who's teaching her how,

while saving a melodramatic outburst for the end of the next couplet:

> Wonder who's looking into her eyes,
> Breathing sighs, telling lies;

They conclude with the ultimate turn of the tables:

> I wonder who's buying the wine
> For lips that I use to call mine,

64. For accounts of Howard's inspiration and Orleb's authorship, see "Joe Howard Dies; Vaudeville Star," *New York Times* (May 21, 1961), 87; and "The Myth of Joe Howard Lingers in a Familiar Air," *New York Times* (June 4, 1961), 85.

Wonder if she ever tells him of me,
I wonder who's kissing her now.

While parity has not been achieved, these lyrics make a start. At the same time they mark the explicit ending of the waltz as a serious mainstay for the industry of popular song. From here on it would be used as period piece: a staid, elegant reference to times gone by, and as a symbol of nostalgia. It had served its purpose well, commercializing sexual innuendo in an acceptable way, portraying the urban scene of courtship in the late nineteenth century, and providing songwriters with insight into the workings of the new mercantile system with its millions of customers.

Isidore Witmark offered a rather harsh appraisal of late-nineteenth-century popular song's artistic value, "Its music, generally, is the doggerel of song, as its rhymes are the doggerel of verse."[65] Perhaps he reacted to the constant demand for novelty, which aimed as much at steady obsolescence as it did at large sales. A song had to be disposable, in one sense, for the next hit to supersede it. But the necessity of setting a "hook"—of arresting attention immediately to compel sales—ultimately required the invention of a psychologically effective formula, especially for the music. Motivic economy created through the use of constant sequence lends the tunes both memorability and a pronounced sense of direction. Coupled with a rich harmonic palette, the melodic writing still retains its effectiveness, even today. This music lends itself well to a natural linguistic accent. And the very plainness of the verse, its use of ordinary speech and vocabulary, yields general accessibility.

The content of the lyrics is also engaging to us, but for different reasons than those that caught the attention of the original audience. The texts impart a distinct sense of the period, and amuse later audiences by virtue of the comparison between new and old mores. Not all songs from the nineties participate in the theatrical realism of pieces like "Mother Was a Lady." Occasionally a song like "Come Down, Ma Evenin' Star" (1902) by Robert B. Smith and John Stromberg presents a sentiment worthy of antebellum chivalry. But by and large, most songs about courtship presented everyday people in believable situations often accompanied by apposite music. Witmark may exaggerate when he claims, "[We] were among the first, before Tin Pan Alley was founded, to sense the importance of turning to profit the major happenings of the time."[66] Nonetheless, his sense that popular song had begun to grapple with actual societal situations bears much merit, even if it applies more generally to the last half of the nineteenth century. In some small measure this development indicates a healthy society articulating issues honestly through popular art. Its ability to make a thriving industry of that art stands as a tribute to its ingenuity, as well.

65. *From Ragtime*, 68.
66. Ibid.

3

Familiar Journey

*Protocols of Dying in
the Nineteenth Century*[1]

Of all the subjects regularly entertained in popular song during the last century, none seems so inappropriate to us as death. In her study of sculpture Joy Kasson remarks about the apparent "fascination with death and dying that was reflected in virtually every aspect of American culture: art, literature, and education, as well as religious and social practices."[2] It is tempting initially for modern writers to attribute this seemingly morbid preoccupation to statistics, and it is true that shorter life expectancy in the nineteenth century played some role in the frequency of songs about dying (especially in the case of children). But a moment's reflection will remind us that death was no more common in the nineteenth century than at any other time. Put simply, just as many people die as are born in the long run. Numbers alone offer very little by way of explanation about a society's view of death.

The answer to the nineteenth century's apparent "fascination with death" lies, instead, mostly in the way we frame the question. The large number of popular songs on dying may not reflect preoccupation so much as familiarity—more first-hand experience. For where the twentieth century has developed a whole set of institutions, medical and mortuarial, to hold the end of life at a technical distance, people had little in the way of professional help during the previous century to insulate them from the events surrounding the passing of their fellow human beings. Death usually occurred in the home, not in a hospital; doctors could do little more for those who were dying than family members; and relatives or friends often took on the tasks surrounding burial, even

---

1. This topic originated in the work of Nan McMurry, a student in my seminar on American popular song during the early 1980s. I have borrowed some organization for this chapter from her paper, which she later expanded for " 'And I? I am in a consumption': The Tuberculosis Patient, 1780–1930'' (Ph.D. dissertation, Duke University, 1985).

2. *Queens and Captives: Women in Nineteenth-Century American Sculpture* (New Haven and London, 1990), 102.

83

in urban settings. Lewis Saum summarizes a typical nineteenth-century encounter with death:

> In February of 1846 Brigham Nims of New Hampshire recorded what may have been his first full participation in the handling the dying and the dead, and he did so in a straightforward way that suggests the routineness of the function. On the night of the 10th he "watched with Seth Towns he was very wild the fore part of the night, more calm toward morning." Nims visited Seth again on the 11th, and, when word came that all was over, he returned to prepare the deceased for burial: "I went and helped Lay him out, and shaved him the first person that I tried to shave."[3]

Nims apparently took pride in performing these social tasks, as if they marked a rite of passage. After viewing several other such accounts, Saum goes on to comment, "People knew [death] by its existential proximity as well as by its actuarial presence."[4]

Because many people could not escape direct confrontation with the whole process of dying, popular song took on the subject more as a necessity than as a macabre obsession. And for this reason such pieces spoke not only to bereavement but also to the standards of behavior expected of both the dying and those who kept them company in their ordeal. They offered practical instruction in the etiquette of death to an audience that had a real need of edification.

Why Do the Beautiful Die?

While nineteenth-century popular composers mourned all loss, they seemed particularly concerned with death among certain groups of people. They honored the elderly in memory, but their passing came in the logical order of things. The death of children, on the other hand, seemed pointless and especially painful in a period when infant mortality remained quite high. The many songs on the death of children do not represent a fetish but a response to an apparent injustice. One of the most poignant numbers on this subject, "Early Lost and Early Found" (1846) by George W. Bethune and Isaac Baker Woodbury, provides a typical rationale for the death of a young girl. The song narrates a story over four verses, the first of which sets the scene:

> Within that downy cradle there lay a little child,
> A group of hov'ring angels unseen upon her smiled;

3. Lewis O. Saum, "Death in the Popular Mind," in *Passing: The Vision of Death in America,* Charles O. Jackson, ed., vol. 2 of Contributions in Family Studies (Westport, CT, and London, 1977), 69–70.

4. Ibid., 71.

One breathed upon her features, and the babe in beauty grew,
With a cheek like morning blushes and an eye of azure hue. . . .

The child grows until she approaches the threshold of maturity, at which point
the fairest of all the angels who watch suggests:

"You've made her all too lovely, for a child of mortal race,
But no shade of human sorrow, shall darken o'er her face,
Nor shall the soul that shineth so purely from within
Her form of earth-born frailty, e'er know the taint of sin."

This "nobler, brighter" angel turns out to be death in the last verse:

"Lulled in my faithful bosom, I'll bear her far away,
Where there's no sin nor sorrow, nor anguish nor decay;
And mine, a boon more glorious than all your gifts shall be-
Lo! I crown her happy spirit with immortality!"

In this line of reasoning, the beautiful die because their perfection exceeds the
earthly and finds its proper place only in paradise.

Woodbury's setting of this sentiment is remarkable for its relative normalcy.
He does not choose anything unusual like minor mode, a convention for funereal subjects in the nineteenth century, to distinguish this song from any other.
In fact we might designate its style "standard transitional" from the period of
the mid-forties. Some Italianate features, like portamenti (gliding ornaments)
and turns, linger in vocal part, but the melody also has a certain declamatory
plainness of shape (especially in its repeated notes) and rhythmic syncopation
that migrate from minstrelsy as a token of popular accessibility (see Ex. 3.1).
The combination of subject matter and mixture of musical influences particularly reflect the composer's background. Woodbury (1819–58) was born in
Beverly, Massachusetts, and he eventually settled in Boston, where the ubiquitous George Frederick Root made his acquaintance:

> He was two or three years older than myself, and had commenced his musi-
> cal work a year or two before me. He had a small room, also, in Tremont
> Row. He was a most indefatigable student and worker. I think it was during
> my first winter in Boston [1838–39] that he taught a singing-school in Bev-
> erly, and often walked back to Boston, fifteen miles, after nine o'clock at
> night, to be ready for his lessons in the morning. . . . Mr. Woodbury was
> very economical, and in a year or two had saved enough money to go to
> London and take lessons for a few months. . . . Mr. Woodbury was a ge-
> nial, pleasant gentleman, and because he wrote only simple music, never was

EXAMPLE 3.1 Isaac B. Woodbury, ''Early Lost and Early Found'' (Boston: C. Bradlee & Co., 1846)

credited (by those who did not know him) with the musical ability and culture that he really possessed.[5]

He later moved to New York, became editor of the *New York Musical Review,* and died in Columbia, South Carolina.[6] As a singing-school leader and sometime writer of hymns, Woodbury could have invoked a sacred style for ''Early Lost,'' but he avoids even this reference in favor of a more popular synthesis. Death takes the familiar, recognizable form of parlor music in his song.

George F. Root (1820–95) took many early cues from Woodbury, following in his footsteps as a singing master and singing-school leader, as well as specializing in songs about death. Root was raised to more august standards, but admitted later:

> I saw at once that mine must be the ''people's song,'' still, I am ashamed to say, I shared the feeling that was around me in regard to that grade of music. When Stephen C. Foster's wonderful melodies (as I now see them) began to appear, and the famous Christy's Minstrels began to make them known, I ''took a hand in'' and wrote a few, but put ''G. Friederich Wurzel'' (the

5. Root, *The Story of a Musical Life* (Cincinnati, 1891), 21.
6. See Grace D. Yerbury, *Song in America from Early Times to About 1850* (Metuchen, NJ, 1971), 122.

German for Root) to them instead of my own name. "Hazel Dell" and "Rosalie, the Prairie Flower" were the best known of those so written. It was not until I imbibed more of Dr. [Lowell] Mason's spirit, and went more among the people of the country, that I saw these things in a truer light, and respected myself, and was thankful when I could write something that all the people would sing.[7]

"Rosalie" (1859) takes as its popular subject the passing of a child, and to make a greater impact, Root follows a sequence of events that would become standard for such songs. In the first verse he portrays the idyllic life and rural surroundings of "a lovely child" noted for her "blue eyes" and "wavy ringlets of flaxen hair." Like the child in "Early Lost," Rosalie exhibits unearthly beauty in Root's second verse:

> When the twilight shadows gathered in the west,
> And the voice of nature sunk to rest,
> Like a cherub kneeling seemed the lovely child,
> With her gentle eyes so mild.

Her fate has now been determined:

> But the summer faded, and a chilly blast
> O'er that happy cottage swept at last,
> When the autumn song-birds woke the dewy morn,
> Little prairie flower was gone;
> For the angels whispered softly in her ear,
> "Child, thy Father calls thee, stay not here,"
> And they gently bore her, robed in spotless white,
> To their blissful home of light.

The chorus provides the consolation that Rosalie is still "blooming in a fadeless bower" far away. Root's music for this widely admired number (it would sell over 100,000 copies) reflects the next stylistic stage after Woodbury's synthesis for "Early Lost." Root's phrases are shorter and reciprocate predictably (see Ex. 3.2). He also eliminates vocal ornamentation and includes the four-part chorus that becomes fashionable in parlor songs during the fifties—songs on dying generally adopt the current style.

Many other pieces about the death of children appeared during this period, providing yet another index of the topic's continued appeal. The catalogue includes "The Dying Boy" (1850) by Mrs. Larned and Lyman Heath, "The Dying Child" (1852) by Theodore A. Gould and L. V. H. Crosby, "Three Angel Visitants" (1857) by Chauncey M. Cady (of publishing fame), "The

---

7. *The Story*, 83.

EXAMPLE 3.2   George F. Root, "Rosalie, the Prairie Flower" (Boston: Henry Tolman & Co., 1859)

Emigrant's Dying Child" (1861) with a waltz accompaniment by Henry D. L. Webster (lyricist for "Lorena"), "Little Maggie Dale" (1863) by W. Dexter Smith, Jr., and Frederick Buckley (of minstrel fame), "Weep No More for Lily" (1864) by Mrs. E. A. [Susan] Parkhurst, "Where the Little Feet Are Waiting" (1868) by Dexter Smith and Joseph Philbrick Webster (an unrelated friend of Henry's), and "Gone to Heaven" (1869) by James R. Murray.

Throughout these several decades the basic rationale for the death of a child changed very little, as we see in "Beyond the Clouds" (1870) written by its publisher, Charles A. White (1829–92). This is admittedly a rather bad song—not nearly as good as White's better-known "Marguerite," "The Poor Drunkard's Child," or "When 'Tis Moonlight."[8] The text is flat, but to the point:

> Mother, where is Minnie now,
> Minnie whom we lov'd so well,
> Will she never more return,
> Has she gone beyond the clouds to dwell?
> The angels wanted her to come,

8. For an account of his songs see Sigmund Spaeth, *A History of Popular Music in America* (New York, 1948), 214–16.

> We made for her a snow-white shroud,
> And then they took her home to dwell
> With them, beyond the clouds.

Children die because they are beautiful and because they are innocent, things the young questioner understands, even though he does not comprehend why his sister cannot return. Such a loss comes particularly hard to the parent:

> Minnie, mother's wept all day,
> And her head with grief is bowed,
> Now on bended knee we ask
> To meet once more beyond the cloud.

Songs invoking this identical conceit remain popular to the end of the century. After "Beyond the Clouds" we find numbers like "Our Angel Baby" (1879) by Dean Howe and Charles Dockstader. "Little Maggie Magee!" (1891), by Loren Bragdon, takes up the subject in the reigning nineties style of "Tempo di Valse." And as late as 1903 Charles K. Harris contributes "Always in the Way," which tells the story of a little girl who dies of longing for her deceased mother.[9]

Beautiful young women comprised the other group most frequently summoned to paradise in song, and their memorials sometimes became very popular indeed. For reasons no longer clear most of them had double names: "Lilly Dale" (1852) by H. S. Thompson, "Cora Lee" (1853) by J. W. Beazell and H. B. Brown, "Ida May" (1853) again by Thompson, "Annie Ray" (1853) by Andy W. Francisco and Stewart Macaulay, "Allie Lee" (1854) by H. S. Cornwall and W. Howard Doane, "Eva Clair" (1854) by H. Avery, "Bell Brandon" (1854) by T. E. Garrett and Francis Wolcott, and "Ida Fay" (1857) by Frank Myrtle and F. W. Smith. There was obviously a replicative industry in these songs, and the trade could produce classics like "Annie Lisle" (1857)[10] by the very prolific H. S. Thompson. He follows a standard, almost ritualized plot that relates Annie's death in stages. The first verse intimates Annie's beauty and provides a probable cause for her death by describing her innocence:

> Pure as the forest lily,
> Never thought of guile

9. Harris leaves an account of writing the song in *After the Ball: Forty Years of Melody* (New York, 1926), 142–45.

10. A facsmile of the sheet music in a British edition attributed to "W. H. Thompson" appears in Nicholas Tawa's *American Solo Songs Through 1865,* vol. 1 of *Three Centuries of American Sacred and Secular Music,* Martha Furman Schleifer and Sam Dennison, eds. ([Boston], 1989), 353–58.

Had its home within the bosom
Of loved Annie Lisle.

Like children, young women's perfection often exceeds the earthly. In the second verse Thompson relates the beginnings of Annie's final trial as she lies "on a bed of pain and anguish," while he concentrates in the third verse on her delirious perception of "forms clad in heavenly beauty, waiting for the longing spirit." In the fourth verse she speaks her last words:

Raise me in your arms, dear Mother,
Let me once more look
On the green and waving willows,
And the flowing brook;
Hark, those strains of angel music
    From the choirs above;
Dearest Mother, I am going,
    Truly, "God is love."

Thompson's story is extensive and relatively complete: Annie lives a blessed life, she begins to fail, she beholds a vision of angels, and she dies at home. The chorus then provides the conclusion:

Wave willows, murmur waters,
    Golden sunbeams smile;
Earthly music cannot waken
    Lovely Annie Lisle.

The progression from beauty and innocence to suffering, resignation, and death produces a kind of beatification (emphasized here by a repeat of the chorus *pianissimo*). But Thompson's tune, while very lovely, has no particularly sacred overtones. It could have been written as a sentimental ballad for the minstrel stage, especially in its repeated-note chorus (see Ex. 3.3). "Annie Lisle" occupied a central place in the nineteenth-century repertory, and its melody is still so popular that it appears retexted in various school songs, most notably in "High Above Cayuga's Waters" or "Hark! The Sound of Tarheel Voices."

Thompson went on to produce a song about the death of a beloved young woman even more popular than "Annie Lisle"—"Down by the River Lived a Maiden" (1863), better known under the title "Oh My Darling Clementine" (credited incorrectly to Percy Montrose; 1884).[11] The republication of the song twenty years after its first appearance testifies to continued interest in the sub-

---

11. A facsimile of this edition appears in Richard Jackson's *Popular Songs of Nineteenth-Century America* (New York, 1976), 148–51.

EXAMPLE 3.3   H. S. Thompson, ''Annie Lisle'' (Boston: Oliver Ditson, 1857)

ject. Thompson does not beatify the young beloved in ''Clementine,'' but after setting the obligatory scene in the first verse, relates the story of her demise, beginning with its improbable cause:

> She drove her ducklets, To the river,
> Ev'ry morning just at nine;
> She stubb'd her toe, against a sliver,
> And fell into the foaming brine.

Clementine's last moments are equally unromantic:

> I saw her lips above the water,
> Blowing bubbles soft and fine;
> Alas for me, I was no swimmer,
> And so I lost my Clementine.

Thompson marks the well-known tune "Tempo di Mazurka," and it may seem to us inappropriate as a setting for a text on this subject. But the use of the dance is not intended ironically. Rather it provides yet another indication of the nineteenth century's intimacy with dying: death can be treated like any other topic because it is ordinary in the literal sense of word. In fact, Thompson's chorus almost lends a matter-of-fact tone to the narrator's mourning:

> Oh my darling, oh my darling,
> Oh my darling Clementine,
> You are lost and gone forever,
> Dreffel sorry, Clementine.

What was familiar to the nineteenth century is foreign to us and therefore takes on a wry tone.

The litany of titles bearing the name of the dying or expired beloved goes on endlessly. Stephen Foster contributes "Cora Dean" (1860) in this tradition, with exactly the same progression of verses as Thompson's "Annie Lisle." In the last,

> Eyes bedimmed with tears are streaming,
> Round her deserted home,
> Silent stars are nightly beaming,
> Lending sadness to the gloom.
> While the winds of summer dying,
> Borne from the deep dark wave
> O'er the land in dirges sighing,
> Murmur with sorrow round her grave.

We also find "Lizzie Lee" (1858) by George P. Graff, "Laura of the Dell" (1859) by S. Wesley Martin, "Ella May" (1860) by Charles Hess, "Bright Eyed Little Nell of Narragansett Bay" (1860), arranged by George F. Root, "Ally Ray" (1864) by William S. Pitt, "Elsie Vane" by G. A. Veazie, Jr., and a quodlibet of many previous songs, "Shall I Never More Behold Thee" (1870) by J. E. Crowden and W. A. Carey, featuring "Bonny May" as the beloved. As late as 1886 "Angel Violet" (by Theodore D. C. Miller and Joseph W. Turner) dies following the same basic plot as her predecessors. Women's innocence and purity, which had been exaggerated in songs of courtship before the Civil War, provided the reason for their passing and made paradise their logical abode.

Nineteenth-century lyricists and composers viewed the death of young men as tragic, but they accounted for it more rationally: men died from their activities in the brutal outer world. In "The Maniac Song!" (ca. 1821) by G. W. Smith and C. F. von Bonnhorst, a woman becomes deranged over the death of a lover gone to sea:

> Gently flow ye swelling billows,
> O'er my Edwin's Ocean bed;
> Soft the azure wave that pillows,
> On its breast my lover's head,
>   The Syrens' songs
>   His sleep prolongs,
> His bridal couch the Sea nymphs spread.

The second verse depicts in detail his watery grave:

> Softly breathe ye sighing gales,
> Lightly o'er his death bed sweep:
> Hark! the Mermaids' song bewails,
> See around him Naiads weep;
>   They have made his grave,
>   In Ocean's cave,
> And there I'll to his bosom creep.

Edwin summons his beloved in the third verse, and she then commits suicide. For Smith's miniature drama Bonnhorst provides a suitably operatic accompaniment from the common stock of the 1820s (see Ex. 3.4). Its trills, turns, and cadenzas match the high speech of the lyrics in a manner that would be equally appropriate in a song of courtship. The composer simply does not differentiate in his music between the two kinds of event.

Because the death of young men required some external cause, songs about their dying flourished mainly during wartime. For this reason, such pieces enjoyed their largest nineteenth-century vogue during the Civil War. Almost all of them concern a soldier's last words, often addressed to his mother. Though the narrator in George F. Root's "Just Before the Battle, Mother" (1863)[12] does not actually die in our sight, he contemplates the prospect in all three verses as well as in the chorus. These Root mixes with patriotic sentiments like those in the third verse:

12. Ibid., 102–5.

EXAMPLE 3.4   C. F. Bonnhorst, "The Maniac Song!" (Philadelphia: G. E. Blake, [ca. 1821]; Wolfe No. 962)

Hark! I hear the bugles sounding,
'Tis the signal for the fight,
Now may God protect us Mother,
As He ever does the right.
Hear the "Battle-Cry of Freedom,"
How it swells upon the air;
Oh, yes we'll rally round the standard,
Or we'll perish nobly there.

The repeated chorus then takes up the same theme:

Farewell Mother, you may never
Press me to you heart again;
O, you'll not forget me, Mother,
If I'm numbered with the slain.

94

EXAMPLE 3.5   George F. Root, "Just Before the Battle, Mother" (Chicago: Root & Cady, 1863)

Root had an interest in the firm that published this song,[13] and his pragmatism extended to advertising in its lyrics another of his very popular Civil War ballads, "The Battle-Cry of Freedom." He provides this note of explanation: "In the Army of the Cumberland, the Soldiers sing the Battle-Cry when going into action, by order of the Commanding General." This shrewd sense of the market also marks his musical style, which is distinctly American in its short phrases, unaffected melody, four-part chorus, and occasional syncopations. Root uses this last device very cleverly by pairing syncopes with appoggiaturas on words like "Mother" (see Ex. 3.5) to suggest pathos. Employed in this way, appoggiaturas are translated from Anglo-Italian vocabulary into a distinctly American argot. Root sensed nothing ghoulish in using a song about death to advertise, simply because songs on this subject were not extraordinary. No special rules attached to them.

Dying soldiers usually express thoughts very similar to those in "Before the Battle," and many of their last moments have much in common with those of the dying beloved. "Comrades, I Am Dying" (1864)[14] by Thomas Manahan and B. Sontag is unusually vivid in its first verse:

> Comrades, comrades, I am dying!
> See the crimson fountain flow!
> Sick and wounded, I am dying
> On the field among the foe.
> But the angels hover round me,

13. He was the older brother of Ebenezer T. Root, who founded the concern with Chauncey M. Cady. See Dena J. Epstein, *Music Publishing in Chicago Before 1871: The Firm of Root & Cady 1858–1871*, vol. 14 of Detroit Studies in Music Bibliography (Detroit, 1969), 17–30.

14. A facsimile appears in Richard Crawford's *The Civil War Song Book* (New York, 1977), 78–81.

EXAMPLE 3.6   G. Gumpert, "The Dying Volunteer" (Philadelphia, G. André, 1861)

> They will guard me while I sleep;
> Comrades onward to the battle,
> Do not for the soldier weep.

Aside from the graphic depiction of the wound, however, the sequence of events presents a variation on the plot of "Annie Lisle." Mothers also attend the death of their sons, but they cannot actually hold soldiers in their arms on the battlefield. For this reason Manahan gives us to know that this dying soldier's mother is already dead, and can visit him, therefore, in angelic form to guide him into paradise. The soldier in G. Gumpert's "The Dying Volunteer" (1861),[15] being a bit older, addresses his last message to his wife:

> Care for my boy, and when I die,
> Beneath that starry flag,
> Oh! watch him with a mother's eye,
> His courage will not lag.

This turns out to be a plea for continuing a family tradition: the dying man enlisted following the admonition of his fallen father to defend the Union (we are informed by the preface to the sheet music). The music for the piece, arranged by F. Lossé, contains the exception that proves the rule. Almost alone among Civil War songs about dying, "Volunteer" is accompanied by a funeral march in minor mode (Ex. 3.6). Audiences must have understood this cliché of mourning, and therefore, the choice of most composers to use a standard rather than a special musical style for songs about death is all the more significant. A composer better attuned to the popular market such as Henry Clay Work selected common style to accompany death in his Civil War songs,

15. Ibid., 91–95.

which included "Our Captain's Last Words" (1861) and "Sleeping for the Flag" (1863).

Songs from the Civil War often combined death on the battlefield with the tragic death of children to create numbers like "The Drummer Boy of Shiloh" (1863)[16] by William Shakespeare Hays. Hays (1837–1907), a Louisville journalist with Union sympathies, replicates the usual plot. After setting the scene, Hays beatifies the dying child by portraying his piety:

> "Look down upon the battle field,
> Oh, Thou our Heavenly Friend!
> Have mercy on our sinful souls!"
> The soldiers cried—"Amen!"
> For gathered round a little group,
> Each brave man knelt and cried;
> They listened to the drummer boy,
> Who prayed before he died.

Eventually, like all soldiers, the child calls out:

> "Oh, Mother," said the dying boy,
> "Look down from heaven on me,
> Receive me to thy fond embrace—
> Oh take me home to thee.
> I've loved my country as my God;
> To serve them both I've tried,"
> He smiled, shook hands—death seiezd [sic] the boy
> Who prayed before he died.

In the fourth verse the troupe, substituting for the family, buries their comrade, and Hays depicts the coming of angels in the last stanza. His music for this story falls in common time, but it does not even hint at a march, let alone a funereal one. The melody is notable, instead, for its extremely prominent and relatively frequent syncopations right out of the minstrel tradition.

Stephen Foster and George Cooper contributed a song in this same vein, "For the Dear Old Flag I Die!" (1863),[17] "the last words of a brave little drummer boy who was fatally wounded in the battle of Gettysburg." His address also adopts the formula: "Farewell mother, Death's cold hand weighs upon my spirit now. . . ." Foster's "last musical idea," at least according to the sheet music, set a variation on "Dear Old Flag" entitled "Give This to Mother" (1864), with words by S. W. Harding.[18] In the first verse the dying

---

16. Ibid., 82–86.

17. See the facsimile in *The Music of Stephen Foster*, Steven Saunders and Deane L. Root, eds. (Washington and London, 1990), II, 321–24.

18. Ibid., 391–94.

boy feels his life ebbing away, in the second he hears angel voices, and in the refrain he expresses his last wish, "Take this locket, soldier, brother, Don't forget, give this to mother." Cooper and Foster reverse this scene in "My Boy Is Coming from the War" (1863)[19] by proceeding from the mother's point of view. We finally learn in the last verse:

> My boy is coming from the war
> The mother fondly said,
> While on the gory battle plain
> Her boy was lying dead!

Even Henry Clay Work contributed to the sub-genre with "Little Major" (1863). Hays, Foster, Work, and the others wrote such songs in answer to a real situation, not as idle exercises in the lugubrious.

After the Civil War, composers had little reason to take up the death of young men until the end of the century, when Charles K. Harris revived the genre with "Break the News to Mother" (1897).[20] The song tells the story of a soldier who volunteers to save his regimental flag in the midst of battle. Successful in his mission but mortally wounded, he is carried back by his comrades:

> From afar a noted general had witnessed this brave deed.
> "Who saved our flag? speak up lads; 'twas noble, brave indeed!"
> "There he lies, sir," said the captain, "he's sinking very fast";
> Then slowly turned away to hide a tear.
> The general in a moment, knelt down beside the boy;
> Then gave a cry that touch'd all hearts that day.
> "It's my son, my brave, young hero; I thought you safe at home."
> "Forgive me, father, for I ran away."

The chorus then begins with the phrase that forms the title of the song, set to music adopting the sentimental tone of the period (Ex. 3.7).

Fittingly enough, Harris took the melodramatic plot for "Break the News" from a scene in a play. He immediately tested the song on his brother:

When I had sung it for him I was rewarded with a loud guffaw. Harry's contention was that there had been no war since 1864 *[sic]*, that the memories of that were fast fading away, and that undoubtedly another war was a long way off—so why a soldier song?[21]

19. Ibid., 355–58.
20. Reprinted in Robert A. Fremont's *Favorite Songs of the Nineties* (New York, 1973), 47–51.
21. *After the Ball*, 134.

CHORUS.

Very slow.

Just break the news to moth- er, She knows how dear I love her, And

tell her not to wait for me, For I'm not com - ing home;

rit.

EXAMPLE 3.7   Charles K. Harris, ''Break the New to Mother'' (Milwaukee: Charles
K. Harris, 1897)

In its first performances ''Break the News'' did fail to catch, not because the
song was too sentimental but because audiences saw no immediate reason to
pay attention. But Harris persisted, offering the song to Julia Mackey for her
first appearance at Koster & Bial's, a New York music hall:

> That night the battleship Maine was blown up in Havana harbor. [Meyer]
> Cohen immediately inserted into the opening of the orchestration a few bars
> of The Star-Spangled Banner. When Julia Mackey made her entrance and the
> orchestral played the introduction the audience broke into an uproar. . . .
> When she went into the story the audience seemed deeply impressed. . . .
> My rival publishers said: ''Harris luck; it took war to make his song
> popular.''[22]

As a result of being directly involved with the passing of their relatives and
friends, listeners demanded relevance from songs on death. Last words on the
battlefield were appropriate only under certain conditions. When war broke out,
the soldier's dying utterance took its rightful place in the repertory of perfectly
suitable fare.

22. Ibid., 142.

The Etiquette of the Deathbed

Nineteenth-century popular song laid out a relatively consistent and thorough account of how people should behave when either they or their friends and relatives were about to die. It was important, first, to die at home, a recurrent theme emphasized particularly by songs about children. Isaac Woodbury's "Take Me Home to Die, or The Last Request" (1850)[23] presents the sentiment typically:

> This land is very bright, mother,
> The flowers are very fair,
> There's magic in the orange groves,
> And fragrance in the air;
> But take me to my dear old home,
> Where the brook goes babbling by,
> Let us go back again, mother!
> Oh! take me home to die.

For this plea Woodbury selects the same musical style seen above in his "Early Lost." Some composers dramatized this theme by adding a race against time to the formula, as in Florence Vane's "Are We Almost There!" (1845), varied in James H. Brown and I. B. Woodbury's "We Are Almost There" (1847), and repeated yet again in "Mother, I Am Weary" (1858) by Mrs. S. E. Dawes and Joseph Philbrick Webster. Older people also expressed the wish to die at home in songs like Leonard Grover's "Carry Me Home to Die" (1856).

In such familiar surroundings friends and relatives were expected to gather around the dying person, and in fact, attending such occasions was considered a social privilege.[24] In Woodbury's "Take Me Home" the child specifically requests the gathering:

> Let my father's hand but rest, mother,
> In blessing on my head,
> Let my brothers and my sister dear,
> But throng around my bed;
> Oh! let me feel that lov'd ones near
> Receive my parting breath,
> When I bid you all goodnight, mother,
> And sleep the sleep of death.

In Irish-born Patrick Sarsfield Gilmore's "Sad News from Home for Me" (1854), the narrator laments his inability to observe the death of his father and

23. Facsimile in Tawa, *Solo Songs*, I, 265–69.
24. See Saum, "Death in the Popular Mind," 81–82.

console his mother. And at least one verse in many of the songs mentioned already, among them "The Dying Boy," "The Dying Child," "Annie Lisle," and "Lilly Dale," make some mention of the gathering. For instance, Thompson begins "Lilly Dale" (1852):

> Twas a calm, still night,
> And the moon's pale light,
> Shone soft o'er hill and vale,
> When friends mute with grief
> Stood around the death bed
> Of my poor lost Lilly Dale.

The rest of the story then features other vignettes from the standard plot.

When death overtook somebody away from home, etiquette demanded that anyone in the vicinity perform the duty of holding a vigil in place of the family. We have seen this custom observed in songs about the death of soldiers, where comrades took the place of relatives. We learn in the later verses of George N. Allen's "The Ocean Burial" (1850)[25] that the young man dying on board ship is far from his mother, sister, and sweetheart (his father has gone before him). He does not expire in solitude, however:

> "O! bury me not in the deep, deep sea";
> The words came low and mournfully,
> From the pallid lips of a youth, who lay,
> On his cabin couch at close of day.
> He had wasted and pined 'till o'er his brow,
> The deathshade had slowly passed, and now,
> Where the land and his fond loved home were nigh,
> They had gathered around him to see him die.

The lyrics actually came from an 1839 poem by Edwin H. Chapin, and in a contrafacted version later became "Oh! Bury Me Not on the Lone Prairie."[26] Allen sets the text with a tune that demonstrates the melding of various traditions in American popular song. On the one hand he offers a number of two-note melismas on words like "pallid" and "youth" (Ex. 3.8) that lend the melody a certain grace and hark back to the Anglo-Italian tradition. On the other hand he indulges occasional syncopated declamation on words like "wasted" that answers a demand for natural speech. Here we find a synthesis of Italianate and minstrel elements normal for the period. The tragedy of the piece lies not so much in the death of the youth—this would not have been

---

25. Reprinted in Jackson's *Popular Songs*, 139–43.
26. Ibid., 276.

EXAMPLE 3.8   George N. Allen, ''The Ocean Burial'' (Boston: Oliver Ditson, 1850)

uncommon—as in the failure of the onlookers to grant his last wish. The whole song bespeaks the dying man's desire to be buried on land, but

> They gave no heed to his dying prayer;
> They have lowered him slow o'er the vessel's side,
> Above him has closed the dark cold tide. . . .

One of the reasons for the gathering, aside from providing company, was to speak with the mortally stricken. Those who attended were often rewarded with words of comfort from the dying. In *Uncle Tom's Cabin* (1852) Harriet Beecher Stowe follows standard protocols at the death of Little Eva. The child summons all her black servants, for instance, and then declares:

> Listen to what I say. I want to speak to you about your souls. . . . Many of you, I am afraid, are very careless. You are thinking only about this world. I want you to remember that there is a beautiful world where Jesus is. I am going there, and you can go there. It is for you as much as me. But, if you want to go there, you must not live idle, careless, thoughtless lives. You must be Christians. You must remember that each one of you can be-

come angels, and be angels forever. . . . Try to do the best you can; pray every day; ask Him to help you, and get the Bible read to you whenever you can; and I think I shall see you all in heaven.[27]

At this everybody says "amen" and breaks into sobs. Stowe was repeating part of the usual plot in this scene. For example, in "The Dying Child" (1848) by Theodore B. Gould and C. C. Wentworth, the boy consoles his mother with the prospect that he will see his dead sister in heaven, while the expiring boy in a song by G. P. Burnam and Frederick Buckley admonishes, "Mother Do Not Weep" (1857). The dying person often comforts the gathered witnesses by revealing his ability to view paradise, as he does in "Angel Forms Are O'er Me Bending" (1873) by George W. Persley. The child sees heavenly figures and hears voices, while it repeats in the chorus:

> Going home, Going home,
> I am only going home.
> Cease your weeping, weary Mother,
> I am only going home.

This same theme repeats in J. W. Turner's "Tread Softly, the Angels Are Calling" (1875).

If the angelic figure turned out to be somebody familiar, the gathered relatives took even more consolation. The preface to "Papa, Help Me Across" (1870) by A. Templeton Gorham explains, "A beautiful little girl, residing in Ithaca N.Y., while lying upon her death bed, just before she breathed her last, exclaimed, 'Papa, take hold of my hand and help me across.' Her father had died about three months before." Gorham employs an age-old metaphor for the experience of dying:

> Down by the dark rolling River
> Papa, I'm waiting for you,
> Let your strong arms now uphold me,
> Sing while you carry me through,
> Sing of the joys that await me
> In the bright home of the blessed;
> Bear me above the chill waters,
> Close to your own faithful breast.

Gorham's musical style in this chorus (Ex. 3.9) could have been borrowed from any number of songs by Henry Clay Work or George Root: it features the close part-writing and the chromaticism at cadences that we find in many songs

27. Harriet Beecher Stowe, *Uncle Tom's Cabin* (New York, 1952), 285.

EXAMPLE 3.9   A. Templeton Gorham, "Papa, Help Me Across" (Chicago: Root & Cady, 1870)

of the late sixties, the seventies, and the early eighties. No special style attached to this vision.

The single most important reason for the gathering was to record last wishes. Many songs bear these in their titles, as "Break the News to Mother" or "Take Me Home to Die" do. "Lelia Grey" (1845), by Miss. S. C. Edgarton and I. N. Metcalf, asks her suitor to visit her grave in a beautiful churchyard where they courted; the child in "Take Me Home" also requests a churchyard with a "mossy bank"; the adult in "Carry Me Home" wants to buried in New England, while the speaker in one of Gus Williams's songs merely asks, "See That My Grave Is Kept Green" (1876). The child in Samuel N. Mitchell and Charles E. Pratt's "Put My Little Shoes Away" bequeaths its toys to playmates and its shoes to a sibling, while one little boy in a song by Carrie Brainerd and John Budau tells his mother he is dying and then makes the title request, "Kiss Me Mother Ere I Die" (1875). Sometimes the last wish will be for special remembrance, as it is in "The Little Green Leaf in Our Bible" (1879) by Edward Harrigan and David Braham; the family complies by taking time every Sunday evening to recall a departed mother.

By the end of the nineteenth century, the ceremony surrounding the death watch was already becoming passé. Mark Twain tells a story in his autobiography of a matron on her deathbed: "The lady lay pale and still, with her eyes closed; about the bed, in the solemn hush, were grouped the family softly sobbing, some standing, some kneeling." But they do more than simply watch: in true modern spirit they summon a doctor. To the outrage of the gathering, he decides that the dying woman is a "humbug," and treats her to "an explosion of profane abuse." The breach of etiquette in "the chamber of death" is too great:

> Then the dying woman rose up in bed and the light of battle was in her eye. She poured out upon the doctor her whole insulted mind—just a volcanic irruption, accompanied by thunder and lightning, whirlwinds and earthquakes, pumice stone and ashes. It brought the reaction which he was after and she got well. . . .[28]

Hidden behind the irony of the doctor's method lay a significant change in circumstance: the family summoned a professional because they thought he might produce a positive effect. In most of nineteenth-century literature and popular song doctors generally did not attend the gathering, presumably because they were relatively powerless to help. Eventually deathbed scenes would progress from a family bedroom to a hospital, where the ministrations of science would occupy the last moments of life. The gathering would continue, but much of its ritual would disappear.

28. *The Autobiography of Mark Twain*, Charles Neider, ed. (New York, 1959), 9–10.

The Beautiful Grave

If family and friends gathered in part to hear dying wishes, this last request in popular song often specified the place of burial (as we have seen in many examples above). Descriptions of these locations accordingly had a long history. Pieces about the burial place often share both common features and standard plots that appear early in numbers like "High O'er the Grave Where Mary Sleeps" (ca. 1808) by Samuel Priestly Taylor. The first stanza in the lyrics describes the grave, situated in a rural setting, shaded by a tree (usually a willow), and attended by the sounds of nature:

> High o'er the Grave where MARY sleeps,
> Releas'd by death from ev'ry care,
> The silver willow hangs and weeps,
> And pity's bird sings dirges there.

The second stanza depicts the arrival of a mourner, a man in the case of a dead beloved:

> There at the soft and pensive hour
> Of evening lost to all repose,
> Her lover seeks the lonely bow'r,
> That sweet complainer joins his woes

The third and fourth strophes find him placing flowers on the grave, where he lingers almost perpetually in sorrow. Despite his mention of "dirges," Taylor sets all this in the same musical style he uses for other courtship songs (compare Ex. 3.10 to Ex. 1.4 above). Songwriters use the same basic scheme for men. "William the Brave" (1823), by "a young lady of KY" and Charles Gilfert, dies at the battle of New Orleans, but his anonymous admirer devotes her lyrics to the description of his grave. It lies next to a stream overhung with willows, and each evening "Sweet Mary" visits it, drenching flowers with tears to his memory.

George F. Root, publishing under the pseudonym "Wurzel," repeated the traditional elements of the burial song many years later in "The Hazel Dell" (1853),[29] which traveled the country with Wood's Minstrels. In his first verse Root intensifies the lyrics' sentimental effect by employing a common variation on the usual plot: the beloved lies buried where the narrator of the song courted her:

> Here in the moonlight often we have wander'd
> Thro' the silent shade,

---

29. Facsimile in Tawa, *Solo Songs*, I, 363–66.

EXAMPLE 3.10   Samuel Priestly Taylor, ''High O'er the Grave Where Mary Sleeps''
(New York: J. & M. Pfaff and J. Hewitt, [ca. 1808]; Wolfe no. 9300)

> Now where leafy branches drooping downward,
> Little Nelly's laid.

In place of birds, the ''silent stars'' weep over the grave in the second stanza,
and the third ends typically:

> Now I'm weary, friendless and forsaken,
> Watching here alone,
> Nelly thou no more will fondly cheer me,
> With thy loving tone;
> Yet forever shall thy gentle image
> In my mem'ry dwell,
> And my tears thy lonely grave shall moisten,
> Nelly dear, farewell.

As we can see in the chorus (Ex. 3.11), Root stays well within the bounds
prescribed for popular songs of his day. His two concessions to pathos are the
repeat of the chorus *pianissimo* and the syncopated leap of an octave upward
on ''Nelly'' in the penultimate measure. But this comes from the nostalgic
stock of Irish melodies used commonly in songs on many other subjects around

EXAMPLE 3.11   George F. Root, "The Hazel Dell" (New York: William Hall & Son, 1853)

this time. Root's other "hit" along these lines, "The Honeysuckle Glen" (1859), simply replicates the same story in different words.

Root's frequent choice of death as the subject of his songs was no morbid aberration on his part, but confirms, instead, his place in the mainstream. Significantly, "The Hazel Dell" occasioned a lengthy discussion in Root's autobiography of the qualities attaching to a successful popular song. And his account may be the most enlightening of any published during the nineteenth century:

> Friends used to say: "Root, why don't you do something better than 'Hazel Dell,' and things of that grade?" I used to answer: "If you and other musicians wished to use songs of a higher grade, either for teaching or for your own singing, do you suppose you would take mine when you could get Schubert or Franz, or even Abt, at the same price or less?" They were generally silent at that, and then I would tell them that in the elementary stages of music there were tens of thousands of people whose wants would not be supplied at all if there were in the world only such music as they (the critics) would have; but
>
> > "Convince a man against his will—
> > He's of the same opinion still."
>
> So they continued harping upon the well-worn subject. At last I thought I would publish a song or two above the grade of the "People's song." It was much easier to write where the resources were greater; where I did not have

to stop and say, "That interval is too difficult," or "That chord won't do," and I produced two or three that I knew would never be wanted to any extent. But they gave me the opportunity, when the old question came, "Why don't you do something better?" to say "Have you ever seen or heard of 'Gently, Ah, Gently,' or 'Pictures of Memory?' " To which they would have to answer "No," and I could say "That is why I do not write 'something better,' as you call it. Neither you nor any one else would know anything about my work on that grade, and I should be wasting my time in trying to supply the wants of a few people, who are already abundantly supplied by the best writers of Europe." Then they would say, "Well, it is nothing to write those little songs." I remember one, especially, then an eminent musician in New York, who said: "I could write a dozen in a day," and thinking there might be money in it, he did try under a *nom de plume*. But his dozen or less of "simple songs" slumbered quietly on the shelves of a credulous publisher until they went to the paper mill. It is easy to write correctly a simple song, but so to use the material of which such a song must be made that it will be received and live in the hearts of the people is quite another matter.[30]

Both Charles Hamm and Lawrence Levine suggest that the distinction between art and popular music was blurred in the first half of the nineteenth century, but Root informs us that the division was already well established by the time he published "The Hazel Dell" in 1853.[31] Even more important, the composer uses a song about burial as his quintessential example of a typical popular song.

One nineteenth-century song about burial, in fact, will still be familiar to many audiences today. Entitled "Listen to the Mocking Bird" (1855),[32] it came from the pen of Septimus Winner, writing under the pseudonym of Alice Hawthorne. In early editions Winner claimed credit as lyricist and arranger only, attributing the tune to Richard Milburn, a black musician who had taken employment in Winner's music store. The melody is truly infectious, with a strong hint of dance rhythm (polka or quadrille) and a tendency toward repeated pitches in the chorus suggesting minstrel style (see Ex. 3.12). The lyrics seem to confirm a blackface association, in spite of the missing dialect: the beloved "Hally" gathered cotton with her lover during their courtship. Otherwise, "Mocking Bird" follows the prescribed plot about the place of burial:

30. Root, *The Story*, 96–97.
31. Charles Hamm classifies Franz Abt, for instance, as a "popular composer," something that Root specifically denies. See " 'When the Swallows Homeward Fly'; or, German Song in Nineteenth-Century America," in *Yesterdays: Popular Song in America* (New York, 1979), 187–200; and Lawrence W. Levine, *Highbrow/Lowbrow: The Emergence of Cultural Hierarchy in America* (Cambridge, MA, and London, 1988). Levine relies on Hamm for support in some of his arguments about music.
32. Reprinted in Jackson, *Popular Songs*, 110–14.

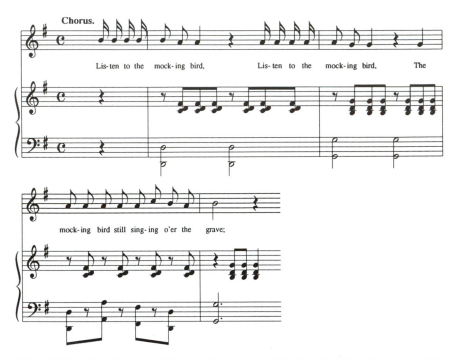

EXAMPLE 3.12 Septimus Winner, "Listen to the Mocking Bird" (Philadelphia: Winner and Shuster, 1855)

> I'm dreaming now of Hally, sweet Hally,
> For the thought of her is one that never dies:
> She's sleeping in the valley,
> And the mocking bird is singing where she lies.

In the last verse his perpetual grief overcomes him:

> When the charms of spring awaken,
> And the mocking bird is singing on the bough,
> I feel like one forsaken,
> Since my Hally is no longer with me now.

In its sprightliness this tune bears a distinct kinship to that in "Oh My Darling Clementine." Both share a memorability based on the immediate, compelling repetition of motives, as well.

The constant appearance of idealized, rural surroundings in songs about burial may reflect the nineteenth century's new concern about the beauty of cemeteries. American popular song was usually fashioned by city dwellers mainly for the consumption of other urbanites. And in the urban parts of early America, interment had traditionally been in churchyards, which became increasingly crowded and provoked concern about public health. For instance, almost 100,000 New Yorkers had been buried on the grounds of Trinity Church by 1800, causing the churchyard to rise perceptibly above the level of the surrounding streets.[33] Starting in the 1830s cemeteries moved into suburban surroundings where there was ample space, and they were landscaped to resemble parks. The first of these was Mount Auburn in Cambridge, and it was followed by Greenwood in Brooklyn, Green Mount in Baltimore, the Woodlands and Laurel Hill in Philadelphia, Harmony Grove in Salem, and the Albany Rural Cemetery:[34] The accent fell on nature in the suburban mortuarial park. Nehemiah Cleveland defended the unassuming gateway to Brooklyn's Greenwood Cemetery: "If the artificial portal be deficient in dignity, not so will you find that of Nature. You are now in a vestibule of her own making. Its floor is a delicious greensward; its walls are the steep hillside; lofty trees with their leafy capitals, form its colonnades. . . ."[35] Perhaps this is why Joseph P. Webster remembers "Willie's Grave" (1857) for its lovely stand of grass, or why in "Carrie Lee" (1860) by H. Angelo and Carroll Clifford, "They made her a grave in the wild wood." John P. Ordway clearly instructs mourners to plant flowers in "O'er Graves of the Loved Ones" (1868). And "In Her Little Bed We Laid Her" (1870) by Charles A. White describes a child's burial next to her mother where the birds sing. Some mourners even gather mementos from lovely mortuarial parks, as does the child who picks "A Violet from Mother's Grave" (words and music by Will H. Fox, 1881): "While life does remain, In memoriam I'll retain, This small violet I pluck'd."

Codes of conduct for the living apply strictly in the precincts of the dead. "Our Mother's Grave" (1863) by Frank Howard depicts a customarily rural scene demanding behavior seen frequently in other songs on the same subject:

> Where the murm'ring breezes gently sigh
> And the drooping willows spread,
> Lies our mother dear, whose soul's on high—
> She's sleeping with the dead.
> Oh! that sacred spot is to us so dear;
> There in sweet commune we stray;
> And o'er her grave drops the silent tear,
> As beside the mound we pray.

It is tempting to dismiss Howard on the basis of these lyrics, and his music for this song is similarly undistinguished. But he must have had his finger on the

---

33. David Charles Sloane, *The Last Great Necessity: Cemetaries in American History* (Baltimore and London, 1991), 19–20.

34. Ibid., 44–64.

35. Neil Harris, "The Cemetary Beautiful," in Jackson, ed., *Passing*, 105.

pulse of popular appeal, for his "When the Robins Nest Again" (1883) became one of the early national hits that suggested specialty publishing of popular songs to Willis Woodward.[36] These same sentiments echo through many other songs, including "Under the Willow She's Sleeping" (1860) by Stephen Foster, "She Was All the World to Me" (1864) by Foster and George Cooper, "Shedding Tears O'er Mother's Grave" (1883) by R. W. Rose and George A. Cragg, and even "Here Lies an Actor" (1889) by Paul Dresser. The thespian's burial is attended by his only child, who makes the appropriate gestures of scattering flowers and praying.

The stereotypical narrative for songs about burial just barely survived the beginning of the twentieth century in one strikingly successful example, "In the Shade of the Old Apple Tree" (1905) by Harry H. Williams and Egbert Van Alstyne.[37] Most listeners will remember the waltz chorus from this song, and it seems to express only nostalgia at first:

> In the shade of the old apple tree,
> Where the love in your eyes I could see,
> When the voice that I heard, like the song of the bird,
> Seem'd to whisper sweet music to me;
> I could hear the dull buzz of the bee,
> In the blossoms as you said to me,
> With a heart that is true, I'll be waiting for you,
> In the shade of the old apple tree.

These are, in fact, last words. The explanatory tale resides in the verse, as it does in almost all Tin Pan Alley songs. To begin the story, a lover gives an account of courtship in the spring, ending mysteriously, "I only pray we'll meet another day." To hold our interest to the end, Williams delays the outcome until the second verse:

> I've really come a long way from the city,
> And though my heart is breaking, I'll be brave,
> I've brought this bunch of flow'rs, I think they're pretty,
> To place upon a freshly mounded grave;
> If you will show me, father, where she's lying,
> Or if it's far, just point it out to me,
> Said he, "she told us all when she was dying,
> To bury her beneath the apple tree."

36. Hamm, *Yesterdays*, 285; Isidore Witmark claims that Howard purchased the rights and authorship for this song from Barney Fagan (Isidore Witmark and Isaac Goldberg, *From Ragtime to Swingtime* (New York, 1939), 180–81).
37. Reprinted in Fremont *Favorite Songs*, 161–65.

"In the Shade" summarizes a century of songs about burial by including the standard elements: fond reminiscences of the happy courtship, the last wish to repose in the beautiful, rural place where romance began, the faithful mourner who returns to the grave. As with most other songs about death, the moral has been set in the current style here: the waltz so often associated around the turn of the century with frustrated or failed romance.

Mourning and Memorials

Though death in the nineteenth century may have been perceived in a much different way than it is today, mourning is understandably a constant feature of encounters with dying. Songs about mourning generally took up the dual themes of loss and fidelity, and none was so poignant as the first success in this genre, "The Old Arm Chair" (1840) by Eliza Cook and Henry Russell. Cook (1818–89) was a British poet of no small reputation. Daughter of a tradesman, she taught herself letters, and she wrote for the *Weekly Dispatch* and the *New Monthly* for years. She later published volumes of her collected poetry, the first and most famous being *Melaia, and Other Poems* (1838). Russell (1812–1900) was also British and began his career as a member of "The Children's Opera Company" at the Drury Lane Theater. In 1825 he departed for Bologna to study at the conservatory there, since Italian opera was all the rage in London at the time. He claims to have pursued composition with Rossini and to have made the acquaintance of Bellini and Donizetti. He came away with a good command of the prevailing Anglo-Italian idiom of his time and emigrated to Canada, settling later in Rochester, New York, during the 1830s. He stayed in the United States just long enough to take the pulse of American popular song, and before he returned to London in 1842, he produced many early hits.[38] In fact, he was probably the most influential songwriter of his generation, as George F. Root attests:

> . . . the most important event to me, in the way of public performances, in those days (1839), was the singing of Henry Russell, an English Jew, who composed and sang "The Ivy Green," "Our Native Song," "A Life on the Ocean Wave," "The Old Sexton," "Wind of the Winter Night," and many other songs of that grade. He had a beautiful baritone voice and great command of the keyboard—played his own accompaniments, gave his concerts entirely alone, and in a year in this country made a fortune.

Russell tended toward highly Italianate melody and intricate accompaniments, but he seems to have toned down his usual style for "The Old Arm

---

38. All this information comes from the composer's autobiography, *Cheer! Boys, Cheer! Memories of Men and Music* (London, 1895).

EXAMPLE 3.13   Henry Russell, "The Old Arm Chair" (Boston: Oakes & Swan, 1840)

Chair," as if he knew he would attract a wider American audience in this way. The song has an extremely controlled melodic ambitus (it focuses on almost one note for much of the verse; see Ex. 3.13) and syncopated declamation, as well as a very plain accompaniment.

   Russell presumably read Cook's poem in a journal or in *Melaia,* and since he was living at the time in the United States, he must have calculated its appeal to American tastes. The "Arm Chair" reminds the speaker of her mother:

> I love it, I love it, and who shall dare
> To chide me for loving that old arm chair,
> I've treasured it long as a holy prize,
> I've bedew'd it with tears, and embalmed it with sighs;
> 'Tis bound by a thousand bands to my heart;
> Not a tie will break, not a link will start.
> Would ye learn the spell, a mother sat there,
> And a sacred thing is that old arm chair.

Fidelity is served by the preservation of the object because it stands specifically as a *memento mori:*

I sat and watch'd her many a day,
When her eye grew dim, and her locks were grey,
And I almost worshipp'd her when she smil'd,
And turn'd from her bible to bless her child.
Years rolled on, but the last one sped,
My idol was shatter'd, my earth star fled:
I learnt how much the heart can bear,
When I saw her die in that old arm chair.

The success of the song generated "A Reply to the Old Arm Chair" (ca. 1841) by John H. Warland and T. Bissell, and Root updated the theme for the Civil War in "The Vacant Chair" (1862). Later variations included "The Old Wooden Rocker" (1878) by Florence Harper, "Cradle's Empty, Baby's Gone" (a variation adapted to children, 1880) by Harry Kennedy, "Grandma's Old Arm Chair" (1880) by Frank B. Carr, "There's No Baby Face in the Cradle" (1881) by Thomas Westendorf, "The Little Old Red Shawl My Mother Wore" (1885) by Charles Moreland, "The Old Spinning Wheel" (1886) by Ike Browne, and "Baby's Rattle" (1888) by I. G. Withers. Even Edward Harrigan and David Braham indulged a light dose of this nostalgia in "My Dad's Dinner Pail" (1883).

So important was the function of memorialization in the nineteenth century that even the friendless had to have mourners. In Henry Russell's "The Poor Man's Friend" (ca. 1840) lyricist Eliza Cook tells of a pauper's funeral:

No sable pall, no waving plume,
No thousand torchlights to illume,
No parting glance, no struggling tear
Is seen to fall upon the bier.
There is not one of kindred clay
To watch the coffin on its way;
No mortal form, no human breast
Cares where the poor man's bones may rest.

But the burial is attended, nonetheless, by an "old, grey dog," who stands at the grave long after prayers have finished. The story has an egalitarian moral that must have been much prized by Americans:

The passing gaze may coldly dwell
On all that polished marbles tell,
For temples built on churchyard earth
Are claimed by riches more than worth.
But who would mark with undimm'd eyes
The mourning dog that starves and dies,

> Who would not ask, who would not crave,
> Such love and faith to guard his grave.

Russell's setting, by far more Italianate than his music for "The Old Arm Chair," seems somewhat at odds with these sentiments about equality.

Composers and lyricists reminded their audience about the egalitarian nature of death as a way to provide comfort in songs of mourning. Russell's unusual minor-mode setting for "The Old Sexton" (1841), with words by Benjamin Park, is more successful than his accompaniment for "The Poor Man's Friend" in engaging this theme, because it is plainer. The title character notes that death does not respect age, and calls himself the "king of the dead," singing the refrain, "I gather them in! I gather them in!" J. S. Cox articulates this same message in "A Few Feet of Clay" (1867), and Charles A. White comes close to lifting it wholesale in "I've Gathered Them In, or The Old Grave Digger" (1873).

The best songs joining death to equality, however, came from the pen of Henry Clay Work. "When the 'Evening Star' Went Down" (1866)[39] chronicles the wreck of ship in its first verse. The second verse supplies the essential message:

> Sail'd ever a ship from her quay,
> So heavily laden as she,
> With folly and fame, with hope and shame,
> With vanity, mirth and glee?
> But in the dark moment that came,
> How useless were rank and renown!
> And honors of earth, what were they worth,
> When the "Evening Star" went down.

To which the chorus adds by way of reinforcement, "They sleep in a fathomless grave, The guest and the mariner brave. . . ." In his accompaniment the composer uses the rocking motion of 6/8 time often associated with songs about ships on the sea. Work's most famous music associated with this subject, for "The Ship That Never Returned" (1865),[40] has no such onomatopoetic intent, however. The story is less explicitly egalitarian than in "Evening Star," but the three verses see every estate of humankind represented. The chorus (Ex. 3.14) gives the moral of fidelity to the departed. This tune became so famous that it worked its way into the oral tradition, rather like "Oh! Susanna." From there it surfaced in the mid-twentieth century as a clever parody performed by the Kingston Trio, called "M.T.A." (chorus: "Did he ever return, no, he

---

39. Reprinted in Henry Clay Work, *Songs,* Bertram G. Work, ed., vol. 19 of Earlier American Music (New York, 1974), 103–6.
   40. Ibid., 91–94.

EXAMPLE 3.14 Henry Clay Work, "The Ship That Never Returned" (Chicago: Root & Cady, 1865)

never returned, and his fate is still unlearned"). Indicative of modern tastes, this later version deflects Work's original focus on death, replacing it with a humorous theme.

Isaac Woodbury suggests in "Strike the Harp Gently" (1849) that song itself preserves images of those who lie "beneath the green turf"; they live in paradise and enjoy the company of other souls there. Many songs adopt the same strategy of intimating an afterlife to console the living. In "Forget Not the Dead" (1847) George Clark, Jr., and Lyman Heath advise that spirits of the departed surround us and console us if we cherish their memory; they watch over the living in Clinton Rose's and William S. Pitt's "Art Thou Watching O'er Me, Mother" (1866). Fanny Crosby and Susan Parkhurst left one of the clearest expressions of these sentiments in "There Are Voices—Spirit Voices" (New York: Horace Waters, 1864):[41]

> There are voices, spirit voices
> In the whisper of the breeze,
> When it wakes the infant blossoms,
> When it sighs among the trees,
> And the forms of those that love us
> On their viewless wings are nigh,
> In the wreathing clouds that linger
> On the blue ethereal sky.

Parkhurst provides a four-part chorus with standard syncopations to make the message perfectly clear:

> Spirit voices, hear the echo,
> They are calling us away.
> Where the roses never wither,
> Where the crystal fountains play.

The usual metaphor for a journey into the afterlife appeared frequently in songs like "Over the River They Beckon Me" (1859) by A. Whitney or "Hope on the Unseen Shore" (1869) by P. S. Pennell and Joseph P. Webster. Webster's undying classic in this vein was "Sweet Bye and Bye" (1868), with lyrics by S. Fillmore Bennett. The cover of the sheet music shows the angelic host hovering in the background sky, while an angel beckons the soul into a boat with a mast surmounted by a cross, and a figure reminiscent of the archangel Michael (or the Greek Charon?) prepares to row. The second verse enlightens us:

41. Reprinted in Judith Tick's *American Women Composers Before 1870* (Ann Arbor, MI, 1983), 208–10.

> We shall sing on that beautiful shore,
> The melodious songs of the blest,
> And our spirits shall sorrow no more—
> Not a sigh for the blessing of rest.

Another famous song in this genre was "Beautiful River" (1866)[42] by Robert Lowry, in a sheet-music arrangement by E. Mack. Death is not explicitly named in the lyrics, but they certainly concern the afterlife in their mention of the stereotypical journey:

> Soon we'll reach the shining river,
> Soon our pilgrimage will cease;
> Soon our happy hearts will quiver
> With the melody of peace.
>
> *[Chorus:]*
> Yes, we'll gather at the river,
> The beautiful, the beautiful river,
> Gather with the saints at the river,
> That flows by the throne of God.

Various descriptions of paradise recur in popular song to the end of the century; "The Beautiful Isle of Somewhere" (1897) by Mrs. Jessie Brown Pounds and J. S. Fearis may have been the last prominent example.

Some popular songs about mourning begin to reveal a changing attitude toward the place of death in American life at the end of the nineteenth century. Paul Dresser's "On the Banks of the Wabash Far Away" (1897)[43] deals with mourning, but avoids any direct confrontation with dying. The first verse, after recalling happy scenes of childhood, laments a deceased parent:

> But one thing there is missing in the picture,
> Without her face it seems so incomplete,
> I long to see my mother in the doorway,
> As she stood there years ago, her boy to greet.

While the second verse mourns a failed courtship and lost beloved:

> Long years have passed since I strolled thro' the churchyard,
> She's sleeping there my angel Mary dear,
> I loved her but she thought I didn't mean it,
> Still I'd give my future were she only here.

42. Reprinted in Jackson, *Popular Songs,* 26–69.
43. Facsimile in Fremont, *Favorite Songs,* 230–34.

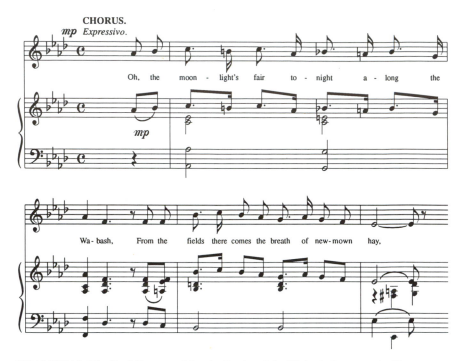

EXAMPLE 3.15   Paul Dresser, "On the Banks of the Wabash Far Away" (New York: Howley, Haviland & Co., 1897)

Dresser (1857–1906) uses these figures to generate longing for rural innocence rather than to confront the tragedy of death.[44] A vaudevillian from Indiana, he wrote the tune and lyrics on a Chicago tour according to Max Hoffmann:

> I went to his room at the Auditorium Hotel. . . . It was summer; all the windows were open and Paul was mulling over a melody that was practically in finished form. But he did not have the words. . . . He had a sort of dummy refrain, which he was studying; but by the time he finished what he was writing down to my playing it was an altogether different lyric.
>
> When Paul came to the line, "Through the sycamores the candle lights were gleaming [sic]," I was tremendously impressed. It struck me, at once, as one of the most poetic inspirations I had ever heard.
>
> I have always felt that Paul got the idea from glancing out of the window now and again as he wrote, and seeing the lights glimmering out on Lake Michigan.[45]

44. Charles Hamm gives this analysis of Dresser's song, *Yesterdays,* 302–8.
45. Witmark, *From Ragtime,* 170–71; Vera Dreiser gives a very different account of the lyrics' composition in *My Uncle Theodore* (New York, 1976), 75–78.

Dresser may well have seen the lights flickering from the Indiana shore; the song presents another "realistic" account of a city dweller's longing for the country. When it followed the second verse, the chorus of "In the Shade of the Old Apple Tree" had related directly a beloved's last words, but Dresser's chorus here (with one of the most beautiful melodies ever created out of descending sequences in the Tin Pan Alley mold; see Ex. 3.15)[46] has become completely detached from any such narrative. It merely bespeaks nostalgia:

> Oh, the moonlight's fair tonight along the Wabash,
> From the fields there comes the breath of new-mown hay,
> Through the sycamores the candle lights are gleaming,
> On the banks of the Wabash, far away.

Dresser's narrator cannot even visit the grave of his mother or beloved; he mourns from a distance which is, in a certain sense, the modern remove from the particulars of death.

Modern aversion to the subject of death and modern embarrassment about discussing it may account for the strange reaction with which we greet nineteenth-century popular music on the subject. Present-day listeners tend to find these lyrics at best amusing, at worst unbearably saccharine. But the songs may have something to teach us besides a comparative lesson about our own prejudices and assumptions. The people who died in each of the scenes we have viewed represented more than medical cases to be treated by science until its battery of techniques was exhausted. In nineteenth-century popular song the most important needs of the dying remained familial warmth and spiritual comfort. And for those who beheld death, the primary emphasis fell on consolation. All the formulaic and seemingly exaggerated etiquette surrounding the deathbed aimed at preserving the humanity of the dying and spectators alike. Even if we are unlikely to adopt the tone of nineteenth-century songs about death, we might consider their preoccupation with compassion and dignity, something our aversion and embarrassment often relegate to secondary concerns in the last hours of life.

46. Charles K. Harris, among many others, thought particularly well of "On the Banks of the Wabash"; see *After the Ball*, 135–37.

4

The Social Faith

Popular Views of Technology

On some very few occasions a popular song captures a cultural nexus where the values of a period reveal themselves to us in a combination of elements that forms an interleaved commentary. Perhaps the most striking instance from the nineteenth century appeared in Jesse L. Hutchinson's "Get Off the Track" (1844),[1] a song of such fervent abolitionist sentiments that it sometimes provoked theater riots during the family singers' performances:

> The *Express* warned us we should lose our popularity if we sang such songs as "Get Off the Track," and our friends advised us not to sing it. New York, as well as the rest of the country, was very tender on the subject of slavery at this time . . . Well, our first concert came off in Niblo's, on the 19th [of March, 1845]. We gave a second on the 24th, and two days later sang in Palmo's Opera House. When we sang "Get Off the Track," the audience hissed; then some began to cheer, and there was a tug of war; finally, the cheers prevailed.[2]

The controversy surrounding the song stemmed not only from its inflammatory words but also from its appropriation of a tune recently popularized in performances by the Virginia Minstrels under the title "Old Dan Tucker" (see Ex. 5.5 below). Old Dan was at once a kind of bare-fisted, populist hero ("De watchman was a runnin roun, cryin Old Dan Tucker's come to town") and a blackface clown ("Tucker is a nice old man, He use to ride our darby ram"), and the irony of using a tune in this tradition as an abolitionist anthem would

---

1. Reprinted in Nicholas Tawa's *American Solo Songs Through 1865,* vol. 1 of *Three Centuries of American Sacred and Secular Music,* Martha Furman Schleifer and Sam Dennison, eds. ([Boston], 1989), 131–34.

2. John Wallace Hutchinson, *Story of the Hutchinsons* (Boston, 1896), I, 138. Additional reactions to the Hutchinsons' performances of "Get Off the Track" appear in Dale Cockrell's edition of *Excelsior: Journals of the Hutchinson Family Singers, 1842–1846,* vol. 5 in Sociology of Music Series (Struvesant, NY, 1989), 252–56, 301–3, 308–11.

not have been lost on contemporary northern audiences, especially in New York City where group minstrelsy began.[3]

The most remarkable feature of "Get Off the Track," though, was incidental to the abolitionist message intended by its author, and that was Jesse's representation of social progress through a metaphor of technological progress. The lithograph on the cover (Illus. 4.1) depicts the content of the text precisely: the railroad car of "Immediate Emancipation," bearing the banners "Herald of Freedom" and "American Standard," "rides majestic" behind the engine "Liberator," while "Repealer" pulls the heavy freight of "Liberty Votes and Ballot Boxes." In the background

> All true friends of Emancipation
> Haste to freedom's railroad station;
> Quick into the cars get seated,
> All is ready and completed.
>   "Put on the steam," all are crying,
>   And the liberty flags are flying.

In the third through fifth verses Hutchinson admonishes merchants, editors, physicians, lawyers, priests, and politicians to join the procession. He threatens the last with electoral revenge, damning Henry Clay by name and Martin Van Buren by nickname for their various compromises in verse six:[4]

> Rail Roads to Emancipation
> Cannot rest on *Clay* foundation
> And the *tracks* of *"The Magician"*
> Are but Rail Roads to perdition.
>   Pull up the Rails! Emancipation
>   Cannot rest on such foundation.

In these clever lyrics the railroad became a symbol of irresistible social change ten years before tracks even reached the eastern bank of the Mississippi:[5]

> Hear the mighty car wheels humming!
> Now look out, the engine's coming!
> Church and statesmen, hear the thunder!
> Clear the track or you'll fall under.
>   "Get off the track!" all are singing
>   While the Liberty Bell is ringing.

---

3. A more complete discussion of the song and the Virginia Minstrels follows in Chapter 5.

4. Abolitionists denied Van Buren the nomination in 1844 for his earlier support of Jackson's pro-slavery stance. As a result Van Buren changed his tune and led the Free Soilers in 1848; see James M. McPherson, *Battle Cry of Freedom: The Civil War Era* (New York, 1988), 60–64.

5. See Robert Edgar Riegel, *The Story of the Western Railroads* (New York, 1926), 6.

Appeals to abolitionist sentiment often included some concept of inevitable progress, but they were usually grounded in militant religion, like this alternate text for the Methodist hymn "Say, Brothers Will You Meet Us?":

> Mine eyes have seen the glory
> of the coming of the Lord:
> He is trampling out the vintage
> where the grapes of wrath are stored;
> He hath loosed the fateful lightning
> of His terrible swift sword:
> His truth is marching on.[6]

By reaching into a secular realm for the imagery of inexorable power, "Get Off the Track" in turn sanctified technology, as N. P. Rogers revealed in the *Herald of Freedom* after hearing the Hutchinsons in June, 1844:

> Their outburst at the convention, in Jesse's celebrated "Get off the track," is absolutely indescribable in any words that can be penned. It represented the moral railroad in characters of living light and song, with all its terrible enginery and speed and danger. And when they came to the chorus-cry that gives name to the song—when they cried to the heedless pro-slavery multitude that were stupidly lingering on the track, and the engine "Liberator" coming hard upon them, under full steam and all speed, the Liberty Bell loud ringing, and they standing like deaf men right in its whirlwind path,—the way they cried, "Get off the track," in defiance of all time and rule, was magnificent and sublime.[7]

This piece presents an unusually exalted use of technological symbolism. It would be fair to say that most American popular songs from this period dealt with machines directly and saw immediate social benefits arising from technology. Despite these more mundane associations, songs in this genre were some of the best-loved and most enduring of all the music of their time.

The Perfect Automaton

To judge from nineteenth-century popular songs, the most admired of all machines in America was the clock. It represented, as Lewis Mumford observes, "the paragon of automatons: almost all that we can achieve and all that we can

6. Julia Ward Howe, "Battle Hymn of the Republic" (Boston: Oliver Ditson & Co., 1862), reprinted in Richard Jackson's *Popular Songs of Nineteenth-Century America* (New York, 1976), 22–25. The tune is usually attributed to William Steffe.

7. Hutchinson, *Story,* I, 117.

expect in automatons was first worked out in the clock.''[8] Not only was the clock "the first automatic machine applied to practical purposes; the whole theory of *production and regular motion* was developed through it,'' according to Karl Marx in 1863.[9] Chronometers also had the potential to bind society together:

> The machine that mechanized time did more than regulate the activities of the day: it synchronized human reactions, not with the rising and setting sun, but with the indicated movements of the clock's hands: so it brought exact measurement and temporal control into every activity, by setting an independent standard whereby the whole day could be laid out and subdivided.[10]

Reflecting this special power over human activity, lyricists commonly addressed clocks as if they were sentient beings. For Eliza Cook and Henry Russell the temporal order imposed by "The Old Clock" (ca. 1837) is the least of its features:

> Clock of the household, the sound of thy bell,
> Tells the hour and to many 'tis all thou can'st tell;
> But to me thou can'st preach with the tongue of a sage,
> And whisper old tales from life's earliest page.

Cook focuses on the clock's endurance, aesthetic beauty, and above all, its promotion of social continuity. Because the old clock runs unceasingly as well as regularly, its beautiful chimes mark holidays in the first verse, and its relentless ticking recalls the "loved and lost" in the second:

> Thou hast broke on my ear through the dead of the night,
> 'Till my spirit outwearied has pray'd for the light;
> When thy echoing tone and a Mother's faint breath,
> Seem'd the sepulchre tidings that whisper'd of death.

Perhaps Cook speaks to the clock in elevated second person because she credits it with immortality (verse three):

> My race may be run when thy musical chime,
> Will be still ringing out in the service of time;
> And the Clock of the household will shine in the room,
> When I the forgotten one sleep in the tomb.

The clock is, in a certain sense, more perfect than humankind.

8. *The Myth of the Machine: Technics and Human Development* (New York, 1966–67), 286.
9. Ibid.
10. Ibid.

To accompany Eliza Cook's vision of the clock Henry Russell provides a musical suggestion. Though the melody of "The Old Clock" follows his usual operatic style (see Ex. 4.1), the inner voices of the piano part move constantly in eighth notes alternating between two pitches, a counterpart to the ceaseless motion of the automaton itself. The redundant bass notes reinforce this mechanistic impression. And the beauty of *bel canto* flourishes highlight the silver tones of the "carol chimes." Russell's indirect suggestion of machinery, limited mostly to the accompaniment and even then to general movement rather than explicit imitation, has subtlety and even a certain elegance, but it starts down the slippery slope his successors would find irresistible.

Quite a number of songs followed the example of "The Old Clock" and may have directly imitated Cook and Russell. For instance, Leigh Cliff and J. Long's "The Old Church Clock" (ca. 1840) also muses on the notion that people age while machines endure, and sees the clock as providing social continuity by its associations with the important events of the past. This perfection ultimately serves as a chilling reminder of mortality in Henry Wadsworth Longfellow's "The Old Clock on the Stairs," set by T. Bricher (1846):

> Half way up the stairs it stands,
> And points and beckons with its hands;
> From its case of massive oak
> Like a monk who under his cloak
> Crosses himself, and sighs alas!
> With sorrowful voice to all who pass:
> Forever—never!

Longfellow comes very close to imitating the sound of the clock in his last line, but Bricher follows Russell's quiet practice of providing just a hint of regular motion in the accompaniment to intimate the relentless mechanism.

Inevitably both lyricists and composers succumbed to the temptation of onomatopoetic allusion, usually in "ticking" choruses or refrains that featured alternation of short repeated pitches. This happened early in songs like A. Sedgwick's "Household Clock" (1853), or in Charles Swaine and James L. Molloy's "The Old Cottage Clock" (ca. 1868), which expresses the stereotypical sentiments. Molloy chooses a compound meter uncharacteristic in this genre to set Swaine's tale (see Ex. 4.2), but in all other respects the song unfolds normally. The first verse stresses the constancy and permanence of the clock as well as attributing a kind of intelligence to it:

> The old, old clock of the household stock,
> Was the brightest thing and the neatest;
> Its hands tho' old had a touch of gold,
> And its chime ran still the sweetest:

Tempo marcato con espressione

EXAMPLE 4.1 Henry Russell, "The Old Clock" (New York: Jas. L. Hewitt, [ca. 1837])

127

Tick, tick it said,   Quick, quick to bed, For   ten   I've giv'n   warn - ing;

EXAMPLE 4.2   James L. Molloy, "The Old Cottage Clock" (Boston: Oliver Ditson, [ca. 1868])

> 'Twas a monitor too, though its words were few,
> Yet they lived though nations altered;
> And its voice still strong warn'd old and young,
> When the voice of friendship faltered.

The second verse endows the clock with a personality: it smiles during the day but speaks more sternly in the morning to wake sleepers. The third verse, marked *più lento,* takes up the more somber traditional theme of "old friends lost forever":

> Its heart beats on though hearts are gone,
> That warmer beat and younger;
> Its hands still move though hands we love
> Are clasped on earth no longer.

The lyrics of the third "ticking" refrain adapt these gloomy thoughts to parallel the form of the first two:

> Tick, tick it said.
> To the churchyard bed,
> The grave hath giv'n warning,
> Up, up and rise,
> and look to the skies,
> And prepare for a heavenly morning.

The perfect machine, admirable though it might be, provided but grim comfort as it marked the passing of time.

This melancholy view found its strongest expression in Major J. Barton's "Our Old Clock" (arranged by M. H. McChesney, 1872), in which ticking

EXAMPLE 4.3   J. Barton, "Our Old Clock" (Chicago: Root & Sons, 1872)

serves as a counterpoint to the disintegration of the narrator's family. Praised for its constancy in verse one of this standard narrative, the clock stands as witness in verse two:

> Its blackened hands still creeping,
> Creeping as they go,
> Unmindful of life's passing scenes
> Of sorrow, sin, and woe,
> Of hearts once light, now weary,
> Of joys forever fled,
> Of homes now sad and dreary,
> Of lov'd ones long since dead.

The ticking chorus (Ex. 4.3) just adds to the misery, and the third verse makes things no better:

> Our little band is scattered,
> The dear ones they are gone,
> Our household idols shattered,
> Have vanished one by one. . . .

To Barton, as to Cook, Longfellow, Sedgwick, and Swaine before him, technology is not insidious—he closes by extolling the constancy of "our dear old wooden clock." But set against human frailty, mechanical immortality proved the source of invidious comparison, and songs emphasizing this depressing inequity had only limited appeal.

Henry Clay Work, a firm believer in social progress from abolition to temperance, took a very different view of the clock: he capitalized on the tradition in popular song by borrowing many of its clichés, but rearranged them to sketch a more humane portrait. His "Grandfather's Clock" (published the same year as the Centennial Exhibition, 1876)[11] comfortingly resembles its owner:

> My grandfather's clock was too large for the shelf,
> So it stood ninety years on the floor;
> It was taller by half than the old man himself,
> Though it weighed not a pennyweight more.

Nor does it provide a foil for human mortality:

> It was bought on the morn of the day that he was born,
> And was always his treasure and pride;
> But it stopp'd short never to go again
> When the old man died.

The clock provides not only order but a kind of friendship: "In childhood and manhood the clock seemed to know and to share both his grief and his joy. For it struck twenty-four when he entered the door with a blooming and beautiful bride." Its running becomes the symbol of constant fidelity rather than a reminder of relentless aging:

> My grandfather said that of those he could hire,
> Not a servant so faithful he found;
> For it wasted no time, and had but one desire—
> At the close of each week to be wound.
> And it kept in its place—not a frown upon its face,
> And its hands never hung by its side. . . .

The puns in this verse give some idea of the song's cheerfulness, reflected also in the famous "ticking" chorus (Ex. 4.4) which proceeds directly from earlier examples of the genre. Work's version may not be as elaborate as Barton's, but its onomatopoeia and clever rhymes—"Ninety years without slumbering, tick, tick, tick, tick, His life seconds numbering, tick . . ."—prove far more memorable.

In "Grandfather's Clock" Work also hit at the end of his career on the

---

11. Reprints appear in Jackson's *Popular Songs,* 76–79, and in Henry Clay Work's *Songs,* Bertram G. Work, ed., vol. 19 of Earlier American Music (New York, 1974), 177–80.

EXAMPLE 4.4 Henry Clay Work, "Grandfather's Clock," chorus (New York: C. M. Cady, 1876)

EXAMPLE 4.5   Henry Clay Work, "Grandfather's Clock," verse (1876)

melodic formula that Tin Pan Alley would later adopt to ensure the success of its songs. The melody of the verse consists of variations on a short motive—the three notes on the word "watching its" (Ex. 4.5)—which the composer repeats in sequence once and then inverts (with the second note rising rather than falling) for a third repetition. The combination of arresting music and witty, positive lyrics had predictable results: in 1879 George Birdseye claimed that "Grandfather's Clock"

> is without doubt the most popular song in this country. . . . [It] was first sung in public in New Haven, by Sam Lucas, in the Hyer Sisters Combination, a genuine colored minstrel troupe, and was a decided hit from the start. Now, it is sung, it might be said without much exaggeration, simultaneously every night by half the minstrel companies in the United States, to say nothing of being played by orchestras, bands, and musical instruments of every description anywhere and everywhere.[12]

Work's vision of the clock as a humane servant generated parodies numbering "upwards of twoscore," according to Birdseye, who exaggerated little in this case. Alice Dale and George W. Morgan copied Work's song immediately

---

12. "America's Song Composers. IV. Henry Clay Work," *Potter's American Monthly* 12 (1879), 286.

in "Grandmother's Clock" (1876) which also provides companionship (she talks to the machine throughout) and dies with its owner. B. M. McWilliams came very close to plagiarism in "The Clock That Struck When Grandpa Died" (1880). And Work himself tried to capitalize on his success with "Sequel to 'Grandfather's Clock' " (1878), in which a relative returns to the old man's house and watches the useless machine chopped up for kindling. It is replaced by a wall clock (ticking in chorus) which its owner dislikes. A few songs continued the older theme of human mortality, including J. W. Turner's "The Old Kitchen Clock" (1879) and Frank Dumont and W. S. Mullaly's "The Old Cuckoo Clock" (1882), written for performance by the San Francisco Minstrels. In spite of their onomatopoetic choruses, none of these had the impact of Work's original which firmly established automatons as friends and companions of humankind.

The Virtues of Mobility

Where songs about clocks appreciated the inherent properties of machines, songs about transportation usually addressed the benefits accruing to society from the workings of technology. When Stephen Foster writes in "The Glendy Burk" (1860)[13] of speed, it serves merely to send the main character on his way:

> De Glendy Burk is a mighty fast boat,
> Wid a mighty fast captain too;
> He sits up dah on de hurricane roof
> And he keeps his eye on de crew.
> I can't stay here, for dey work too hard;
> I'm bound to leave dis town;
> I'll take my duds and tote 'em on my back
> When de Glendy Burk comes down.

The second verse also paints a specific picture of the machine, burning wood, smoking, roaring, reciprocating, but this is just atmosphere: Foster uses the song to rehearse the standard phrases of minstrelsy. In fact, songs about steamboats were rare, despite the crucial role river travel played in opening the west. For some reason this technology did not resonate in popular song.

Railroads, on the other hand, immediately captured the public imagination (as "Get Off the Track" attests), perhaps because the very enterprise of their

13. Facsimile in *The Music of Stephen Foster,* Steven Saunders and Deane L. Root, eds. (Washington and London, 1990), II, 93–96.

construction engendered civic virtue. To somebody of Ralph Waldo Emerson's erudition and Protestant values,

> The benefaction derived in Illinois and the great West from the railroads is inestimable, and vastly exceeding any intentional philanthropy on record. What is the benefit done by a good King Alfred, or by a Howard, or Pestalozzi, or Elizabeth Fry, or Florence Nightingale, or any lover, less or larger, compared with the involuntary blessing wrought on nations by the selfish capitalists who built the Illinois, Michigan, and the network of the Mississippi-valley roads; which have evoked not only all the wealth of the soil, but the energy of millions of men. It is a sentence of ancient wisdom that "God hangs the greatest weights on the smallest wires."[14]

A handful of popular songs actually echoed Emerson's praise of building railroads as a magnificent enterprise and accomplishment. Stephen C. Massett dedicated his "Clear the Way" (1868) to "The President Director & Company of the Great Pacific Railroad" before congressional investigations in 1873 revealed the scandal surrounding Credit Mobilier.[15] A better-known song lauding both the western railroad and the wonders of transcontinental adventure is Henry Clay Work's "Crossing the Grand Sierras" (1870).[16] Written for a vocal quartet (Ex. 4.6), it sometimes imitates the rumbling noise of a railroad car in the lower voices (as opposed to the imitation of steam escaping an engine found in "Get Off the Track"). In the confident march rhythm Work reserves for songs about progress, he hails the realization of manifest destiny in a duet and chorus:

> Forgetting far Atlantic,
> And midway scenes romantic,
> We scale the peaks gigantic,
> which guard the Land of Gold. . . .
>
> [Chorus:]
> We sing a wond'rous story,
> No nation sang before!
> A Continental Chorus,
> That echoes either shore:
> We sang it on the summit!
> We sing it on the plain!
> We've climbed the Grand Sierras
> With the Lightning Palace Train.

14. Ralph Waldo Emerson, *The Conduct of Life* (Boston and New York, 1909), 243–44.

15. Dee Brown gives an extensive account of corruption in the building of the first transcontinental railroad in *Hear the Lonesome Whistle Blow: Railroads in the West* (New York, 1977), 58–77.

16. The sheet music appears in Work's *Songs*, 145–53.

EXAMPLE 4.6   Henry Clay Work, "Crossing the Grand Sierras" (Chicago: Root & Cady, 1870)

Attesting to the seductiveness of Work's vision, just a few years later Henry C. Jarrett and Harry Palmer organized a special "Lightning Train" of "hotel" cars to travel from New York to Sacramento in three days.[17] Will S. Hays wrote a similarly laudatory ballad to an engine, "Number Twenty Nine" (1871), with verses on the speed, power, and beauty of the machine to a repeated-note melody meant to suggest its action. And nature itself rejoiced in man's ability to change the environment in T. M. Dewey's "Tunnel Song" (undated) about the building of the Hoosic Tunnel.

In the end, though, the wonders of trains or the miraculous logistics of railroad construction had to take mere supporting roles in the drama of technology, which was mainly a morality play about the promotion of republican egalitarianism. By shrinking the distances separating various localities in a vast American nation, railroads promoted one kind of social intermixing. And the actual design of American railroad cars facilitated another. Europeans took the mail coach as their model and separated the ever-increasing length of cars into compartments for a limited number of passengers. Americans, on the other hand, eventually adopted the plan of the packet boat, with its long aisle running down the center of a common room.[18] Even first-class Pullman sleepers had rows of seats by day and placed berths along a central aisle. The arrangement had the effect of throwing all types of humanity together, a situation noted early in "Riding on a Rail" (1853) by Charlie Converse. He devotes the first verse with its peculiar monotone imitation of mechanism (see Ex. 4.7) to the wonders of the technology, but he gets down to business in the second:

> Men of different stations,
> In the eye of fame,
> Here are very quickly
> Coming to the same;
> High and lowly people,
> Birds of every feather,
> On a common level,
> A travelling together.

He goes on to present a humorous catalogue of human peccadillos, including a man who snores, a woman with a crying baby, a woman guarding eggs taken to market, and a nervous spinster who becomes the object of a double entendre:

> Ancient maiden lady,
> Anxiously remarks,

17. Brown, *Lonesome Whistle*, 218–20.
18. Wolfgang Schivelbusch suggests that American railroad cars were designed specifically to promote interaction between people of various stations (*The Railway Journey: The Industrialization of Time and Space in the 19th Century* (Leamington Spa, Hamburg, and New York, 1986), 103–7).

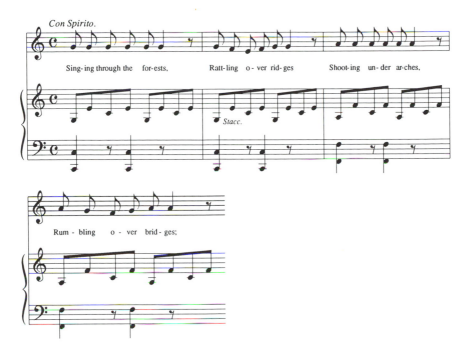

EXAMPLE 4.7   Charlie Converse, "Riding on a Rail" (Boston: Oliver Ditson, 1853)

That there must be peril
'Mong so many sparks;
Roguish looking fellow,
Turning to a stranger,
Says it's his opinion
She is out of danger.

Converse obviously takes no real offense at these social irritations, finding
them salutary for their entertainment as well as for the social intermixing from
which they result. Both the punning and the musical onomatopoeia indicate the
ease with which Americans embraced the revolution of railroad travel.

American songwriters employed this same relaxed jocularity in treating the
amorous encounters that inevitably developed from social interaction. C. D.
Lakey and H. M. Higgins tell the story of a successful romance in "The Celebrated Railroad Song" (1866), using the metaphors of train travel to outline
the ensuing stages of marriage. T. S. Lonsdale, writing in the new spirit of
postbellum romantic frankness, relates the tale of widower who begins a romance while on a journey with his small son in "Tommy Make Room for Your
Auntie" (1875). The little boy balks at his father's familiarity, and the female
speaker complains in the dialogue printed after the first verse:

137

Yes, the confounded young urchin caused me a great deal of pain, and sorrow; and the widower, his Father, introduced me to the little boy as his auntie, and during the whole of the journey the father had to say. . . .

The chorus then serves as punchline,[19] "Tommy make room for your Auntie. . . . " Humorous though the song may be, it delivers a serious message, for "Miss Fitzwilliam of Union Square" does not herald from the privileged classes:

> When first I met this Widower
> 'Twas on my journey down
> To spend a day at Long Branch,
> Just like a swell from town,
> The Widower loved romantic scenes,
> And a squeeze on the sly.
> But when his arm went round my waist,
> The boy began to cry!

The boy constantly invokes a sense of propriety which the social interaction of the railroad car assaults. The train passes conveniently through a tunnel at the end of the third verse, temporarily solving the lovers' problem. Lonsdale sets this story in a "lively" 6/8 (see Ex. 4.8), and he may have designed it for a burlesque routine, since the singer claims in the first verse that "when . . . dressed, of gents she knows a few." The jocularity employed by the author intimates acceptance, even approval of different classes intermingling.

The results of chance mixing during travel were even more diverting when they went awry. W. J. Florence's "Ridin in a Railroad Keer" (ca. 1859) takes place on a western rail journey, where "Slim Jim" meets "Suke Sattinet" (apparently not a blackface character, despite her name) and becomes completely infatuated, only to be chased away with a shotgun by her father. W. H. Cove offers a more demonstrative caution in "The Charming Young Widow I Met in the Train" (ca. 1865), which unfolds to a tune faintly like an Irish jig. The woman riding in first class gives the male speaker her baby to hold, deftly lifts his watch, wallet, and ticket, and sneaks off the train at the next stop. Only later does he discover the fact that the baby is only a doll and that he has been robbed.

Henry Clay Work offers a variation on Cove's theme in his "Buckskin Bag of Gold" (1869),[20] reversing the feminine and masculine roles of Cove's version:

> Last night I met him on the train—
> A man with lovely eyes;

---

19. The technique of inserting spoken dialogue seems to grow out of a desire to reproduce aspects of a particular performer's act. The best examples come from Gus Williams's German dialect songs; see Chapter 8.

20. Reprinted in Work, *Songs*, 48–51.

EXAMPLE 4.8   T. S. Lonsdale, "Tommy Make Room for Your Auntie" (New York: C. H. Ditson, 1875)

> And he gave me such a searching glance
> Of sweetly charm'd surprise!
> I knew 'twas he the lady meant,
> Who once my fortune told,
> By his jet black eyes, his grand moustache,
> And his buckskin bag of gold.

Work teases out the remainder of the story over the course of three more verses, ending with the young woman's fruitless search for her admirer at the hotel in her home town:

> How can I seek a name unknown?
> Oh, tell me where he went!
> What is this I read! why, Papa's bank
> Is robb'd of ev'ry cent!
> The thief, it seems, left town last night,
> Well, well! I'm nicely sold!
> He had jet black eyes, a grand moustache,
> And his buckskin bag of gold.

EXAMPLE 4.9 Henry Clay Work, "Buckskin Bag of Gold" (Chicago: Root & Cady, 1869)

Work does not adopt the moralistic tone in "Buckskin Bag" that he does for "Come Home, Father!" or "When the Evening Star Went Down." A boisterous polka (see Ex. 4.9) forms the basis of his setting, and his choral writing seems to imitate the chuffing of a steam engine. This musical banter supports the comic reversal in the last verse. Work took a benign view of social intermixing on trains, suggesting that only the naïve were at risk.

Even when the technology of railroading ran amok in the nineteenth century, the fault always lay in human error, not in the machine itself. In Artie Kellog's "The Railway Wreck" (1887) the awful crash and fire result from failure of the engineer to observe a proper speed. More often than not, in fact, technolog-

EXAMPLE 4.10   J. W. Bischoff, "Saved from Death" (Cincinnati: J. Church, 1874)

ical mishap served to call forth heroism. George William Hersee and J. W. Bischoff's "Saved from Death" (1874) tells the story of a child playing on the tracks, about to be run over by an oncoming train. The composer sets the lyrics in an old-fashioned style, more reminiscent of Henry Russell in the forties than of anybody from the seventies: Bischoff uses no syncopation, no four-part chorus, and chooses a melodic shape and rhythm in the style of a *romanza* (Ex. 4.10). The four verses unfold in predictable form, the first outlining the situation, the second telling of the mother's anguish, and the third recording the engineer's sudden discovery of impending disaster. He saves the day by slowing the train and leaving the controls:

> And as he feels his way along,
> And on the pilot stands,
> The mother moans, "God give you strength,"
> Then falls upon the sands.
> His eye is quick, his nerve is great,
> His soul knows no alarms,
> O, God, that wheel will crush the child!
> No, no, 'tis in his arms!

At no time does Hersee question the general good of technology. Its dangers, rather, elicit exemplary social behavior.

The two themes of societal intermixing and appropriate social response combined forces in the most famous railroad song of the nineteenth century (perhaps of all time), Gussie Lord Davis's "In the Baggage Coach Ahead" (1896).[21] Davis (1863–99) was one of the rare African-American composers before World War II to have his music accepted in the non-ethnic canon of popular song. A native of Cincinnati, he received an informal education in music and some private lessons at the Nelson Musical College while working as a janitor (he was refused admission as a student on racial grounds). He moved to New York around 1887, just in time to witness the birth of Tin Pan Alley as a force in the publication of popular song, and he soon became one of its most famous composers, contributing a song still heard occasionally, "Irene, Good Night." Edward Marks called him a "mainstay" of Joseph W. Stern & Co.[22]

"Baggage Coach," Davis's best-known composition, usually receives attention for its sentimentality, and Marks reprints a maudlin poem that supposedly served as a model for the lyrics (a Pulman porter claimed to have written the verses and shown them to Davis when he was similarly employed).[23] But while the story of a widowed father caring for his child wears its heart on its sleeve, the cover bears no *memento mori*. Instead a picture of a train with the caption "The Empire State Express of the New York Central.——Fastest Train in the World" (see Illus. 4.2) suggests a different focus. Davis begins by establishing the conditions to which American carriages expose the traveler:

> On a dark stormy night, as the train rattled on,
> All the passengers had gone to bed,
> Except one young man with a babe in his arms
> Who sat there with a bowed-down head,
> The innocent one began crying just then,
> As though its poor heart would break,
> One angry man said, "Make that child stop its noise,
> For its keeping all of us awake,"
> "Put it out," said another, "Don't keep it in here,
> We've paid for our berths and want rest,"
> But never a word said the man with the child,
> As he fondled it close to his breast. . . .

21. A copy of the original sheet music appears in Robert A. Freemont's *Favorite Songs of the Nineties* (New York, 1973), 152–56.

22. Edward B. Marks and Abbott J. Liebling, *They All Sang, from Tony Pastor to Rudy Vallée* (New York, 1934), 81. Eileen Southern reprints a good many contemporary articles on Davis, "In Retrospect: Gussie Lord Davis (1863–1899), Tin Pan Alley Tunesmith," *Black Perspective in Music* 6 (1978), 188–230.

23. *They All Sang*, 82–83; for a purely sentimental Davis song about trains, see "Just Set a Light" with words by Henry V. Neal (New York, Howley, Haviland & Co, 1896).

EXAMPLE 4.11   Gussie Lord Davis, "In the Baggage Coach Ahead" (New York: Howley, Haviland & Co., 1896)

All this unfolds to the strains of a waltz (Ex. 4.11), exhibiting here one of its several connotations: nostalgic reminiscence of frustrated romance.[24] In the second verse a passenger learns that the child's deceased mother lies "In the Baggage Coach Ahead," and the moral of the story ensues:

> Ev'ry woman arose to assist with the child,
> There were mothers and wives on that train,
> And soon was the little one sleeping in peace,
> With no tho't of sorrow or pain,
> Next morn at a station, he bade all goodbye,
> "God bless you," he softly said,
> Each one had a story to tell in their home,
> Of the baggage coach ahead.

Davis not only commends patience and charity to the listener in such communal situations, he speaks also of what we gain from traveling: it exercises our reflexes for tolerance.

24. Both "After the Ball" and "In the Shade of the Old Apple Tree," for instance, feature this association.

143

Where train travel promoted social virtue, other technologies of travel increased individual freedom with unexpected results. The most revolutionary of these seems to have been the bicycle, though its ability to change social custom was not immediately apparent when it came on the American scene from France around 1869. In "The New Velocipede" (1869) E. H. Sherwood discusses little more than the speed of the contraption, comparing it to the rapidity of lightning, a woman's tongue (the author was obviously no feminist), or finally in the chorus:

> It goes some like the railroad
> That you will always find
> To run ahead of any train,
> And also run behind.

Frank Wilder's "The Great Velocipede" (1869) also limits comment to the thrill of speed, but it implies a further allure and social significance by sporting a picture of a girl in bloomers on the cover. O. H. Harpel and Henry Atkins spell out another such implication of the bicycle for courtship in the five verses of their "Velocipede Jimmy" (1869): the first introduces the new invention, the second relates how it attracts women, the third explains its operation, the fourth its speed compared to the horse, and the fifth of an accident caused by showing off for a girlfriend.

The bicycle craze took until the 1890s, however, to overwhelm both the songwriter and the general public. Edward Marks credited a British bicycle number, "Daisy Bell" by Harry Dacre (also known as "A Bicycle Built for Two," 1892),[25] with nothing less than launching the vogue of the waltz song.[26] The amorous associations of the dance join the virtues of the machine in the famous chorus:

> Daisy, Daisy,
> Give me your answer, do!
> I'm half crazy,
> All for the love of you!
> It won't be a stylish marriage,
> I can't afford a carriage,
> But you'll look sweet on the seat
> Of a bicycle built for two!

The link to courting was no mere gimmick. "Velocipedes" granted new mobility to young people and became the vehicle of choice for courtship among couples of moderate means. Nineteenth-century songs about courting often

25. Sheet music in Fremont, *Favorite Songs*, 64–67.
26. *They All Sang*, 71.

stressed the prying eyes of parents, and those unable to afford a horse and buggy found it difficult to escape the family parlor. The comparatively cheap bicycle enabled couples to find privacy more easily. Americans picked up this theme in songs like J. M. Richards's "Bicycle Episode" (1897), in which the narrator meets his girl while riding in the park. He promptly recommends the machine as a progressive form of transportation for the purpose of winning fair lady.

The newfound freedom of mobility also liberated women in the eyes of most male lyricists and composers. Avery Oddfellow and F. W. Meacham's "The Bicycle Girl" (1895) adopts the stylish waltz meter for a description of the modern woman who is not the least shy in her manner. The first verse deals with speed and independence, while the second talks with unease about the implications:

> Oh, the bicycle girl is the latest thing out,
> Just published by Women and Co.
> Of their notable rights, in a very loose form,
> In short, without covers, you know, that's no go,
> In short, without covers, you know!
> But the rights of the bicycle girl are all wrongs,
> She's no more or less than a thief;
> She has stolen our collars and caps, and she thinks,
> We'll throw her the handkerchief!

Oddfellow's connection between the bicycle and women's growing independence was not an amusing exaggeration, moreover. Marks actually wrote of Tin Pan Alley during this time, "The rapid change in the types of songs confused the old-line publishers. The bicycle craze hurt their business because it took girls away from the piano."[27] The theme surfaced in Edward Harrigan and David Braham's "The Girl That's Up to Date" (1894), in A. A. Condon's "The Latest Fad" (1895), in O. A. Hoffmann's "Have You a Wheel?" (1895), and in Nellie Burt's "Dora Brown" (1897). George Lowell Tracy and James C. Dunn stated quite baldly that the vehicle would cause "men to cook the meals" while women roam the public domain freely in "The New Columbia Wheel" (1898). And Philip Wales portrayed a father so suspicious of his daughter's freedom, he insisted on riding along with her in "My 'Cycle Gal" (1899).

None of the later bicycle songs achieved the popularity of Dacre's original (many seem to have been published as novelties by their composers), but they all agreed on the social effects of this technological development. Moreover, songs about bicycles set the precedent for automobiles, when they gained cur-

27. Ibid., 73.

rency just after the turn of the century. The amorous waltz proves the immediate style of choice for pieces like "In My Merry Oldsmobile" by Vincent Bryan and Gus Edwards (1905),[28] which offers yet another way to free couples from parental supervision:

> Come away with me Lucille
> In my merry Oldsmobile,
> Down the road of life we'll fly,
> Automobubbling you and I.
> To the church we'll swiftly steal,
> Then our wedding bells will peal,
> You can go as far as you like with me,
> In my merry Oldsmobile.

Giddy Communication

Though all the innovations of nineteenth-century technology elicited humor from lyricists and composers, songs about the new developments in communication, the telegraph and telephone, tended to fall mostly in a comic vein. The workings of a clock, bicycle, or train were visible and relatively easy to apprehend through common sense. But it seemed incredible to contact somebody tens, or hundreds, or thousands of miles away almost instantaneously by means of a completely invisible force. One favorite manifestation of this incredulity takes the form of an impossible telephone call in songs like Charles H. Hoyt and Charles Reed's "Telephone in de Air" (1887). Hoyt (1860–1900) would go on to great fame as the author and lyricist of *A Trip to Chinatown,* a musical comedy that ran hundreds of performances in New York during the early 1890s.[29] This earlier example of his work comes from the long tradition of pseudo-spirituals and has their standard musical features (see Ex. 4.12): call-and-response verse, prominent syncopation, and duple meter, all part of the "realism" which permeated song on various levels after the Civil War. This style generaly connotes an exaggerated rural religiosity, and the comic tone in the dialect lyrics comes from obvious absurdities (called impossibilia) customarily associated with minstrelsy:[30]

> When I close dese earthly books,
> Telephone up dar!

28. Sheet music in Fremont, *Favorite Songs,* 148–51.
29. A short summary of its history appears in Stanley Appelbaum's *Show Songs from "The Black Crook" to "The Red Mill"* (New York, 1974), xxix; and Gerald Bordman gives a lengthier account in *American Musical Theatre: A Chronicle,* 2nd ed. (New York, 1992), 113–15.
30. Impossibilia are discussed in Chapter 5; the history of the pseudo-spiritual in Chapter 6.

EXAMPLE 4.12   Charles Reed, "Telephone in de Air" (Chicago: Bowen & Schleif-farth, 1887)

I want to hang on Gabriel's hooks,
    Telephone up dar!
I fix my seat wid carpet tacks,
    Telephone up dar!
Please do send an answer back
    Telephone up dar!

[Refrain:]
Don't you hear dem bells aringin',
'Way up in de sky?
I know dey means to hab me near,
So I'll bid you all goodbye.
I leave you all my real estate,
For dose I doesn't care;
I'se got de latest news jes now,
Telephone up dar!

Even the minstrel narrator probably knows that telephone lines do not run to paradise, but his faith, both spiritual and technological, would have it other-wise. The joke is revealing, nonetheless: the new invention seems to reach

147

everywhere, why not heaven? In the second verse the narrator calls Noah, and the third verse offers a political jest at the expense of the high and mighty in true minstrel fashion:

> Oh Mr. Cleveland's President now;
>   Telephone up dar!
> De clouds am hangin' on his brow,
>   Telephone up dar!
> His frien's are boun' to fall in line,
>   Telephone up dar!
> Will he get dar a second time?
>   Telephone up dar!

The conceit about the telephone's ubiquity was not confined to blackface. It appeared in songs like Frank N. Scott and D. L. White's "I've Heard from the Man in the Moon" (1893), a version of the same theme in waltz time. And in the twentieth century Charles K. Harris parlayed it into a major success, "Hello Central, Give Me Heaven" (1901), though this variation turned sentimental.

If "Telephone in de Air" and "I've Heard from the Man in the Moon" indicated by exaggeration the reach of the telephone, many other songs showed how extended communication combined social interaction with privacy in a way much akin to the bicycle. Hugh Morton and Gustave Kerker contribute a waltz song about a courtship conducted over the wires in "Oh, My Estelle" (1898), a number from *The Telephone Girl*.[31] And the classic of this genre is the well-known "Hello! Ma Baby" (1899) credited on its cover to Ida Emerson and Joseph E. Howard (some attribute the song to Howard alone, but Andrew Sterling later claimed to be the lyricist).[32] Howard (1867–1961) was a talented vaudeville singer who toured far and wide (with Emerson as his sometime partner). His output reflected his eclectic talents for capitalizing on every popular idiom that came along (Marks calls him an "opportunist of song"),[33] and at the end of the century that meant ragtime. Even if we did not know the title of this song, we would still recognize the elements of vocal ragtime: a suggestion of "alternating" bass (octaves leaping back and forth in the lowest voice of the accompaniment) and a bit of syncopation confined here to the chorus (Ex. 4.13), as well as a little chromaticism in the verse to add extra spice. In mild dialect the lyrics display the newly extended scope of social interaction:

31. See Appelbaum, *Show Songs*, for a brief discussion of the show and an additional number, "Little Birdies Learning How to Fly," xxxiii and 111–15.

32. The original sheet music appears in Fremont's *Favorite Songs*, 108–12; Marks lists Emerson as part of the vaudeville act premiering the song (*They All Sang*, 235), a possible explanation for the appearance of her name on the sheet music. Alec Wilder reports Sterling's assertions in *American Popular Song: The Great Innovators, 1900–1950* (New York and Oxford, 1972), 12.

33. Ibid., 92.

EXAMPLE 4.13   Joseph Howard, "Hello Ma Baby" (New York: T. B. Harms, 1899)

> I'se got a little baby, but she's out of sight,
> I talk to her across the telephone;
> I'se never seen my honey but she's mine all right;
> So take my tip, an' leave this gal alone.
> Ev'ry single morning you will hear me yell,
> "Hey Central! fix me up along the line."
> He connects me with my honey, then I rings the bell,
> And this is what I say to baby mine. . . .

The famous chorus is a masterpiece of Tin Pan Alley's motivic craft, which sets the conceit of remote courtship by machine to a descending sequence:

> Hello! ma baby,
> Hello! ma honey,
> Hello! ma ragtime gal,
> Send me a kiss by wire,
> Baby, my heart's on fire!
> If you refuse me,
> Honey, you'll lose me,
> Then you'll be left alone;
> Oh baby, Telephone
> And tell me I'se your own.

This infatuation at a distance does not follow in the least the frustrated romantic course of pre-Civil War songs: the speaker eventually secures the name and address of his beloved in the second verse. Such romances can also turn sour, as one does in H. M. Saumenig and A. B. Sloane's "Ring Off, Coon!" (1899) about infidelity pursued over the phone. But this song still shares with "Hello! Ma Baby" the links between ragtime style and astonished bemusement about the possibilities of the new technology.

Ragtime developed a distinct association with modern technology, and none other than George M. Cohan (1878–1942) used the connection to generate his first big hit. "I Guess I'll Have to Telegraph My Baby" (1898) is a "coon song" that documents, in an extremely interesting twist, the effects of modern transportation and communication on the entertainment industry itself. Born into a theatrical family, Cohan made his initial fame on a vaudeville circuit that resulted, as we have seen earlier, from rapid national rail travel between short runs, combined with the use of telegraph to book a complicated schedule of individual acts. In "Telegraph My Baby" Cohan takes up the fate of a black minstrel:

> A coon he left his happy home
> to go upon the stage,
> He joined a colored minstrel troupe,
> he thought he'd be the rage,
> He left the nicest little gal
> in Memphis Tennessee,
> And just because an actor man
> this coon desired to be;
> He thought he was a corker,
> dat Williams and Walker
> Would soon have to take off
> their hats and salaam.
> In a town they landed, troupe disbanded,
> Coons all stranded empty handed,
> Big black actor said to him,
> "What will you do now Sam?"
> He sighed and cried,
> and then he replied. . . .

The chorus, with its sporadic syncopations (see Ex. 4.14), answers the tag line. In the second stanza the situation worsens: the hotel bill comes due, and with no paycheck the actor lands in jail—another cause to send a wire. Technology has disrupted society—through the offices of rail travel the performer is stranded far from his home, his friends, his family—and technology also provides the solution to the ills it creates. The song does not reveal, however, whether this faith is rewarded.

Will A. Heelan and Harry Von Tilzer keep the faith in their "direct answer to the phenomenal success, 'I Guess I'll Have to Telegraph My Baby' " entitled "I've Just Received a Telegram from Baby" (1899). Von Tilzer naturally selects ragtime to accompany Heelan's sequel:

> A coon sat in his lonely cell, he couldn't sit outside
> Until he paid his little fine; to raise it he had tried.

EXAMPLE 4.14   George M. Cohan, "I Guess I'll Have to Telegraph My Baby" (New York: George L. Spaulding, 1898)

He'd been out with a minstrel show, got mixed up in a fight,
And telegraphed his baby for some coin on Saturday night.
On Sunday and Monday that coon he had the blues,
'Twould double his trouble if baby should refuse;
But the next day just at noontime, he was singing songs in coontime,
And he said, "I've got more money now than I know how to use."

The chorus gives the happy ending:

For I've just received a telegram from Baby,
An answer to the one she got from me.
I found she was a most obliging lady,
Just as I expected her to be.
I knew my baby wouldn't disappoint me,
I never gave her cause to turn me down;
She wired me on a twenty,
and I guess that will be plenty,
For to take me back to town.

The connection between overtly racist, socially regressive "coon songs" and technological progress seems at first to contradict the promise held out by "Get Off the Track." But the rude comedy of blackface lent itself well to the flippant ease with which Americans had customarily regarded machines in popular song. And ragtime, the standard music of "coon songs," was not only a stylistic novelty—progressive by definition at the end of the nineteenth century—it had also entered mainstream culture at an event dedicated to technological

151

advancement, the Columbian Exposition of 1893.[34] The characters in ''Hello! Ma Baby,'' ''Ring Off, Coon!,'' ''Telegraph My Baby,'' and ''Telegram from Baby'' are sophisticated city dwellers in depictions like that for Emerson and Howard's song (Illus. 4.3). These characters deal confidently with modern developments, and their ragtime music is avant-garde chic.

Questioning the Faith

The giddiness of popular songs about new inventions may also reflect a nervous disbelief that American society might be so quickly rearranged by seemingly innocuous devices like the telephone. John Kasson suggests that ''a retreat from technological America was expressed in the pervasive nostalgia for the homogeneous, pre-industrial village culture of the early nineteenth century,''[35] and as we shall see later, early minstrelsy contains elements of just such a revolt, usually expressed negatively in the form of rural longing. But explicit complaints about technology per se are rare in nineteenth-century popular song, and when writers do object, they initially cite the disparity between the promise of modern inventions to improve the social order and the propensity of industrial civilization to create social chaos.

At the end of the century the urban landscape most graphically displayed the dazzling progress of technology to most Americans. In his novel *Sister Carrie* written just at the end of the nineteenth century Theodore Dreiser (brother of songwriter Paul Dresser) described the expansion of Chicago in terms of ''great industries,'' transportation, and public utilites seeming to grow in the middle of the empty prairie. The city at night especially exhibits this magic to Dreiser:

> . . . the approach to a great city for the first time is a wonderful thing. Particularly if it be evening—that mystic period between the glare and gloom of the world when life is changing from one sphere or condition to another. Ah, the promise of the night. What does it not hold for the weary! What old illusion of hope is not here forever repeated! Says the soul of the toiler to itself, ''I shall soon be free. I shall be in the ways and the host of the merry. The streets, the lamps, the lighted chamber set for dining, are for me. . . . ''[36]

The allure of an urban night, however, could prove dangerous, as it does in ''The Bowery'' (1892)[37] by Charles H. Hoyt and Percy Gaunt, which hints

34. See Edward F. Berlin's *Ragtime: A Musical and Cultural History* (Berkeley, Los Angeles, London, 1980), 25–29, or the longer exposition on ragtime songs in Chapter 6.
35. *Civilizing the Machine: Technology and Republican Values in America, 1776–1900* (New York, 1976), 188.
36. *Sister Carrie* (New York, 1957), 9.
37. Reproduced in Fremont, *Favorite Songs*, 42–46.

especially in its first verse at some discontent with technology. The show for which the number was written, *A Trip to China Town,* revolves around the city, and the "rube" in this song is initially drawn into a series of misadventures there by mechanical glitter:

> Oh! the night that I struck New York,
> I went out for a quiet walk;
> Folks who are "on to" the city say,
> Better by far that I took Broadway;
> But I was out to enjoy the sights,
> There was the Bow'ry ablaze with lights;
> I had one of the devil's own nights!
> I'll never go there any more!

But most of the lyrics concern the dangerous climate of a raucous neighborhood, not the general problems of urban disorder.

The Columbian Exposition of 1893 provides a better foil for failed social expectations in Charles K. Harris's "After the Fair" (1893). Though the sheet music lists Press Eldridge as lyricist, Harris explains in his memoirs:

> During the World's Fair in Chicago, Jack Haverly, of minstrel fame, opened Haverly's Casino Theater in that city, where he used a stock minstrel company. . . . A friend of mine, Tom Lewis, was also playing there, and he introduced me to [William] Windom. . . . Lewis also introduced me to the entire company, which included Banks Winters, author of *White Wings*; Castell Bridges, a featured singer; Press Eldridge, monologist; Billy Rice, comedian and end man; and Charles Shattuck, the interlocutor. . . . And so it came about that I furnished Banks Winters with *Kiss and Let's Make Up*; Bridges with *Creep, Baby, Creep*; Press Eldridge with a parody on *After the Ball* called *After the Fair*; and Billy Rice with *Hello, Central, Hello!* This representation, together with Will Windom's singing of *After the Ball*, gave me much prestige with Haverly's various companies.[38]

Minstrelsy provides the traditional venue for common-sense skepticism about grandiose endeavors:

> A little maiden climbed an old man's knee,
> Begged for a story, do uncle please,
> Tell of Chicago, that wondrous town,
> With its tall buildings, they're world renowned.
> Soon the great World's Fair will be at its height,
> Prices of all things will go out of sight;

38. *After the Ball: Forty Years of Melody* (New York, 1926), 114–15.

They'll charge for ev'rything but the air,
But just watch the difference after the Fair.

[Chorus:]
After the Fair is over, just watch the rents come down,
When all the rubes and hayseeds have skipped away from town;
Many a man will be busted, people will tear their hair,
Hyde Park will be dead and buried after the Fair.

The remaining verses and choruses (each supplied with different lyrics) give concrete examples of inflation and overcrowding, relying on the interplay between implicit assumptions about progress manifested in the Fair's exhibitions and disappointment over the disorder it causes in the city. Among other things, this means a very different view of the intermixing facilitated by improved transportation:

Oh, what a picnic this fair will be
What wondrous people at it we'll see;
Indians from Indianapolis, Japs from Japan,
Mr. Joe Bunko and the three card Monte man.
Turks, French and Arabs and Esquimaux,
Buffalo Bill and his great Wild West show;
Things will be lively, money to spare,
But oh, what a diff'rence after the Fair.

The parody entailed another level of irony, as well. For "After the Ball" was the song that first used the national system of marketing made available by the combined technological developments of mass printing, fast transportation, and telegraphy, that is, the whole apparatus of specialty publishing and advertising. Performers from John Philip Sousa to William Windom plugged the song incessantly at the Columbian Exhibition. Will Rossiter, who billed himself on the cover of "After the Fair" as "The Popular Song Publisher," made deliberate light of the new mass commercialization with a note, "Song Pirates are hereby notified that this song is Copyright," while adding on the first page, "If desired this song can be sung to the tune of 'After the Ball.' "

The discontent with industrialization gained momentum at the beginning of the twentieth century in popular song. William Jerome and Jean Schwartz's "Rip Van Winkle Was a Lucky Man" (1901)[39] uses a sprightly declamatory patter to list the modern ills Rip escapes in his long absence:

He never had to ride around in overcrowded cars,
    Or smoke those generously good infantile Child cigars,

39. A copy of the music appears in Appelbaum's *Show Songs,* 165–69.

Eat Dennett's cakes, or buckwheat flakes,
He never had to listen to those ragtime organs play,
   Or read about two hundred thousand extras every day,
Omega oil is very good for shoes.

In other verses and choruses the authors decry at some length the cramped new residential flats in Harlem, protest all manner of commercialization, and even question that ultimate wonderland of popularized gadgetry, the amusement park. The symbol of disillusionment is, logically enough, an old Dutch figure of folkish legend from pre-industrial New York. Jerome's chorus asserts over Schwartz's impish alternating bass:

Rip Van Winkle was a lucky man,
   Rip Van Winkle took the cake,
Never had to eat any homemade pies like mother used to make,
   How lucky,
Rip Van Winkle knew a thing or two,
   Deny it no one can,
He never seen the women
   Down at Coney Island swimming,
Rip Van Winkle was a lucky man.

Condemnation of technology itself in American popular song would wait another decade, until songs like Irving Berlin's "Keep Away from the Fellow Who Owns an Automobile" (1912);[40] the driver runs out of gas on a date. A related misfortune plagues the man in "He'd Have to Get Under, Get Out and Get Under (to Fix Up His Automobile)," with lyrics by Grant Clarke and Edgar Leslie, music by Maurice Abraham (1913). Where "My Merry Oldsmobile" had listed the advantages of courtship in the car, "Get Out and Get Under" speaks in a specifically ragtime voice of two romances frustrated by "the old machinery":

He'd have to get under, get out and get under
To fix up his little machine,
He was just dying to cuddle his queen,
But ev'ry minute when he'd begin it,
He had to get under, get out and get under,
Then he'd get back at the wheel.
A dozen times they'd start to hug and kiss.
And then the darn old engine it would miss.
And then he'd have to get under, get out and get under,
And fix up his automobile.

40. My thanks to Charlotte Greenspan for bringing this song to my attention.

Here a musical style once associated with jocular amazement about the power of technology in songs like ''Hello! Ma Baby'' now serves the ends of mildly comic derision. Though some twentieth-century songs continue to profess faith in technology and its potential for social good, songs like ''Rip Van Winkle'' and ''Get Out and Get Under'' reveal cracks in what had previously been a popular orthodoxy.

PART II

5

Antebellum Minstrelsy and the Carnivalesque

Nothing amidst the array of American culture so appalls and fascinates as nineteenth-century blackface, that improbable entertainment featuring performers who darkened their faces with burnt cork. Minstrel songs have elicited an astonishing range of contradictory interpretations from modern authors,[1] and Bayard Taylor's contemporary description of a sojourn in the saloons of California provides a key to understanding the wide range of later reaction:

> Some of the establishments have small companies of Ethiopian melodists, who nightly call upon ''Susanna!'' and entreat to be carried back to Old Virginny. These songs are universally popular, and the crowd of listeners is often so great as to embarrass the player at the monte tables and injure the business of the gamblers. I confess a strong liking for the Ethiopian airs, and used to spend half an hour every night in listening to them and watching the curious expressions of satisfaction and delight in the faces of the overland emigrants, who always attended in a body. The spirit of the music was always encouraging; even its most doleful passages had a grotesque touch of cheerfulness—a mingling of sincere pathos and whimsical consolation, which somehow took hold of all moods in which it might be heard, raising them to the same notch of careless good-humor. The Ethiopian melodies well deserve to be called, as they are in fact, the national airs of America. Their quaint, mock-sentimental cadences, so well suited to the broad absurdity of the words—their reckless gaiety and irreverent familiarity with serious subjects— and their spirit of antagonism and perseverance—are true expressions of the

---

1. Not surprisingly more recent authors have tended to focus disapproval on the institution of blackface. Sam Dennison in *Scandalize My Name: Black Imagery in American Popular Music* (New York and London, 1982) disagrees strongly with the views presented by Carl Wittke in *Tambo and Bones: A History of the American Minstrel Stage* (Durham, NC, 1930) and by Hans Nathan in *Dan Emmett and the Rise of Early Negro Minstrelsy* (Norman, OK, 1962).

more popular sides of the national character. They follow the American race in all its emigrations, colonizations and conquests, as certainly as the Fourth of July and Thanksgiving Day. The penniless and half despairing emigrant is stimulated to try again by the sound of "It'll never do to give it up so!" and feels a pang of home-sickness at the burthen of the "Old Virginia Shore." [2]

Taylor's description outlines the three primary themes that pervade American blackface from the mid-1820s to the end of the nineteenth century and beyond. The first element in Taylor's account stresses minstrelsy's invocation of the ethnically and racially exotic, represented here by the term "Ethiopian." In assuming these "African" identities the players proclaim the folkloric tone of the entertainment and appeal to the audience's fascination with and attraction to what they perceive to be *primitive*. Equally important, Taylor plainly refuses to take this exotic art literally. The songs are "absurd" and "mocking," "irreverent" and "reckless," "antagonistic" and "grotesque," in short, a manifestation of a *carnivalesque* world. The performers are maskers whose assumed disguises facilitate ironic poses that paint figurative portraits. And for the overland emigrants in Taylor's memoir the most potent of the many symbols in minstrel entertainment consists of a lost *rural* paradise (here "The Old Virginia Shore") inevitably regarded with longing. For as strange as it may seem, Taylor and the forty-niners of his story identify strongly with the primitive characters who populate the entertainment. The mechanism of this empathy with "Ethiopian" figures lies at the heart of understanding the institution of American blackface.

Solo Minstrelsy and Jacksonian Populism

The history of isolated blackface performances in British and American ballad operas surfaces frequently in many scholarly accounts of minstrelsy,[3] and eighteenth-century English and early American performances displayed many features found in later entertainments.[4] But the continuous American tradition

2. William Austin reprints this passage in *"Susanna," "Jeanie," and "The Old Folks at Home": The Songs of Stephen Foster from His Time to Ours* (New York, 1975), 29–30. I quote from Bayard Taylor's *Eldorado; or, Adventures in the Path of Empire: Comprising a Voyage to California, via Panama; Life in San Francisco and Monterey; Pictures of the Gold Region, and Experiences of Mexican Travel,* 18th ed. (New York 1864), 275.

3. Wittke begins *Tambo and Bones* this way, 3–14. Nathan provides the most concise narrative in *Dan Emmett,* 3–49, which ripples through authors like Dennison, *Scandalize My Name,* 3–35, and Charles Hamm, *Yesterdays: Popular Song in America* (New York and London: 1979), 109–17.

4. In " 'Backside Albany' and Early Blackface Minstrelsy," *American Music* 6 (1988), 1–27, William J. Mahar observes qualities in one of these early blackface songs which we might in retrospect call carnivalesque. The African-American figure derides the failure of the British on Lake Champlain during the War of 1812. And it may be no coincidence that this song appears

of blackface really began with solo acts at the very end of the 1820s and the early '30s. They shared with their earlier relations certain underlying traits of the carnivalesque, a term that finds its roots in the activities surrounding festivities like Mardi Gras.

In its most narrow sense carnival is an anti-holiday (literally an unholy feast) during which the populace at large frees itself from strictures invoked all the more severely in Lent. "As opposed to the official feast," Mikhail Bakhtin writes, "one might say that carnival celebrated temporary liberation from the prevailing truth of the established order; it marked the suspension of all hierarchical rank, privileges, norms and prohibitions."[5] Normally temperate during the year (and sometimes abstemious during Lent), people become intoxicated during carnival; normally chaste (and perhaps celibate during Lent), they enjoy sexual license; normally orderly in the streets, crowds overwhelm the thoroughfares, producing a kind of chaos. Carnival is a populist activity, which celebrates an inversion between the rulers and the ruled.

The "carnivalesque" constitutes "a potent, populist, critical inversion of *all* official words and hierarchies,"[6] and its artistic history is long and prominent. Many examples of carnivalesque art appear from the sixteenth century onward in popular broadsheets which depict a "World Upside Down." The humorous scenes usually come in such groupings as the horse riding the jockey, the rabbits hunting the hounds, the wife beating the husband, the peasant ruling the noble, and so forth.[7] The last two instances suggest that the inversion often comments on an injustice, protests disenfranchisement, or displays the desire for power by the powerless. Scenes of the low dominating the high are frequently made risible by grotesque images in broadsheets such as an ass driving a donkey cart pulled by teamsters or oxen guiding a plow pulled by yoked farmers. These come from a tradition of "impossibilia" and medieval *drôlerie* like those found in the *Roman de Fauvel*.[8] Such images show inanimate objects as alive or animals behaving as human beings.

Well-known examples of the carnivalesque in the theater include musical plays like *The Beggar's Opera* by John Gay, in which the "high" entertainment of Italian *opera seria,* with its elaborate music and sets inhabited by the royalty or nobility, is inverted by use of "low" popular ballads sung in the

---

around the election of 1824 in which Jackson won a plurality but lost the presidency in the Congress.

5. *Rabelais and His World,* H. Iswolsky, trans. (Bloomington, IN, 1984), 10. I became aware of Bakhtin's writing through Peter Stallybrass and Allon White, *The Politics and Poetics of Transgression* (Ithaca, NY, 1986). I have relied in certain respects on their introduction to the carnivalesque, 6–26. My thanks to colleague Robert Allen for bringing this study to my attention and for allowing me to see a draft of his book, *Horrible Prettiness: Burlesque and American Culture* (Chapel Hill, NC, 1991), before its publication.

6. Stallybrass and White, *Transgression,* 7.

7. See Eric Kunzle's "World Upside Down: The Iconography of a European Broadsheet Type," in Barbara A. Babcock, ed., *The Reversible World: Symbolic Inversion in Art and Society* (Ithaca, NY, and London, 1978), 39–94.

8. Ibid., 59–61.

backstreets of a city peopled by thieves, prostitutes, and pimps. These low characters specifically deride the ruling classes in homilies like the opening song of the fence and informer Peachum: "And the statesman because he's so great / thinks his job as honest as mine." Carnivalesque art, be it the ballad opera or broadsheet of the inverted world, arises in many cases from political discontent.[9] Gay, a member of the opposition party, intended *The Beggar's Opera* as an attack on the ethics of Walpole's government. Significantly, he carried out his assault indirectly by aiming his theatrical entertainment against the aristocratically supported Italian opera.

Indirection in the form of mummery also abets rebellion against authority in the time of carnival. Maskers can manifest their transient power in several ways, either by donning the garb of an aristocracy to which they do not belong (the kings and queens of Mardi Gras) or putting on the rags of low figures (pirates, hoboes, and the like) to take over the streets. All these costumes are examples of transvesting, which simply means wearing the clothes and therefore taking on the identity of somebody else (sexual reversal is merely one particular form of the charade). Transvesting not only exemplifies an inverted world (the common man suddenly made king, the low ruling the streets, a male as a female), it also permits the mummer to disguise his identity from those in power who might punish his rude defiance.

Blackface was a variation of mummery, and practitioners often created (or were surrounded by) elaborate myths claiming that their stage performances and published music offered authentic imitations of African-American culture. They adopted these poses in order to deflect objections by the various parties they criticized, though apart from the appropriation of superficial characteristics, the claims of authenticity were exaggerations. Such a myth of folkloric realism, for instance, surrounded the music and performances of Thomas Dartmouth Rice (1806–60), who created perhaps the most famous of nineteenth-century blackface figures in the person of Jim Crow. Depending on the version of the story, "Daddy" Rice, the "father of minstrelsy," was working in the theater of some urban center in the Ohio valley (Louisville, Cincinnati, Pittsburgh) during the last years of the 1820s. Upon beholding variously a black stevedore, stableman, or teamster, the actor learned to impersonate his peculiar song and dance.[10] A version of this story, to give just one specific example, appears in the autobiography of a contemporary actress, Clara Fisher Maeder, decades after the fact. In spite of her personal acquaintance with the actor, the exact derivation of Rice's character remains vague:

> I first met Mr. Thomas D. Rice in Cincinnati early in the thirties, and on several occasions he played with me in various Western theaters. He had

9. Ibid., 61–72.

10. Compare the several accounts in "Stephen Foster and Negro Minstrelsy," *Atlantic Monthly* 20 (1867), 608–9; S. Foster Damon, ed., *Series of Old American Songs* (Providence, RI, 1936), no. 15; Hans Nathan, *Dan Emmett*, 50–52; and Carl Wittke, *Tambo and Bones*, 21–29. James H.

been with Ludlow's company in Mobile and Montgomery and other towns on the Southern circuit, and when I met him at Ludlow's Cincinnati Theater he had picked up a song somewhere in the South called "Jim Crow," with which he made quite a hit between plays. He was not much of an actor, but a very industrious young man and a good mimic. My mother, who liked and often talked to him both at the theater and the hotel, said to him: "Why don't you give up acting and devote yourself entirely to negro characters— you sing and dance this odd negro stuff so well—and go to the larger cities, where it will be a novelty?" . . . Not long after we heard of his writing and playing negro pieces, introducing "Jim Crow" and other melodies to crowded houses at the Walnut Street Theater, Philadelphia.[11]

In other words, Rice himself authored much of his role ("writing and playing negro pieces"), relying on a certain talent for imitation to sustain an illusion. He hailed from a northern, urban background like many of his successors,[12] and was less concerned with authenticity than with assuming the mask of the folkloric. In fact, the humor of Rice's charade depended precisely on the spectator's knowledge of his disguise.[13] The cover of an early edition (ca. 1832)[14] informed the purchaser that this was "Mr. T. Rice as . . . Jim Crow." The audience had to be made aware that the elaborately engraved black character on the cover was really a transvested white man (Illus. 5.1). The exaggerated features of his disguise bear all the marks of counterculture: he is not only poor, but his extremities and facial features protrude (as they do in all subsequent depictions of minstrel figures) in ungainly ways meant to confront the smooth regularity of idealized gentility.

Just as the illustration intimates a carnivalesque masquerade, the lyrics of the song conduct the listener into a fantastic and grotesque realm which at the same time is rustic and folkloric. The sheet music first establishes in the opening stanza (Ex. 5.1) that the character is rural and western (from Kentucky), and it confirms Jim's "low" nature with a dialect that imitates some superficial as-

---

Dormon gives what may be the most accurate account of Rice's early years, "The Strange Career of Jim Crow Rice," *Journal of Social History* 3 (1969–70), 109–11.

11. *Autobiography of Clara Fisher Maeder* (New York, 1897), 37–38.

12. Ibid.

13. Charles Haywood writes on this point in "Negro Minstrelsy and Shakespearean Burlesque," in *Folklore & Society: Essays in Honor of Benj. A. Botkin,* Bruce Jackson, ed. (Hatboro, PA, 1966), 77.

14. See the facsimile in Nicholas Tawa, *American Solo Songs Through 1865,* vol. 1 of *Three Centuries of American Sacred and Secular Music,* Martha Furman Schleifer and Sam Dennison, eds. ([Boston], 1989), 95–97. There are many other editions, some without attribution to any songwriter, others naming George Washington Dixon as author. Dating the sheet music is problematic, and many assign early copies to 1828, the date of Rice's first appearances as this character. But Rice presented Jim Crow for the first time in New York theaters during the fall of 1832, and the political topics in most editions of the song also suggest a date around 1832. For Rice's career on stage see George C. D. Odell, *Annals of the New York Stage* (New York, 1928), III, 631–36.

EXAMPLE 5.1   Thomas Dartmouth Rice, "Jim Crow" (New York: E. Riley, [ca. 1832])

pects of African-American English.[15] We learn in the third verse that Jim Crow lives along the Ohio or Mississippi and has experience as a boatman:

> I git 'pon a flat boat,
>   I cotch de Uncle Sam,
> Den I went to see de place
>   Wher dey kill'd Packenham.

Having identified the character, the lyrics then spin out two interrelated kinds of tales, one showing all manner of absurdity, the other portraying Jim Crow as larger than life. Gestures of the first kind depict a "World Upside Down" by means of folklike impossibilia:

> Dere's Possum up de gumtree,
>   An racoon in de hollow,
> Wake Snakes for June bugs
>   Stole my half a dollar.

or:

> Oh de way dey bake de hoecake
>   In old Virginny neber tire,
> Dey put de doe upon de foot,
>   An hole it to de fire.

15. William Mahar recounts the various linguistic traits of blackface songs and speculates about their authenticity, in " 'Backside Albany,' " 11–13.

Gestures of the second type extend inverted relationships to Jim. He is a kind of superman:

> I wip my weight in wildcats,
>   I eat an Alligator,
> And tear up more ground
>   Dan kifer 50 load of tater.

For this reason, when he comes to the urban east, he bests all the city folk in drinking, brawling, and wooing. He has complete contempt for urban life, deriding its foppish ways. He visits a museum,

> An dare is daddy Lambert,
>   An a skeleton on he hunkie,
> An likeness of Broadway dandy,
>   In a glass case of monkies.

> De Broadway bells,
>   When dey carry full sail,
> Around dem wear a funny ting,
>   Just like a fox tail.

The sophisticated denizens of Philadelphia, Hoboken, "Weehawk," Brooklyn, and New York all come in for derision from this country bumpkin in a world turned upside down.

The character of Jim Crow comes straight out of Jacksonian populism, and he shares many virtues with the western hero whose famous battlefield (outside of New Orleans "wher dey kill'd Packenham") he visits early in the song. Jackson, a westerner, was portrayed as a simple "ploughman," one of "nature's noblemen," who led a group of unsophisticated backwoodsmen, the "Hunters of Kentucky," to victory over a professional British soldiery. His was a triumph of "wisdom" over "learning," of the rural over the urban, and when Jackson died, one eulogy proclaimed:

> Behold, then, the unlettered man of the West, the nursling of the wilds, the
> farmer of the Hermitage, little versed in books, unconnected by science with
> the tradition of the past, raised by the will of the people to the highest pinna-
> cle of honour, to the central post in the civilization of republican freedom,
> to the station where all the nations of the earth would watch his actions—
> where his words would vibrate through the civilized world, and his spirit be
> the moving-star to guide the nations. What policy will he pursue? What wis-

'dom will he bring with him from the forest? What rules of duty will he evolve from the oracles of his own mind?[16]

According to this view Jackson was primitive in a positive sense of the word (though the vision comes to a certain extent from political propaganda, which interpreted loosely the facts surrounding the Battle of New Orleans, Jackson's background, and his occupation).

A figure from the age of Jackson, Jim Crow is a political symbol and his song in part a political tract touting Jacksonian positions. After the large number of verses establishing Jim's credentials as primitive rustic in an inverted world, talk turns to subjects like nullification, part of the dispute between southern and northern states over federal tariffs to protect manufacturing. Because these favored the North, the South maintained that individual states could "nullify" tariffs, but as President, Jackson supported federal prerogatives. The issue intensified during the summer of 1832 right before elections:

> De great Nullification,
> And fuss in de South,
> Is now before Congress,
> To be tried by word of mouth.
>
> Wid Jackson at de head,
> Dey soon de ting may settle,
> For ole Hickory is a man,
> Dat's tarnal full ob mettle.

The Bank of the United States was another favorite target of Jim's scorn in a version of the song titled "Jimmy Crow" (ca. 1832).[17] Jackson had long despised the private national bank as anti-democratic, an institution favoring wealthy and powerful easterners. When the Bank's president, Nicholas Biddle, requested a bill to renew its charter in January, 1832, Jackson mounted a campaign against it. And when Congress renewed the charter over Jackson's opposition, he vetoed the bill, citing its propensity to make "the rich richer and the potent more powerful" while "farmers, mechanics, and laborers . . . have a right to complain of the injustice . . . . "[18] Jimmy Crow does just this:

> O den I go to Washington,
> Wid bank memorial;

16. George Bancroft reprinted in B. M. Dusenbery, comp. *Monument to the Memory of General Andrew Jackson: Containing Twenty-five Eulogies and Sermons Delivered on the Occasion of His Death* (Philadelphia, 1848), cited in John William Ward, *Andrew Jackson, Symbol for an Age* (New York, 1962), 73.

17. Published in New York at Atwill's Music Saloon and reproduced in S. Foster Damon, *Old American Songs*, no. 15.

18. Robert V. Remini, *Andrew Jackson and the Course of American Freedom, 1822–32* (New York, 1981), 368–69.

> But find dey tork sich nonsense,
> I spen my time wid Sal.

The next verse complains of bribes from bank officers, the very chicanery that led to popular resentment:

> I teld dem dare be Ole Nick,
>   Wat wants de bank renew;
> He gib me so much mony,
>   O lor, dey want it too.

Jim, however, is not actually corrupted, and consistent with his western background, he recommends a veto of the recharter to President Jackson, who has asked his opinion. Carnivalesque inversion reigns when the lowest member of society from a group completely disenfranchised ridicules and rules the powerful, fulfilling the fantasies of any listener oppressed by authority.[19] Just as burnt cork and tattered clothes hide Rice's physical identity, comedy cloaks the acid nature of the political protest in this sheet music.

Rice extends the symbolism of Jim Crow's appearance, dialect, and sentiments to the music of his song as well. It constitutes a protest against all the artificial graces of the Anglo-Italian style that dominates genteel contemporary songs. The second verse reminds us of this "scientific" (learned) style by specifically citing a famous Italian virtuoso and implies that Jim's country playing is just as good:

> I'm a rorer on de fiddle,
>   An down in ole Virginny;
> Dey say I play de skientific,
>   Like massa Pagganinny.

This is one clue to the nature of Rice's tune, and another comes in the refrain for every verse:

> Weel about and turn about
>   And do jis so,
> Eb'ry time I weel about
>   And jump Jim Crow.

19. Jules Zanger specifically ties early minstrelsy to the emergence of Jacksonian democracy, but does not elaborate ("The Minstrel Show as Theater of Misrule," *Quarterly Journal of Speech* 60 (1974), 33). Alexander Saxton makes a good case for populist political themes in ensemble minstrelsy from the 1840s to the Civil War in "Minstrelsy and Jacksonian Ideology," *American Quarterly* 27 (1975), 3–28, but for some reason he does not trace it back to its solo roots.

Apparently the music has ties to a tradition of dance music for violin in a folk tradition, and Hans Nathan suggests Anglo-Celtic fiddle music as the most likely candidate.[20] He calls this style "noncantabile" and "unlyrical" because of its short phrases, uneven rhythms, and many repeated notes supporting the incessant patter of the text (Ex. 5.1). Its melodic shape directly inverts the standard arch of *bel canto:* Rice's tune begins and ends in the high range, touching the lowest notes in the middle. This music places the "characteristic" (the piquant, the folkish, the irregular) in opposition to the "classical" (the learned, well formed, cosmopolitan, and even). Anglo-Celtic folk music directly confronts the music of chivalric romance, just as Jim's approach to courtship takes a much more blunt form:

> O den I cast de sheeps eye,
>   Dey all fall in lub;
> I pick my choose among dem dare,
>   An took Miss Dina Scrub.

"Jim Crow" reverses all values, social, political, romantic, and musical. Through a "theater of misrule," Rice articulates "the discontent of a broad section of America with the pieties of genteel American culture" and the inequities of American politics.[21]

Minstrel songs often featured the combination of Anglo-Celtic tune and African-American stage dialect with a narrative about the primitive rural savant who challenges "civilized" urban mores. Rice himself recycled Jim Crow in the character of "Gombo Chaff" (1834) with a tune modeled on the English "Bow Wow Wow."[22] Gombo begins as a slave in Indiana. His master dies and, in the spirit of populist justice, resides in Hell, performing the menial tasks he had assigned to slaves ("For when he live I know, he light upon me so, Now he gone to tote de firewood and water down below"). When the master's widow remarries foolishly ("Den Missis she did marry Big Bill de weaver, Soon she found out, he was a gay deceiver"), Gombo escapes down the Ohio River, eventually landing in New Orleans. He easily outdoes urban rivals in his new role as stevedore, derides the French spoken in Louisiana, declines the learned occupation of clerk, and returns ultimately to the place of true happiness—a farm in the Ohio valley.

A similar character appears in "Sich a Gitting Up Stairs" (ca. 1834), often attributed to Bob Farrell, a blackface entertainer active in the New York theater. He invents a boatman and country fiddler from the Chesapeake Bay rather than from the West (see Ex. 5.2). This primitive migrates logically enough to Washington, where he lampoons genteel objections to drinking and gambling:

20. *Dan Emmett*, 171–72.
21. Zanger, "Misrule," 38.
22. Nathan, *Dan Emmett*, 172–73.

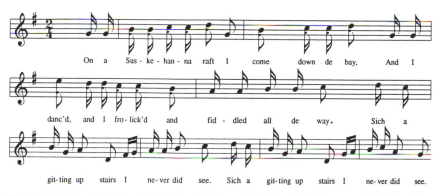

EXAMPLE 5.2 Bob Farrell, ''Sich a Gitting Up Stairs'' (Baltimore: G. Willig, [ca. 1834])

> Oh I is dat boy dat know to preach a sarmount
> Bout Temperance and *seven up* an all dat kind of varmint.

The sheet music also makes fun of recolonization and what would later be called miscegenation:

> Nigger hold a meeting about de Clonization,
> An dere I spoke a speech about Amalgamation.

The newcomer bests a city slicker, ''Joe,'' in a fight for the hand of ''Sal,'' but flees to Baltimore when Joe summons the police. The sheet music takes this opportunity to deride higher learning:

> An den I show my science—prenez gardez vous,
> Bung he eye, break he shin, split de nose in two.

All the verses play out over a repeated-note melody that stems from the boatman's dance:

> Trike de toe an heel—cut de pigeon wing,
> Scratch gravel, slap de foot—dat's just de ting.

Nathan links the tune with an English Morris dance, ''Getting Up Stairs,''[23] and though he may have relied on anachronistic collections for this identification, the melody at least bears a stylistic imprint of folk music for dancing. As a populist symbol for the audience, the alternate musical style is just as im-

---

23. Ibid., 169. The melody also resembles the tune of children's song ''This Old Man.''

portant as the social inversion of a "Suskehanna boy" besting a city dweller and supplanting a learned cleric.

Bob Farrell receives credit on the cover of "Sich a Gitting Up Stairs" for creating the second famous carnivalesque type in solo minstrelsy, the blackface dandy "Zip Coon." Most writers associate this character, however, with George Washington Dixon (d. 1861). Dixon began his blackface career in New York at the Chatham Theater during July of 1828.[24] He often played the role of "Coal Black Rose" in a song about a love triangle parodying "polite" songs of courtship. He may also have created "Long Tail Blue," a song in which the blackface principal bears a strong resemblance to Zip Coon.

Zip is a doubly transvested figure as he appears on the cover of sheet music first published around 1833 (Illus. 5.2).[25] The caption under the engraving informs us that Dixon has disguised himself as a black man, and this "low" figure in turn dons the costume of the urban elite. The first stanza of the song makes it clear that Zip's dress mocks the taste of the town and its intellectual pretension:

> O ole Zip Coon he is a larned skoler. . .
> Sings posum up a gum tree an coony in a holler.

"Larned skoler" is another catchword from the controversy surrounding Andrew Jackson. In June of 1833 Jackson decided to visit Boston, and the overseers of Harvard conferred on him the honorary degree Doctor of Laws, as they had on former Presidents. Many Whigs protested, among them John Quincy Adams, complaining that Jackson could hardly write a grammatical sentence or spell his own name (in fact, Jackson's English left something to be desired). In the aftermath a number of cruel jokes circulated, including a toast to "Andrew Jackson—In War a Hero—In Politics a Statesman; in literature an L.L.D. and an A.S.S." Jacksonian humorists quickly turned the insult into a compliment by rendering A.S.S. as "Amazin' Smart Skoller," and Ward writes, "The people cared so little for formal learning that it was of no purpose to create stories to demonstrate their hero's lack of it; they simply turned them around to reaffirm their belief in the unacquired wisdom of the natural man."[26] It was no accident that many versions of "Zip Coon" ended by praising the General's victory at New Orleans.

In an alternate edition of "Zip Coon" published slightly later (1834),[27] the association with Jacksonian populism becomes even more explicit, duplicating

24. Odell, *Annals,* III, 354.

25. A facsimile appears in Richard Jackson's collection, *Popular Songs of Nineteenth-Century America* (New York, 1976), 258–60.

26. *Symbol for an Age,* 86; my account of this incident follows Ward's in all particulars.

27. New York: Atwill's Music Saloon (copyright by Thos. Birch), facsimile in Tawa, *Solo Songs,* I, 117–19.

many of the sentiments heard in "Jim Crow." One verse takes on the national bank and turns the world upside down at one blow:

> I tell you what will happin den, now bery soon,
> De Nited States Bank will be blone to de moon;
> Dare General Jackson, will him lampoon,
> An de bery nex President, will be Zip Coon.

The song reinforces the inversion by alluding to the real election of backwoodsman Davy Crockett to Congress. Zip associates himself quickly with the populist hero:

> Now mind what you arter, you tarnel kritter Crocket,
> You shant go head widout Old Zip, he is de boy to block it,
> Zip shall be President, Crocket shall be vice,
> An den dey two togedder, will hab de tings nice.

In a version printed just slightly later by Firth & Hall (New York, ca. 1836) the lyrics use the image of Crockett to deride the Congress:

> Dat tarnal critter Crockett, he never say his prayers,
> He kill all de wild cats de Coons and de Bears,
> An den he go to Washington to help to make de laws,
> An dere he find de Congressmen sucking of deir paws.

The ending verse is a litany for Jackson:

> O glory be to Jackson, for he blow up de Banks,
> An glory be to Jackson, for he many funny pranks,
> An glory be to Jackson, for de battle of Orleans,
> For dere he gib de enemy de hot butter beans.

The triumph of the rural, folkloric figure dressed as an effete urbanite finds support in the fiddle tune used for the song, now commonly known as "Turkey in the Straw" (Ex. 5.3). Early histories of minstrelsy claim a western point of origin for this music in a dance played by rivermen, "Natchez Under Hill," and some folklorists suggest a relationship to a reel called "The Rose Tree," which appears as early as 1782 in some collections of fiddle music.[28] Whatever the exact origins of the tune, its uneven rhythms, frequent repeated notes, and angular rather than smooth melodic curves make it the antithesis of Italianate gentility. The contradiction between Zip's music and his attire reemphasizes

---

28. See Chris Goertzen and Alan Jabbour, "George P. Knauff's *Virginia Reels* and Fiddling in the Antebellum South," *American Music* 5 (1987), 125.

EXAMPLE 5.3   George Washington Dixon, "Zip Coon" (New York: J. L. Hewitt, [ca. 1832])

his carnivalesque protest against the pretensions of the rich, the stylish, and the well educated. The twice-transvested dandy as a populist symbol appears in other songs, including "Jim Brown" (1835) and "Jim Along Josey" (1840) by Edward Harper. Many of these songs traded verses and themes, and they seem to have circulated freely among blackface artists like Rice, Dixon, Mr. Leicester, Farrell, Mr. Brower, and a host of others. Publishers regularly pirated each other's versions in recognition of this practice, and the several editions of each song suggest that the sheet music enjoyed no small popularity among the consumers of such wares.

Populist discontent also found expression in solo minstrelsy's creation of imaginary lands where life is idyllic. Many of these songs take place in rustic settings where humorous, folkloric impossibilia indicate an inverted world. "Clare de Kitchen," sung by Thomas Dartmouth Rice (ca. 1832) is one of the sprightliest representatives of this genre. Set specifically in "ole Kentuck," the first verse describes a carefree rural life (Ex. 5.4), and then moves on to all sorts of nonsensical tales. One verse concerns a blind horse and a running commentary by "Jim Crow," who happens along the road:

> My horse fell down upon de spot,
> Says he "dont you see his eyes is sot";

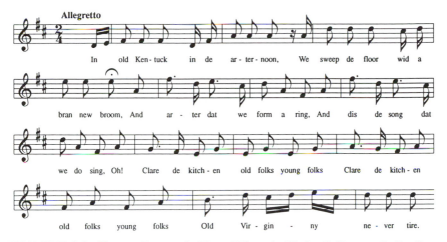

In old Ken-tuck in de ar-ter-noon, We sweep de floor wid a bran new broom, And ar-ter dat we form a ring, And dis de song dat we do sing, Oh! Clare de kitch-en old folks young folks Clare de kitch-en old folks young folks Old Vir-gin-ny ne-ver tire.

EXAMPLE 5.4   Thomas Dartmouth Rice, "Clare de Kitchen" (Boston: C. Bradlee, [ca. 1832])

> So I took out my knife and off wid his skin,
> And when he comes to life I'll ride him again.
>   So Clare de kitchen &c.

The fantastic landscape includes anthropomorphized animals who speak with the narrator:

> A jay bird sot on a hickory limb,
> He wink'd at me and I wink'd at him;
> I pick'd up a stone and hit his shin,
> Says he you better not do dat agin.
>   So Clare de kitchen &c.

Yet another grotesque stanza features crows (like Jim "Crow") frustrating the depredations of their enemies:

> A Bull frog dress'd in sogers close,
> Went in de field to shoot some crows;
> De crows smell powder and fly away.
> De Bull frog mighty mad dat day.

Such verses establish the comically reversed nature of the world inhabited by blackface art, where the folkloric and carnivalesque join as interrelated conceits.[29]

29. Robert C. Toll asserts that this story comes out of African-American folk songs, but all the collections he cites postdate the sheet music. It is possible, then, that the verses actually originated

"Clare de Kitchen" ends with an innocent picture of rural courtship just as it begins with a picture of carefree labor:

> I wish I was back in old Kentuck,
> For since I left it I had no luck;
> De gals so proud dey wont eat mush,
> And wen you go to court 'em dey say O hush.

If rustics who come to the city exhibit more common sense, more fortitude, and more honesty than presumably superior urbanites, then some fundamental virtue must attach to living in the country. In "Clare de Kitchen" the West offers a society uncomplicated in all ways. The tune recalls others in the minstrel repertory: it features many repeated notes, dotted rhythms, and a melodic shape that ends on the second highest pitch of the song. These musical traits, together with dancelike rhythms, connoted folkish style both to the maskers who selected them and the northern urban audiences who bought the sheet music. Other portraits of this fabled land appeared in Rice's "Long Time Ago" (1833) which invokes a country pedigree in its opening line, "O I was born down ole Varginee," and in "Sitting on a Rail" (1836), also titled "The Raccoon Hunt," as sung by "Mr. Leicester."

Most of the songs in early solo minstrelsy take place in settings removed from the urban experience of both performers and audience. And the nature of blackface suggests that while it may appropriate token African-American traits, it borrows them for a charade that makes no thorough attempt at ethnological accuracy. The low black mask merely serves to intensify an attack on high white society. But one song about a fabled land seems to reflect the life of urban blacks with more candor, "Ching Ring Chaw" (ca. 1833).[30] The text speaks in terse musical phrases (Ex. 5.5) of a better country, but not a legendary rural Eden. Instead the narrator admonishes his audience to leave "Bucra" (an African-derived word meaning "white man's") land for "Hetee," where an independent republic of former slaves had been established. Here blacks would no longer be required to perform menial tasks:

> No more carry hod, no more oister opee,
> No more dig de sod, no more krub de shop-e,
> But hab whiskers gran, an promenade de street-e,
> Wid beauties ob de lan, were we in full dress meet-e.

---

in blackface comedy. See *Blacking Up: The Minstrel Show in Nineteenth-Century America* (New York, 1974), 260–61.

30. This song also appears under the title "Sambo's 'Dress to He' Bred'rin'" (New York: Thos. Birch, 1833), "As Sung with the most Enormous Applause, at Mr. Davis' Musical Parties, on Friday Evenings, Broadway House, by Mr Brower . . . ." See the facsimile in Tawa, *Solo Songs,* I, 109–11.

Bro-der let us leabe,

Buc-ra lan for Het-tee.

Dar you be re-ceibe

Gran as La Fay-et-te;

EXAMPLE 5.5 "Ching A Ring Chaw" (Baltimore: Geo. Willig Junr, [ca. 1833])

No more carry bag an wid a nail and tick-e,
Nasty dirty rag, out gutte pick-e,
No more barrow wheel all about de street-e,
No more blige to teal, den by massa beat-e.

No more our sons cry sweep, no more he be de lack-e,
No more our dorters weep, kase dey all call em black-e,
No more dye servant be, no more wash and cook-e,
But ebery day we see em read de novel book-e.

No more wid black and baush make boot and shoe to shin-e,
But hab all things flush, and all ob 'em sublim-e.

The list of occupations—hod carriers, rag pickers, bootblacks, streetsweeps, household servants—squares well with predominant occupations of African-Americans, especially in northern cities.[31]

In the end, though, the song presents a populist fantasy in which the powerless suddenly gain the estate of the powerful, "La Fayette," "Munro," and

31. See Leonard P. Curry, *The Free Black in Urban America 1800–1850* (Chicago and London, 1981), 15–24, 258–66.

175

"Louis Philip." The cover engraving depicts this reversal (Illus. 5.3), as do many other stanzas in the song:

> Oh dat equal sod, hoo no want to go-e,
> Dare we feel no rod, dar we hab no fo-e;
> Dar we lib so fine wid our coach and hors-e,
> An ebery time we dine, hab one, two, three, four corsee-e.
>
> Dar too we are sure to make our dorters de fine lad-e,
> An wen dey husbans take, dey bove de common grad-e,
> An den perhaps our son, he rise in glorious splender,
> An be like Washington, he country's defender.

The licentious, populist protest of carnival was permanently enshrined in the minstrel songs sold as sheet music during the 1830s, and this beginning established the basic tradition of later nineteenth-century blackface. The combined themes of rustic common sense and virility, idyllic, often rural lands, and the simple people inhabiting them hit a deep vein in the American way of thinking. The mask of the African-American provided the perfect disguise because it provoked an immediate association with the least privileged segment of society and because black dialect instantly conveyed an impression of the folkloric. The public sympathized with African-American characters as underdogs and empathized with them as they turned the world upside down to gain power over the ruling elite. At the same time, the identification was ironic, conflicting severely with the white listeners' sense of superiority to African-Americans and their racist disdain for blacks' quaint and risible behavior.

Diversified Practice and Minstrel Ensembles

The 1840s saw a remarkable expansion of minstrelsy based on the precedent established in the 1830s and on the organization of minstrels into troupes of at least four players, often centered around the theaters of the Bowery (though there were ensembles in many cities). These groups sometimes toured, and they made a wider reputation by publishing their songs under the name of their ensembles or leaders. Solo minstrels generally had performed short numbers between the acts of larger plays, but minstrel troupes filled whole evenings at the theater (or at least large segments). Early shows by minstrel bands featured the players seated in a semi-circle on stage performing a loose collection of songs and dances, interspersed with comic banter.[32] Because members of the

---

32. The best study of minstrel theater remains Toll's *Blacking Up*, and he finds in minstrel skits and songs many of the same features I discuss here. For the early history of group minstrelsy, see pages 51–52.

ILLUSTRATION 1.1
A Victorian woman on a crenelated
turret from the cover of James G.
Maeder's *Answer to the Carrier
Dove* (1841), courtesy the Newberry
Library.

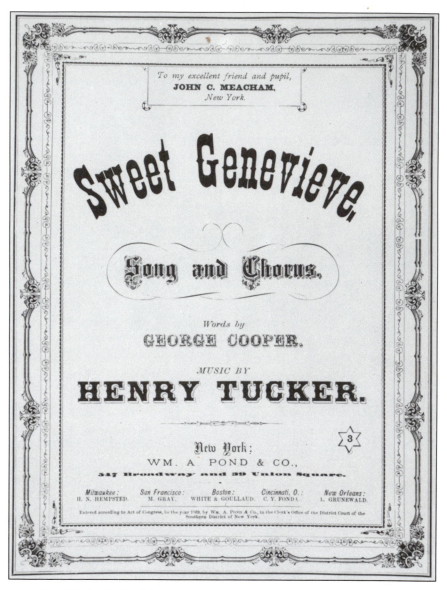

ILLUSTRATION 2.1
Corresponding publishers on the
cover of Henry Tucker's *Sweet
Genevieve* (1869), courtesy the Hill
Music Library.

ILLUSTRATION 2.2
A depiction of the waltz on the cover
of *After the Ball* (later edition, ca.
1902), courtesy the Hill Music Library.

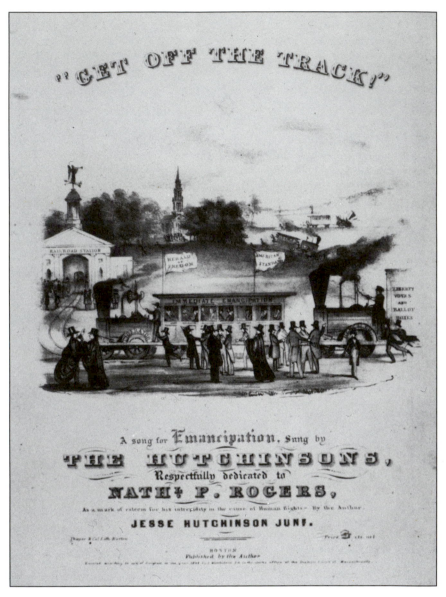

ILLUSTRATION 4.1
Technological progress symbolizing
social progress on the cover of Jesse
Hutchinson's *Get Off the Track*
(1844), courtesy the Newberry Library.

ILLUSTRATION 4.2
The train as symbol of democratic
social etiquette on the cover of *In
the Baggage Coach Ahead* (1896),
courtesy the Hill Music Library.

ILLUSTRATION 4.3
Stylish African-Americans for Emerson
and Howard's *Hello! Ma Baby* (1899),
courtesy the Hill Music Library.

ILLUSTRATION 5.1
Thomas Dartmouth Rice engaged in a picturesque dance as *Jim Crow* (ca. 1832), courtesy the Newberry Library.

ILLUSTRATION 5.2
Sheet music depiction of an early blackface dandy, *Zip Coon* (ca. 1832), courtesy the Hill Music Library.

ILLUSTRATION 5.3
Typical occupations for urban
African-Americans together with
their dreams of elevated status
depicted on the cover of *Ching a
Ring Chaw* (ca. 1883), courtesy the
Newberry Library.

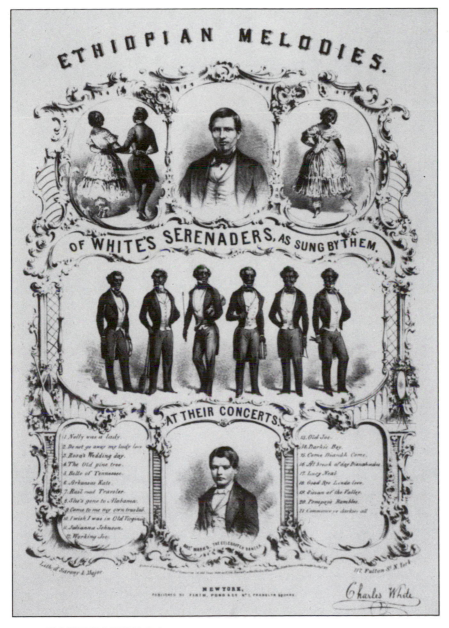

ILLUSTRATION 5.4
General cover for songs performed
by White's Serenaders, showing
their elegant costumes (1849),
courtesy the Newberry Library.

ILLUSTRATION 6.1
Nostalgia for the lost rural paradise
depicted in the engraving for James
Putnam's *My Home in Alabam'* and
H. P. Danks's *My Dear Savannah
Home* (1881), courtesy the Newberry
Library.

ILLUSTRATION 6.2
Scenes of comedy and religious fer-
vor on the cover of Sam Lucas's
Every Day'l Be Sunday By and By
(1881), courtesy the Newberry
Library.

ILLUSTRATION 6.3
The African-American urban dandy translated into a black demon in Sam Lucas's *De Coon Dat Had de Razor* (1885), courtesy the Newberry Library.

ILLUSTRATION 6.4
The violent dandy repeated for *May Irwin's Bully Song* (1896), courtesy the Hill Music Library.

ILLUSTRATION 7.1
A noble savage on the cover of
Russell's *Indian Hunter* (later
edition, ca. 1839), courtesy the
Hill Music Library.

ILLUSTRATION 7.2
The beautiful Indian maiden in
Sullivan's *Blue Juniata* (1844),
courtesy the Hill Music Library.

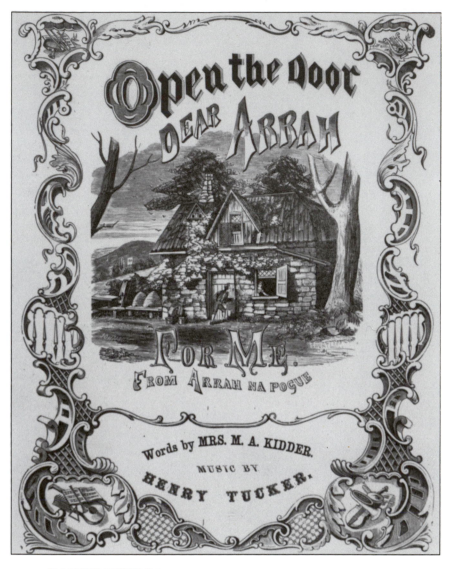

ILLUSTRATION 8.1
A scene of rural Irish courtship for
Open the Door, Dear Arrah, for Me
(1865), courtesy the Newberry
Library.

ILLUSTRATION 7.3
(facing) Stereotypical Indian maid-
en repeated for Tivolie's *Hee-Lah-
Dee!* (1873), courtesy the William
L. Clements Library.

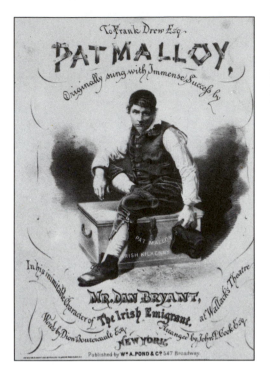

ILLUSTRATION 8.2
An Irish immigrant as played by
Dan Bryant in 1865, courtesy the
Newberry Library.

ILLUSTRATION 8.3
Edward Harrigan and Tony Hart as
members of *The Mulligan Guard*
(1873), courtesy the Hill Music
Library.

company could specialize in particular roles, either as straightmen or gagmen, their songs tended to concentrate on isolated conceits. The themes of the rural, the primitive, and the carnivalesque persisted but were often exposed separately, to be recombined only in certain kinds of ensemble songs. Mention of contemporary political events became less frequent in minstrel sheet music during the 1840s, but the roots of the entertainment still lay in Jacksonian populism.[33]

The Virginia Minstrels generally received credit as the first coherent troupe. It included four members who had been engaged in solo or duo blackface performances for some time: William Whitlock on banjo, Richard Pelham on tambourine, Frank Brower on bones (long castanets played rather like spoons), and Daniel Emmett on fiddle. Speaking through a newspaper reporter, Emmett left a fascinating description of their first audition in 1843:

> All four were one day sitting in the North American Hotel, in the Bowery, when one of them proposed that with their instruments they should cross over to the Bowery Circus and give one of the proprietors (Uncle Nate Howes) a "charivari" as he sat by the stove in the hall entrance. Bringing forth his banjo for Whitlock to play on, Emmett took the violin, Pelham the tambourine, and Brower the bones. Without any rehearsal, with hardly the ghost of an idea as to what was to follow, they crossed the street and proceeded to "browbeat" Uncle Nat Howes into giving them an engagement, the calculation being that he would succumb in preference to standing the horrible noise (for they attempted no tune) they were making with their instruments. After standing it for a while, Uncle Nate said:
>
> "Boys, you've got a good thing. Can't you sing us a song?"
>
> Thereupon Emmett accompanying himself on his violin, began to sing "Old Dan Tucker," the others joining in the chorus. After singing some more songs for him, they returned to the North American, where they resumed their "horrible noise" in the reading-room, which was quickly filled with spectators.[34]

The term "charivari" applies not only to raucous serenade of newlyweds but also denotes the revels of grotesquely masked, noisy roisterers during French carnival. Early bills for this short-lived ensemble (the act survived only a year and a half) advertise the same prevarication used by solo minstrels to establish their folkloric masks:

> . . . [they have been praised for] truly delineating in a masterly and chaste manner, the Sports and Pastimes of the Virginia Colored Race, through the medium of Songs, Refrain and Ditties, as sung by the Southern Slaves, at all

---

33. See Saxton, "Blackface Minstrelsy and Jacksonian Ideology."

34. "The Origin of Minstrelsy: Dan Emmett's History of the Wanderings of the First Troupe," *New York Clipper* 25, no. 8 (May 19, 1877), 61.

their Merry Meetings, such as the gathering of the Cotton and Sugar Crops, Corn Huskings, Slave Weddings and Junketings.

The bottom of the early bill reveals that the principals are really transvested white men: "The harmony and skill with which the banjo, violin, castinets [bones], and tambourine are blended by these truly original minstrels, in their Ethiopian characters, is a redeeming feature of this species of amusement. . . . "[35]

Much debate surrounds the question of authenticity in minstrel presentations. The banjo, for instance, originated in Africa,[36] but its gourd resonator was replaced with a sturdier wood or metal frame by theater performers, and this changed the nature of the sound. Billy Whitlock's obituary claimed that he learned banjo from Joe Sweeney, composer of songs like "Ole Tare River" (1840) and "Whar Did You Come From" (1840).[37] Sweeney in turn is supposed to have learned the banjo from slaves on his family plantation.[38] In fact, Whitlock spent only four days with Sweeney, though later Billy maintained he "would quietly steal off to some negro hut to hear the darkies sing and see them dance" while on tour in the South with the circus. Whitlock and the other performers may well have included elements of African-American performance in their playing, just as they appropriated some features from black dialect for their lyrics. But they borrowed these traits to create a mask: the Virginia Minstrels continued the mummery of solo blackface in a new format.

The song for the Virginia Minstrels' first audition, "Old Dan Tucker," originated in the repertory of solo minstrelsy. Originally published in New York by Millet's Music Saloon in 1842, one early cover shows a black dandy in silhouette.[39] In Emmett's version (1843),[40] however, Old Dan takes the slightly different role of a primitive backwoodsman with awesome abilities, whose arrival in town provokes consternation among the populace (see Ex. 5.6). After supplying this initial information, the words follow the pattern established in earlier blackface songs of presenting comic exaggerations about a grotesque world:

> Tucker is a nice old man,
> He use to ride our darby ram;

35. This flyer for performances by the Virginia Minstrels in Worcester, Massachusetts, March 20–22, 1843, can be found in the Driscoll Collection of Chicago's Newberry Library, Box 306.

36. For the etymology of "banjo," see Deana J. Epstein, "The Folk Banjo: A Documentary History," *Ethnomusicology* 19 (1975), 347–71.

37. "William M. Whitlock. The Origin of Negro Minstrelsy," *New York Clipper* 26, no. 3 (April 13, 1878), 21.

38. The most thorough consideration of banjo style appears in Robert B. Winans, "The Folk, the Stage, and the Five String Banjo in the Nineteenth Century," *Journal of American Folklore* 89 (1976), 407–37.

39. For this anonymous composite edition (cover by Atwill's, plates by Millet's) see Damon, *Old American Songs*, no. 37; Damon repeats an assertion that Dan Emmett wrote the song in 1830, but it seems unlikely it went unpublished for twelve years.

40. "The Original Old Dan Tucker, Words by Old Dan D. Emmit [sic]" appears in Jackson's *Popular Songs*, 160–62.

EXAMPLE 5.6 "Old Dan Tucker" (Boston: Chas. H. Keith, 1843)

He sent him whizzen down de hill,
If he hadn't got up he'd lay dar still.

or:

Tucker was a hardened sinner,
He nebber said his grace at dinner;
De ole sow squeel, de pigs did squall,
He 'hole hog wid de tail and all.

But Emmett does not go on to the next step in the standard narrative, political criticism, leaving only the opposition of rural and urban to hint at a populist context. The cover lithograph "by W. Sharp from a sketch by Johnston" enhances the atmosphere by depicting impossibilia: a blackface character fending off an alligator with a banjo, serenading a rooster with a banjo, holding a bull by wrapping its tail around a banjo. An assortment of revelers also dance to fiddle, banjo, tambourine, and bones.

The musical content of "Old Dan Tucker" hails from the traditional roots of minstrelsy. The instrumental prelude and postlude rely heavily on Anglo-Celtic dance figures. The melody (Ex. 5.6) shares the parlando rhythms of

EXAMPLE 5.7   Dan Emmett, "De Boatman's Dance" (Boston: Chas. H. Keith, 1843)

earlier minstrel songs and punctuates the prosaic declamation with many sylla-bles on one repeated pitch. The tune has a very flat melodic shape suited to its patter, and the refrain emphasizes a relatively new feature in blackface songs, syncopation in the phrase "get *out* de way!"

The Virginia Minstrels also combined the theme of the amazing primitive with dance idiom to produce "The Fine Old Colored Gentlemen" (parody of Henry Russell's famous "A Fine Old English Gentleman"), " 'Twill Nebber Do to Gib It Up So," "De Wild Goose Nation," "Dar He Goes! Dats Him!," and "Dandy Jim from Caroline" (1844; sometimes credited to S. S. Steele and Dan Myers). In one of these songs, "De Boatman's Dance" (1843), Emmett returned to an old standby of solo minstrelsy. The first verse (Ex. 5.7) alludes to the rivermen of the West, but the second may also refer to a Chesapeake boatman:

> De oyster boat should keep to de shore,
> De fishin smack should venture more,
> De schooner sails before de wind,
> De steamboat leave a streak behind.

EXAMPLE 5.8   "Jim Crack Corn" (Baltimore: F. D. Benteen, 1846)

In any event, this boatman has much in common with Jim Crow or the "Suske-hanna boy." He is an audacious brawler, very attractive to the ladies:

> De boatman is a thrifty man,
> Dars none can do as de boatman can;
> I neber see a putty gal in my life
> But dat she was a boatman's wife.

These lyrics unfold, as in other songs of this type, over a punctuated melody very narrow in range, with the exception of the chorus which features violin or banjo arpeggiations (in fact, this music may derive from a fiddle tune published by George Knauff in 1839, called "Ohio River").[41] But while the boatman's music and primitive heroism are familiar from earlier minstrelsy, his song lacks the tones of protest or politics.

The Virginia Minstrel's repertory, however, did not overlook populist inversion altogether. The most famous instance came in " 'Jim Crack Corn' or the Blue Tail Fly," best known in a version published by F. D. Benteen (1846)[42] after the troupe had disbanded in 1844. The first verse presents the narrator as a slave (Ex. 5.8), using the usual parlando style. The ensuing story concerns the master's riding accident:

> One day he rode aroun' de farm,
> De flies so numerous dey did swarm;
> One chance to bite 'im on the thigh,
> De debble take dat blue tail fly.
>
> De poney run, he jump an' pitch,
> An' tumble massa in de ditch,

41. Goertzen and Jabbour, "Knauff's *Virginia Reels*," 133–35.
42. See Jackson, *Popular Songs,* 91–92, 271–72.

He died, an' de jury wonder'd why
De verdic was de blue tail fly.

The slave mourns in facetious tones:

Dey laid 'im under a 'simmon tree,
His epitaph am dar to see:
"Beneath dis stone I'm forced to lie,
All by de means ob de blue tail fly."

The chorus, now written in the four parts facilitated by group minstrelsy, cheers the overthrow of authority: "Jim crack corn I don't care, Ole Massa gone away." The love of the world upside down was still alive and well, even if it did not appear in every minstrel text.

Another famous band, Christy's Minstrels, claimed to have originated ensemble blackface, though reliable accounts place their beginning in 1844 after the first performance of the Virginia Minstrels. Edwin P. Christy, a ballad singer born in Philadelphia, founded his ensemble in Buffalo, New York, apparently in imitation of Emmett's group. Together with his stepson, George Christy, he gravitated to New York City. There Christy's Minstrels set up for a long run in Mechanics' (i.e., "workers' ") Hall from early 1847 to the autumn of 1853, when George's departure broke up the original band. Edwin and George went their separate ways, with Edwin retiring from the stage in 1855, while George continued to be active to the end of his life in 1868.[43]

Christy's Minstrels popularized a great number of songs, including "Stop Dat Knocking at My Door" (1847), "Farewell Ladies" (also known as "Good Night Ladies," 1847), and "Carry Me Back to Old Virginia" (1847). One of their best loved numbers, "Oh! Susanna" (1848),[44] featured the ensemble's name in early editions but made no mention of the song's composer, Stephen Foster. Foster, like Emmett, knew the tradition of solo minstrelsy. He had been impressed by Thomas Dartmouth Rice's portrayal of "Jim Crow" as a child, and submitted some early songs to him in hopes of having them performed.[45] "Oh! Susanna" was probably written for Nelson Kneass, a member of the Sable Harmonists and supplier of the tune for "Ben Bolt."[46] The narrator in "Oh! Susanna" holds many traits in common with the carnivalesque figure

43. See Edward Leroy Rice, *Monarchs of Minstrelsy from "Daddy" Rice to Date* (New York, 1911), 19–20.

44. Reprinted in Jackson, *Popular Songs,* 152–55.

45. Rice's grandson, Dean J. Rice, claims that Foster maintained a friendship with the performer from 1851 to his death in 1860; see the foreword to *Two Stephen C. Foster Songs* (New York, 1931).

46. See John Tasker Howard, *Stephen Foster, America's Troubadour* (New York, 1953), 126–29. E. L. Rice suggests that Kneass adapted a German melody for "Ben Bolt"; see *Monarchs,* 26.

who inhabits earlier blackface compositions. He begins by outlining a series of comic non sequiturs:

> It rain'd all night the day I left,
> The weather it was dry,
> The sun so hot I frose to death;
> Susanna dont you cry.

The next verse continues with a set of impossibilia:

> I jumped aboard de telegraph,
> And trabbelled down de riber,
> De Lectric fluid magnified,
> And killed five hundred Nigger.
> De bullgine bust, de horse run off,
> I realy thought I'd die;
> I shut my eyes to hold my breath,
> Susanna, dont you cry.

In the last verse this archtypical primitive journeys to the urban climes of New Orleans in search of his true love. Foster updates him by choosing recent technology (''de telegraph,'' ''de lectric fluid'') to express the subversion of reality. And just as he modernizes the text's point of reference, Foster translates the musical symbolism of earlier blackface into a newly popular language. He has kept the inclination to repeated notes that set dialect in uneven rhythms (Ex. 5.9). But he selects the contemporary polka to provide the rhythmic underpinnings of the song where earlier composers chose older dances—jigs and reels. Also following the modern practice, Foster supplies the song with a four-part chorus featuring a prominent syncopation on the word ''Susanna.''[47]

After ''Oh! Susanna'' Foster continued to send Christy songs in the comic vein like ''Away Down South'' (1848), ''My Brudder Gum'' (1849), and ''Gwine to Run All Night or De Camptown Races'' (1850).[48] The text of this last composition is particularly rich in impossibilia featuring animals:

> De blind hoss sticken in a big mud hole—Doo-dah! doo-dah!
> Can't touch bottom wid a ten foot pole—Oh! doo-dah-day!
> Old muley cow come on to de track—Doo-dah! doo-dah!
> De bob-tail fling her ober his back—Oh! doo-dah-day!
>
> Den fly along like a rail-road car—Doo-dah! doo-dah!
> Runnin a race wid a shootin' star—Oh! Doo-dah-day!

47. For a discussion of the polka in connection with ''Oh! Susanna,'' see Austin, ''Susanna,'' 8–9.
48. Facsimile in Jackson, *Popular Songs,* 39–42.

EXAMPLE 5.9   Stephen Foster, "Oh! Susanna" (New York: C. Holt Jr., 1848)

In addition to the droll lines about the horse race, the responsorial nonsense syllables give an extra touch of the folkloric.

At the end of the 1840s and throughout the 1850s minstrel troupes expanded greatly, and the minstrel show gradually assumed the three-part form it maintained until the end of the century. The first part took the original practice of early group minstrelsy as its pattern. In the middle of an enlarged semi-circle sat a straightman, or "interlocutor," who spoke in the overly formal tones of a trained thespian and also served as master of ceremonies. At the ends of the semi-circle sat the gagmen, or "endmen," often known as "Mister Tambo" and "Mr. Bones" after the instruments they played. The comic chatter between these players alternated with dances and all manner of songs, both droll and sentimental (a romantic tenor often sang the latter). The second part of the show, called the "olio," featured novelty acts performing in front of the curtain that hid the set-up for the finale. The acts ranged from acrobats to musical saw players to song-and-dance routines (this section was the forerunner of variety). The show concluded with a comic skit or one-act play on any number of subjects, the favorite being plantation life. A skit on a southern subject would often end with the whole cast performing a "walk-around," a spirited song-and-dance number.[49]

49. Toll outlines the structure of the minstrel show in *Blacking Up,* 52–57; and a sample of routines for each part (with most of the racially offensive dialect removed) appears in Dailey

The expanded format, with its intermixture of comic and sentimental elements, produced songs that combined the old themes from solo blackface with stylistic traits from other traditions in American popular song. This synthesis may be the most important of the many significant contributions minstrel ensembles made to the creation of a national style. One such troupe, the Harmoneons, was active in Boston, enlisting the talents of L. V. H. Crosby, the Powers Brothers, and Marshall S. Pike. They became sufficiently famous to perform at the White House for Polk in 1847. Pike (1818–1901), their best-known member, was a minstrel pioneer in "wench" roles, and he would later join John P. Ordway's Aeolians.[50] Pike also composed over 100 songs, and a good example of his minstrel style appears in "I Hab Leff Alabama" (1849). The text strikes a vein of nostalgia for lost rural happiness, tied here to the separation of lovers (see Ex. 5.10). The note of comedy has not entirely disappeared in the female slave's reasons for leaving:

> Oh! Ben was my true lub but de galls all would kiss him,
> And so I got jealous and leff him soon den;
> But soon arter dat my affections did miss him,
> And I must go back to Alabama agen.

But sentimentality prevails:

> Den I'll tell Ben I lub him and he will beliebe me,
> Case he knows dat I tink he's der gemblam ob men;
> And massa will smile and be glad to receibe me,
> When I's home safe back in Alabama agen.

This song strikes a tone of rural longing very different from that in "Clare de Kitchen," partly because Pike has based his melody on a vocal rather than dance tradition (Ex. 5.10). In fact, Pike's tune comes very close to quoting "Believe Me If All Those Endearing Young Charms" from Thomas Moore's *Irish Melodies*. This tradition was not only lyrical, it carried with it distinctly nostalgic associations. Moore's collection did a brisk trade in longing for times past and for a lost, distant country. Pike's move away from the usual musical vocabulary of minstrelsy also seems to exclude the more raucous impossibilia in the lyrics of earlier songs on the same subject.

Large minstrel troupes could afford to indulge elegance, as White's Serenaders did while playing in various Bowery theaters from 1846 to 1854 under the direction of Charles T. White (1821–91). White was so successful that at one time he owned a theater, White's Ethiopian Opera House, where distin-

---

Paskman's *"Gentlemen, Be Seated!": A Parade of the American Minstrels,* rev. ed. (New York, 1976).

50. Rice, *Monarchs,* 28, 44.

EXAMPLE 5.10 Marshall S. Pike, "I Hab Leff Alabama" (Boston: A. & J. P. Ord-way, 1849)

guished minstrels, including Dan Emmett, plied their trade.[51] A lithographed cover for the troupe's songs (Illus. 5.4) gives an idea of its size, refinement, and its use of male juveniles to play travesty roles. The carnivalesque did not entirely disappear in White's minstrelsy, nor did the classic instruments—banjo, fiddle, tambourine, and bones—all depicted in this engraving. But the troupe performed a number of songs in a more genteel vein, including "Do Not Go Away My Lady Love," "Belle of Tennessee," and "Lucy Neal." Their most famous song along these lines was "Nancy Till" (1851), sometimes attributed to White himself,[52] though the title page merely reads "written for and sung by White's Serenaders." Solo minstrelsy had taken a direct, almost ribald approach to courtship, but "Nancy Till" assumes the chivalric stance of polite songs:

> Open de window, love O do;
> And listen to de music, Ise playing for you;
> De whisp'rings ob love, so soft and low:
> Harmonise my voice, wid de old banjo.

51. Ibid., 35; Nathan, *Dan Emmett,* 218.
52. Hamm, *Yesterdays,* 269.

The suitor admires the distant beloved from below and from afar:

> Softly de casement, begin for to rise;
> De stars am a shining, above in de skies;
> De moon am declining, behind yonder hill:
> Reflecting its rays, on you my Nancy Till.

Like her polite predecessors, Nancy remains far beyond the reach of her swain. Yet aspects of the rural and primitive pervade the genteel scene. The suitor is a western boatman singing in obvious dialect:

> [Chorus:]
> Come love come, de boat lies low;
> She lies high and dry on de Ohio:
> Come love come, won't you go along with me;
> I'll take you down to Tenessee [sic].

This last line also alludes just briefly to the longing for a fabled, lost country. The composer of "Nancy Till" has sentimentalized this rural longing in response to his gentle subject.

Just as the text of "Nancy Till" mixes elements of the serenade with the rural and primitive, so the music blends traits from both genteel and populist traditions. The melody for the verse breathes long, graceful lines that rise and fall lyrically (see Ex. 5.11). The rhythms are smoother, more even and regular, than in the parlando style of earlier minstrelsy. Yet the boatman's singing in the four-part chorus returns just a bit to repeated notes and includes a touch of syncopation on the last word, Tennessee.

The combination of lyrical music with texts about rural longing proved irresistible to contemporary audiences. And nobody was better equipped to take advantage of the demand than Stephen Foster, who mastered every stylistic trend of his day. By 1851 the composer had concluded an agreement allowing Christy to sing Foster's minstrel songs before they were published and to have the troupe's name printed on the cover.[53] Going one step further, Foster published "Old Folks at Home," an "Ethiopian Melody as sung by Christy's Minstrels" (1851) under Christy's name.[54] During his lifetime it was Foster's most popular composition by the evidence of royalties,[55] partly because it epitomizes nostalgia for a lost rural past:

> Way down upon de Swanee ribber,
> Far, far away,

53. Howard, *Foster*, 195–201.
54. Facsimile in Jackson, *Popular Songs*, 163–66.
55. Howard, *Foster*, 266–67,

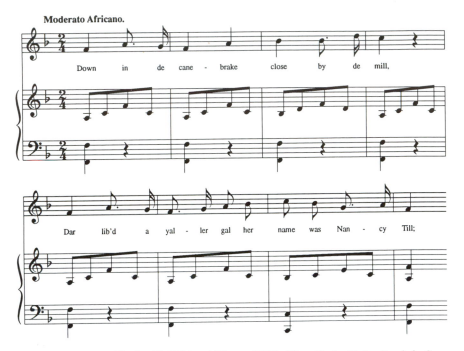

EXAMPLE 5.11 Charles T. White, "Nancy Till" (New York: Firth, Pond & Co., 1851), excerpts of verse and chorus (on facing page)

> Dere's wha my heart is turning ebber,
> Dere's wha de old folks stay. . . .
>
> *[Chorus:]*
> All de world am sad and dreary,
> Ebry where I roam,
> Oh! darkeys how my heart grows weary,
> Far from de old folks at home.

The remaining verses continue with fond remembrances of "de little farm," the "little hut," and familial childhood security which provides another reason for nostalgia. Despite the song's dialect, any immigrant or traveler could empathize with its longing for home. This tune, like Pike's earlier "I Hab Leff Alabama," invokes Moore's *Irish Melodies,* but not by quotation. Foster follows the more subtle approach of imitating the "Irish" style, particularly in the large leap near the beginning of several phrases (Ex. 5.12).[56] To the

56. Charles Hamm discusses the stylistic influence of the *Irish Melodies* on Foster in *Yesterdays,* 55–57.

"Irish" melodic shape Foster adds minstrel touches like the syncopated setting of "ribber" and "ebber," in addition to the short phrases and four-part chorus. The Irish melos here connotes the polite nostalgia of songs like "Gentle Annie"; dialect and situation represent the rural.

"My Old Kentucky Home" (1853)[57] is a more genteel translation of "Old Folks." Foster draws a vivid rural portrait:

> The corn top's ripe and the meadow's in the bloom,
> While the birds make music all the day.

57. Facsimile in Jackson's *Stephen Foster Song Book* (New York, 1974), 67–71.

189

EXAMPLE 5.12   Stephen Foster, "Old Folks at Home" (New York: Firth, Pond & Co., 1851)

> The young folks roll on the little cabin floor,
> All merry, all happy and bright. . . .

But of course this happy land of agrarian splendor is irretrievably lost:

> They hunt no more for the possum and the coon
> On the meadow, the hill and the shore,
> They sing no more by the glimmer of the moon,
> On the bench by the old cabin door.

Foster's text gives the reason for the "darkies" leaving their homeland: they have been sold to the cruel sugar-cane plantations of the lower South. But it is not this depiction of slavery's injustice that engages the empathy of audiences; instead, homesickness forms the touchstone:

> Weep no more, my lady, oh! weep no more today!
> We will sing one song for the old Kentucky Home,
> For the old Kentucky Home, far away.

For this reason, "Kentucky Home" never became a favorite of the abolition movement in the way that militant political songs like "Get Off the Track" or "John Brown" did. Foster's music leads genteel listeners to identify with the text of "Kentucky Home": the tune has gently arched phrases and mostly even rhythms. In fact, the first phrase (Ex. 5.13) seems to quote the beginning of "Nancy Till" (see Ex. 5.11 above), evoking a lyrical melancholy. Many of his other songs assume this posture, including "Old Dog Tray" (1853), "Old Black Joe," and "Down Among the Cane-Brakes" (1860).

Genteel sentimentality did not replace the old minstrel banter, but simply expanded the variety of styles at a troupe's command. The "endmen" always

EXAMPLE 5.13   Stephen Foster, ''My Old Kentucky Home'' (New York: Firth, Pond & Co., 1853)

had sprightly numbers. While Charles T. White featured a refined nocturne like ''Nancy Till,'' other performers might sing ''Cool'' White's ''Lubly Fan Will You Come Out Tonight'' (1844),[58] a more bumptious serenade later known as ''Buffalo Gals (Won't You Come Out Tonight?)'' ''Cool White'' was actually the pseudonym of John Hodges (1821–91), a blackface pioneer who organized the Virginia Serenaders in 1843, the Sable Melodists some years later, and finally Cool White's Broadway Minstrels in 1870.[59] The suitor in White's ''Lubly Fan'' has no time for polite restraint. When he sees a ''pretty gal'' he reacts immediately:

> I lub to taste dem lubly lips,
> > Lubly lips,
> > Lubly lips,
> Oh den I sure would lose my wits,
> An drap down on de floor.

58. Reprinted in Tawa, *Solo Songs*, I, 107–8.
59. Rice, *Monarchs*, 34–35.

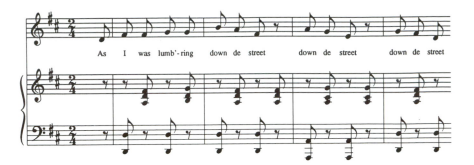

As I was lumb'-ring down de street down de street down de street

EXAMPLE 5.14 "Cool" White, "Lubly Fan Will You Come Out Tonight" (Boston: C. H. Keith, 1844)

Neither does his lady love maintain her chaste distance in the last verse:

> Yes Lubly Fan will cum out to night,
>   Cum out to night,
>   Cum out to night,
> Yes Lubly Fan will cum out to night,
> An dance by de light ob de moon.

The melody for the verse (Ex. 5.14) repeats in the four-part chorus, and it is a model of minstrel style, with the tendency to heavy punctuation, narrow range, and syncopation: "Den Lubly Fan will you come *out* to night, come *out* to night, . . . " The tune for "Lubly Fan," like so many others in the minstrel collection, probably comes from the repertory of fiddle music.[60] This song is made for an earthy, even a rude kind of enjoyment.

On occasion, political humor still worked its way into isolated minstrel songs. One was "Pop Goes the Weasel," which appeared simultaneously in Britain and America during 1853.[61] The American version, published in New York by Berry and Gordon in 1853 and reissued from the same plates by Stephen T. Gordon in 1859, speaks to the dance in its first stanza:[62]

> Ob all de dance dat ebber was plann'd
> To galvanize de heel and de hand,
> Dar's none dat moves so gay and grand
>   As "Pop goes de Weasel."

60. Goertzen and Jabbour, "Knauff's *Virginia Reels*," 133.
61. See James J. Fuld, *The Book of World-Famous Music*, rev. and enlarged ed. (New York, 1971), 440–41.
62. Reprinted in Jackson, *Popular Songs*, 176–79. The "9" in this later printing has been altered by addition of a line to the original numeral "3".

and also at its very end:

> Den form two lines as straight as a string,
> Dance in and out, den three in a ring—
> Dive under like de duck, and sing
>   "Pop goes de Weasel!"

These references continue an established tradition of dance in minstrelsy.

The main body of "Pop Goes the Weasel," however, really concerns the issues of 1853. The second stanza is devoted exclusively to the various defects of Great Britain, beginning with English criticism of American slavery:

> John Bull tells, in de ole cow's hum,
> How Uncle Sam used *Uncle Tom,*
> While he makes some white folks *slaves* at home,
>   By "Pop goes de Weasel!"

Besides condemning English sanctimony, the lyrics also warn Great Britain against supporting Spain on the question of Cuba ("[John Bull] talks about a friendly trip, To Cuba in a steam war-ship"). Sentiment for American purchase, annexation, or outright conquest of the island rose to fever pitch just after the election of Franklin Pierce in 1852, and during the following summer of 1853 a demonstration for a free Cuba "began with a torchlight procession led by the popular Dodsworth's Band from Fulton Street up Broadway."[63] This stanza also warns the British against poaching in the United States' fishing grounds. From the beginning to the end of antebellum minstrelsy, the English provided a good target for anti-authoritarian protest because of their immense economic influence and maritime power. And as an expression of populism, minstrelsy typically exhibited a certain amount of xenophobia. These sentiments obviously persisted, for the 1853 version was reprinted in 1859 when the issue of Cuba resurfaced.

The third stanza in "Pop" concerns the pleasures of this world—drinking, women, and dancing—beginning with the self-deceptions of the temperance movement, a traditional butt of minstrel jokes:

> De Temperance folks from Souf to Main *[sic],*
> Against all liquor spout and strain,
> But when dey feels an ugly pain
>   Den "Pop goes de Weasel!"

63. Charles H. Brown, *Agents of Manifest Destiny: The Lives and Times of the Filibusters* (Chapel Hill, NC, 1980), 119.

The hypocrisy of the genteel always provided good amunition. And so-called "Maine Laws" (named after the 1851 legislation in that state) made prohibition a particularly good subject in 1853 for an entertainment dealing in protest against governmental authority.[64] The emphasis on political subjects, almost to the exclusion of all other concerns, displays the increasing separation of one theme from another in minstrelsy of the period. The topicality in "Pop Goes the Weasel" results in a surprising twist: the narrator defends urban, not rural surroundings, in his praise for the women at the New York World's Fair of 1853.

Rustic themes continued to predominate, however, and in "The Yellow Rose of Texas" (1858)[65] for example, rural longing took a cheerful rather than sentimental form. Rhythms very like the polka in "Oh! Susanna" resound strongly in this spirited tune by the anonymous "J. K.," who composed it for Charles H. Brown of Jackson, Tennessee, according to the cover. While the text contains no dialect, the references to "darkies," a beautiful African-American woman ("yellow rose—the sweetest rose of color"), and the banjo place this song in the domain of blackface, as do the four-part chorus, the uneven vocal rhythms featuring much syncopation, and the staccato accompaniment (see Ex. 5.15). This musical style is tied to comic minstrelsy, and while "Yellow Rose" contains nostalgia for the beauty of the lost country,

> Where the Rio Grande is flowing
> and the starry skies are bright,
> She walks along the river,
> in the quiet summer night;

the song mingles, to use Bayard Taylor's words, "whimsical consolation" with "sincere pathos":

> Oh! now I'm going to find her
> for my heart is full of woe,
> And we'll sing the song together,
> that we sung so long ago;
> We'll play the banjo gaily,
> and we'll sing the songs of yore,
> And the yellow rose of Texas
> shall be mine for evermore.

"Yellow Rose" served as an antidote for those who found "Nancy Till" or "My Old Kentucky Home" too sentimental. But some of gentility rubbed off:

64. See Ian R. Tyrrell, *Sobering Up: From Temperance to Prohibition in Antebellum America, 1800–1860* (Westport, CT, and London, 1979), 252–309.
65. Reprinted in Jackson, *Popular Songs*, 253–57.

EXAMPLE 5.15   "The Yellow Rose of Texas" (New York: Firth, Pond & Co., 1858)

"Yellow Rose" does not contain lyrics that would ruffle feathers in even the most polite parlor, though the musical style and general context remain distinctly populist.

Occasionally a song reversed the growing separation of subjects in minstrelsy, and none provides a better example than Dan Emmett's "I Wish I Was in Dixie's Land" (1860).[66] It gathers many threads from the preceding three decades of blackface. In 1858 Emmett left White's Serenaders to join Bryant's Minstrels.[67] He wrote a good deal for this company established by three brothers, Dan, Jerry, and Neil, who also did immigrant impersonations, especially of Irishmen. "Old K. Y. Ky.," "Dar's a Darkey in de Tent," "Billy Patterson," "Jack on the Green," and "Darrow-Arrow" all came from Emmett's last flowering as a songwriter, and issued during the early 1860s from the presses of Firth, Pond and Company.

"Dixie's Land" first appeared in a program given by Bryant's Minstrels on April 4, 1859, as a "Plantation Song and Dance," following a burlesque of Italian opera and preceding a performance of *Our American Cousin* (ironically, the comedy Lincoln was viewing almost exactly six years later when he was assassinated).[68] The song is literally a pastiche. The initial, well-known verse

66. Sheet music facsimile, ibid., 61–64.
67. Nathan, *Dan Emmett,* 230.
68. Ibid., 246. Nathan recounts at length the dispute between Emmett and Firth, Pond on the one hand and P. P. Werlein of New Orleans on the other concerning the rights to the song which

and the chorus play on a cheerful rural longing much the same as in "Yellow Rose":

> I wish I was in de land ob cotton,
> Old times dar am not forgotten;
>   Look away! &c—
> In Dixie Land whar I was born in,
> Early on one frosty mornin,
>   Look away! &c—

> [Chorus:]
> Den I wish I was in Dixie,
> Hooray! Hooray!
> In Dixie Land, I'll took my stand,
> To lib an die in Dixie,
> Away, Away,
> Away down south in Dixie.

The first line of this verse copies a stock phrase found in songs like "Clare de Kitchen' "'s last verse: "I wish I was back in old Kentuck," or in a well-known title from Charles White's repertory, "I Wish I Was in Old Virginia."

This first verse of "Dixie," with its praise of the rural South, endeared the song to Confederates during the Civil War, but the remaining stanzas suited rebel patriotism less well and were usually omitted (sheet music printed in the South often supplied a different text altogether). Two stanzas express populist resentment of authority, beginning with lines Emmett appropriated from "Gombo Chaff":

> Old Missus marry "Will-de-weaber,"
> Willium was a gay deceaber;
>   Look away! &c—
> But when he put his arm around'er,
> He smiled as fierce as a 'forty-pound'er.
>   Look away! &c—

The slave expands on his criticism of mistress and master:

> His face was sharp as a butcher's cleaber
> But dat did not seem to greab'er;

---

was settled at a meeting of the Board of Music Trade (266–69). More recently Howard and Judith Sacks have tried to show that "Dixie" was written by a family of black musicians living near Emmett's birthplace of Mount Vernon, Ohio, in "Way Up North in Dixie: Black-White Musical Interaction in Knox County, Ohio," *American Music* 6 (1988), 409–27. The appearance of several verses borrowed from minstrel songs of the 1830s argues more for Emmett's authorship than for origins in folkish practice.

Look away! &c—
Old Missus acted de foolish part,
And died for a man dat broke her heart,
Look away! &c—

The next verse rehearses old themes of the admired ladies' man and comedy:

Now here's a health to the next old Missus,
An all de galls dat want to kiss us;
Look away! &c—
But if you want to drive 'way sorrow,
Come an hear dis song to-morrow.
Look away! &c—

The last verse enumerates both folkish cuisine and the traditional dance steps of "walk-arounds":

Dar's buck-wheat cakes an "Ingen" batter,
Makes you fat or a little fatter;
Look away! &c—
Den hoe it down an scratch your grabble,
To Dixie land I'm bound to trabble.
Look away! &c—

Just as the text borrows and recombines, the music synthesizes various traditions. Though at first glance the melody seems to dwell on the repeated-note patter of early blackface songs, the tune ultimately forms an almost Italianate arch moving up the scale and then descending in arpeggios (see Ex. 5.16). Melismas even intrude on the setting ("*I* wish I *was*" or "*In* Dixie *land whar*"). Other features are folkish, including the use of a response ("Look away") that may be reminiscent of African-American folk singing (spirituals often feature call and response, though "Dixie's Land" lays far from the sacred tradition). Additional non-genteel traits include uneven, dance-like rhythms (reminiscent of the polka) and prominent syncopations. W. L. Hobbs, the arranger, provides a fiddle-like postlude to cap the endeavor.

Antebellum minstrelsy's gift to American popular song was nothing less than the synthesis of a distinctive style ("they are in fact, the national airs of America," Taylor writes). The short phrases with their syllabic setting of text, the lack of ornaments, the resulting clarity of declamation, the use of dance rhythms, the sporadic but persistent syncopation, and the references to the melodic shapes of folk music produced a vitality unknown in the predominantly Italianate style during the first four decades of the nineteenth century. By combining this clipped folkloric language with the melodic rise and fall of genteel music, composers such as Stephen Foster produced a hybrid which provided

197

EXAMPLE 5.16   Dan Emmett, "I Wish I Was in Dixie's Land" (New York: Firth, Pond & Co., 1860)

the root stock for a generation of compositions. In addition, while it may not have invented the multi-voice refrain, ensemble minstrelsy enshrined the four-voice chorus in song for at least three decades, and popularized a narrative structure in which a story unfolds in the verse while the chorus provided a moral, commentary, or sentiment. These conventional functions persist in wide currency until the present day.

In its lyrics antebellum blackface was usually a symbolic rather than a realistic art, and for this reason it does not translate literally into easy generalizations about white Americans' attitudes toward African-Americans. Many writers have viewed minstrelsy as an entertainment designed primarily to derogate black people,[69] but transvesting in this particular case served more as a means than an end for composers, performers, and audiences. Much of the humor depended on the knowledge that the players on stage were really white men hiding their irreverence behind masks. Minstrelsy certainly reveals a vein of racism in the primarily northern urban performers who created the genre, and audiences must have shared these feelings. But the use of African-Americans as symbols of rural longing also betrays covert admiration. On the one hand

69. This interpretation forms the basis of Dennison's *Scandalize My Name,* but it also marks to a lesser extent Hamm's *Yesterdays,* chapter 6.

notions of the primitive ("African" or "Ethiopian" in this context) and the rustic invoked by blackface held the tantalizing appeal of the exotic and also bore connotations of unsullied virtue and common sense unclouded by sophistry. On the other hand, all Western societies consider "primitive" people backward, and most urban dwellers looked down to some extent on country folk.

The relationships of authority in minstrelsy display this same deep-seated ambivalence. A good portion of American society seems to have delighted in and identified with the spectacle of powerless blackface characters outsmarting or commanding the powerful. At the same time, the constant use of a single racial group as a symbol of the "low" betrays contempt. The phenomenon of antebellum minstrelsy, then, manifested a combination of curiosity, envy, admiration, compassion, guilt, and aversion on the part of whites toward blacks.

6

Postbellum Blackface Song

Authenticity and the Minstrel Demon

The passing of slavery did not spell the doom of minstrelsy by any means, for the main authors of the entertainment tended to be northerners in search of an exoticism blackface still provided. Troupes, mostly based in large urban centers, expanded yet further to casts numbering as many as sixty or eighty. "Towards the end of the last century," according to James Weldon Johnson, "[minstrelsy] provided the most gorgeous stage spectacle to be seen in the United States."[1] Even when vaudeville largely replaced minstrel troupes on theater stages in the last decade of nineteenth century, individual blackface acts remained highly successful well into the twentieth.

Yet the content of blackface songs changed, responding to the various developments in popular art. The decline of elevated gentility in popular songs after the war removed a primary target, as Edward Marks lamented some years later: "Mock dignity that grew upon its practitioners until it became real; grotesque exaggeration that mocked a vanishing ideal! When manners flourished in America, their amiable parodists were loved. When the substance departed, the shadow might not linger."[2] In place of a primitive sage decrying excesses of power and lampooning upper-class politesse from behind a black mask, composers substituted a "realistic" African-American who represented one ethnic minority among many in an increasingly diverse population. Direct confrontation of new black status might seem a healthy development in popular culture after the Civil War. But the de-emphasis of a symbolic role for blackface characters meant that they could no longer function regularly as protagonists for white audiences. Of the elaborate world created by antebellum minstrelsy, only rural longing remained to elicit empathy from the consumers of sheet music.

1. *Black Manhattan* (New York, 1930), 89.
2. Edward B. Marks and Abbott J. Liebling, *They All Sang, from Tony Pastor to Rudy Vallée* (New York, 1934), 59.

200

The African-American as religious curiosity or as violent urban antagonist became the mainstay of blackface song.

Escapism and Slavery:
Myths of the Rural Past

The connections between pre- and postwar minstrel songs about nostalgia for a lost rural paradise were expressed most vividly in various imitations. A title like "Carry Me Back to Old Virginny" by James A. Bland (1878)[3] took its inspiration from "Carry Me Back to Old Virginia," as arranged and sung by E. P. Christy (1847). Bland (1854–1911), scion of a long line of freemen, was born in Flushing, New York, and moved to Washington, D.C., when his college-educated father received a post as a patent office examiner. After attending Howard University to study law, James decided his talents lay in music. He served an itinerant apprenticeship, later appearing in 1875 as a performer in Callender's Original Georgia Minstrels,[4] and during his early peregrinations he probably heard the antebellum composition that inspired his famous song.

Though Christy's and Bland's versions of "Carry Me Back" share a basic conceit (the nostalgia of old age and the contemplation of death), their texts and music handle the subject differently. In the Christy version, "Virginny" turns out to be a fisherman's boat, most likely plying the Chesapeake Bay:

> The floating scow of Old Virginny
> I work'd in from day to day,
> A fishing 'mongst de oyster beds,
> To me it was but play.

Only in the chorus, somewhat as an afterthought, does Christy's fisherman mention the state in the title:

3. This date comes from the first page of the sheet music published in Richard Jackson's *Popular Songs of Nineteenth-Century America* (New York, 1976), 43–46. Jackson reproduces a reprinting by the Oliver Ditson Company, which took over Perry's firm (and plates) in 1883. Robert Toll, *Blacking Up: The Minstrel Show in Nineteenth-Century America* (New York, 1974), 216, 231–32, contests the date for the first edition, giving 1875 instead. But James J. Fuld confirms 1878 from copyright records in the Library of Congress (*The Book of World-Famous Music, Classical, Popular, and Folk,* 3d ed. (New York, 1985), 164).

4. For a brief outline of Bland's life, see James A. Bland, *Album of Outstanding Songs,* Charles Haywood, ed. (New York, 1946), Foreword, or John Jay Daly, *A Song in His Heart* (Philadelphia, 1951). Toll places Bland in Boston during this period as a performer in the Original Black Diamonds, but his information rests on a hand-dated playbill in the Harvard Theater Collection, *Blacking Up,* 231–32.

201

EXAMPLE 6.1 E. P. Christy, arr. "Carry Me Back to Old Virginia" (New York: Jaques & Brother, 1847)

> But now I'm growing very old,
> I cannot work any more,
> So carry me back to Old Virginny,
> To Old Virginny's shore.

Subsequent verses show scenes of the character when young. He was a primitive hunter who lived off the natural bounty, eating wild game ("'possum, coon"), and who once longed to buy a farm. He resembles the frontier boatman in many other early minstrel songs, and he sings with their repeated-note declamation, in their limited range, to the simplest of accompaniments (Ex. 6.1). He is Gombo Chaff in old age.

Bland's character, on the other hand, longs for a lost youth spent in the specifically agrarian surroundings of the plantation,

> . . . where the cotton and the corn and 'tatoes grow,
> There's where the birds warble sweet in the springtime,
> There's where the old darkey's heart am long'd to go,
> There's where I labored so hard for old massa,
> Day after day in the field of yellow corn,
> No place on earth do I love more sincerely
> Than old Virginny, the state where I was born.

The cover depicts this impoverished African-American gentleman with white hair and beard imagining the slave cabin of yore, where he appears as a young man carrying a hoe in place of the cane which props his old age. Here the blackface character stands as symbol for the dispossessed, torn from familiar roots:

Long by the old Dismal Swamp have I wandered,
There's where this old darkey's life will pass away.
Massa and missis have long gone before me,
Soon we will meet on that bright and golden shore,
There we'll be happy and free from all sorrow,
There's where we'll meet and we'll part never more.

The general melancholy in this song may seem like that in "Old Kentucky Home," but the circumstances are quite different. Foster's slave longs for a life less cruel and laments his separation from his own family, while Bland's slave misses his white master. As a freeman, Bland could not have mourned a slavery he never experienced. The appeal of the plantation to his elderly blackface character lies in its stable hierarchy of social relations. It offers an alternative to the turbulence of the 1870s and '80s:

> Irresponsibility in a disorganized society generated a host of ethical evasions
> no more subtle than the evils they were meant to hide. Some idealized the
> past and the passing. A flood of fiction sighed over the lost virtues of another
> day: the valiant men of the Wild West, the touching warmth between master
> and slave, the quiet peace of the New England village, the happy innocence
> of the barefoot boy with cheek of tan. The peculiar ethical value of an ag-
> ricultural life, long taken for granted by so many Americans, now became
> one of their obsessions.[5]

Bland's music for "Carry Me Back" is equally distinct from Christy's, reflecting instead the synthesis achieved in songs like "Kentucky Home." Bland writes a melody of unmistakably American gracefulness, combining syncopation, a balanced shape, and mainly conjunct motion seasoned by melodic leaps at the ends of alternate lines (Ex. 6.2). The song draws its accompaniment from the generic writing popular during the '70s and '80s. While far from complex, the piano part endows the inner voices more richly than any antebellum minstrel texture, and its harmonies betray the increasingly chromatic vocabulary of this era, especially at cadence points. Without the text, the audience would be largely unable to distinguish this music from a contemporary song on any other theme. Part of the white listener's inducement to empathize with the speaker comes from the completely normal writing, and in turn the presence of this generic style informs the audience that the composer has not attempted a folkish portrait of plantation life.

Bland, like many other composers and lyricists writing in this genre, usually portrays rural America as place of close family ties. "In the Evening by the Moonlight" (1880)[6] speaks of this lost happiness:

5. Robert H. Wiebe, *The Search for Order, 1877–1920* (New York, 1967), 39.
6. Jackson reprints the piece in *Popular Songs*, 87–90.

EXAMPLE 6.2   James Bland, ''Carry Me Back to Old Virginny'' (Boston: J. F. Perry & Co., 1878)

> In de ebening by de moonlight
> when dis darkies work was over,
> We would gather round de fire,
> 'till de hoecake it was done.
> Den we all would eat our supper,
> after dat we'd clear de kitchen,
> Dat's de only time we had to spare,
> to hab a little fun. . . .

Various lines seem to come from minstrel tradition—after eating ''hoecakes,'' the group ''clears the kitchen.'' And there are other archetypical activities in this idyllic land of the preserved family:

> Uncle Gabe would take de fiddle down,
> dat hung upon de wall,
> While de silv'ry moon
> was shining clear and bright,
> How de old folks would enjoy it,

they would sit all night and listen
As we sang in de ebe'ning by de moonlight.

But some unnamed force (death, economic collapse, social entropy) scatters
this closely knitted society:

All dem happy times we use to hab
will ne'er return again,
Eb'ry thing was den
so merry gay and bright,
And I neber will forget it,
when our daily toil was ober,
How we sang
in de ebe'ning by de moonlight.

The series of folkloric references and heavy use of dialect may prompt rever-
sion to a somewhat older minstrel vocabulary. "In the Evening" has a parlando
melody (Ex. 6.3) that is much less tuneful than "Carry Me Back," even if it
is marked "*con dolce maniera.*" But while "In the Evening" features the old

EXAMPLE 6.3 James Bland, "In the Evening by the Moonlight" (New York: Benj.
W. Hitchcock, 1880)

205

theme of rural longing, it prizes social order (represented by a large family gathered in one place) rather than the misrule of inversion.

Rural longing after the Civil War entailed an explicit rejection of urban surroundings as well as the desire for social order, a point made most eloquently in James S. Putnam's "My Home in Alabam' " (1881). The engraving on the cover reveals how its artist viewed this song (as well as Hart Pease Danks's "My Dear Savannah Home" which evidently shared the frontispiece, Illus. 6.1). An impoverished, elderly African-American broods amidst the squalor of a decaying tenement in a less desirable neighborhood of a large city. He holds on his lap the emblem of the folkloric, a five-string banjo, while he dreams an idyllic agrarian scene. The vista offered by the brightly lit fields, the lovely manor in the distance, and the mountains in the background stands in direct contrast to the close room dimly illuminated by one constricted window. The old man imagines a lost youth in better surroundings:

> Pleasant mem'ries take me back, yes many years ago,
> To the dear old spot where I was bred and born,
> How the darkies used to sing, and make the banjo ring,
> When they'd tire from working in the cane and corn,
> But them days won't come again, and it fills my heart with pain,
> I remember well my good old massa Sam,
> And it's ev'ry night I weep as I lay me down to sleep,
> For the dear old home I had in Alabam'.

Putnam's music intermixes some of Bland's declamation from "In the Evening" with a somewhat wider and more arched line. And in the end, it is hard to distinguish this song from any other melancholy number of the period. Putnam uses the increased chromaticism of the prevailing style to good effect in the service of sentiment for lines like ". . . in my sorrow then I cry. . . " (Ex. 6.4). And where half-step motion does not appear in the melody, the accompaniment supplies it at particularly impassioned moments. "Home in Alabam' " seeks to disassociate itself from any realistic view of slavery or from the African-American's life in the South. For this same reason minstrel dialect barely intrudes upon the sentimental phrases of longing.

Escapism of this type repeated many times in songs from the 1870s and '80s, in Will S. Hays's "The Little Old Cabin in the Lane" (1871) or his "I'm a Gwine Down South" (1874), in John Ford's "Away Down South" (1876), in Hart Pease Danks's "De Cabin on de Mississippi Shore" (1879), in Henry Newman's "Dem Good Ole Times" (1877), in Charles A. Williams's "Cabin's Empty, Hannah's Gone" (1881), in Jerry D. McCarthy's "The Banjo Now Hangs Silent" (1881), in Stephen S. Bonbright's "Dar Sleeps Massa and My Missus Side by Side" (1884), in Edward Harrigan and David Braham's "Where the Sweet Magnolia Grows" (1887), and in songs by countless other composers active mostly in northern cities. Though some interpret

For when tear-drops fill my eyes   in my   sor-row then I   cry,   Give me

back the home I had   in   Al - a - bam'.

EXAMPLE 6.4   James S. Putnam, "My Home in Alabam'" (Boston: John F. Perry & Co., 1881)

this theme as a variety of racism which suggests that African-Americans enjoyed life under slavery or should return to it,[7] only an understanding of these songs as symbols of a general nostalgia for an imaginary agrarian past accounts for their enormous popularity. In employing blacks as symbols of rural longing, composers, lyricists, and engravers may have been guilty of thoughtlessness and insensitivity, but rarely of malice. When the institution of slavery formed the explicit focus of their songs, the lyrics usually decried its injustice, as in John Braham and William B. Dever's "Don't Take Me Back to Slavery" (1878), Samuel Butler and James Bland's "De Slavery Chains Am Broke at Last" (1880), or Harrigan and Braham's "Slavery Days" (1876).

The symbolic relationship between master and slave, at the zenith of its popularity in the 1870s and '80s, disappeared by the end of the century, though the obsession with a rustic paradise persisted in the genre of the blackface lullaby. Hattie Starr, so successful financially in writing songs that she aban-

7. Both Sam Dennison in *Scandalize My Name* (New York and London, 1982), 259–63, and Hamm for one case in *Yesterdays* (New York and London, 1979), 270, adopt this point of view. Rare songs do laud slavery itself, like A. von Rochow and Dick Parker's "Darkey's Suffrage" (1868), which speaks against enfranchising blacks, L. M. French and O. R. Beers's "I Lost My Massa When Dey Set Me Free" (1882), or Chas. Yale's "Poor Aunt Chloe" (1881). But these exceptions prove the rule.

doned her career as a singer,[8] contributed "Little Alabama Coon" (1893)[9] to a repertory that idealizes the South,

> I 'member seein' a great big moon!
> I 'member hearin' one sweet song!
> When dey tote me down to de cotton field,
> Dar I roll and I tumble in de sun!
> While my daddy pick de cotton, mammy watch me grow,
> And dis am de song she sung!
> Go to sleep, my little picaninny,
> Brer' Fox 'il catch you if yo' don't. . . .

"Kentucky Babe," with words by Richard Henry Buck and music by Adam Geibel (1896),[10] also participates in the tradition. This "Schottische" has overtones of the ragtime which became quite popular by end of the century and which often accompanied blackface songs (more about this later). The mock "alternating" bass of the chorus in particular, together with sporadic syncopation and uneven rhythms, lends a contradictory note of urban sophistication to the picture of rustic simplicity painted by Buck's "plantation lullaby":

> 'Skeeter's am a hummin' on de honeysuckle vine, . . .
> Silv'ry moon am shinin' in de heabens up above,
> Bob-o-link am pinin' fo' his little lady love, . . .

or:

> Daddy's in the canebrake wid his little dog and gun. . . ,
> Possom, fo' yo' breakfast when yo' sleepin' time is done. . . .

Americans never tired of dreaming about what they imagined as a carefree existence in a rustic state of grace, even as they increasingly abandoned the demanding life of the farm for the opportunity of the city. Titles famous well after the First World War like George Gershwin's "Swanee" stand as monuments to the popularity of the genre. The fantasy came to be closely associated with the South—less industrialized, more agrarian than the North—and with its most exotic denizens, African-Americans. In this theatrical and musical tradi-

---

8. Isaac Goldberg, *Tin Pan Alley: A Chronicle of the American Popular Music Racket* (New York, 1930), 99.

9. Facsimile in Nicholas Tawa, *American Solo Songs 1866 Through 1910*, vol. 2 of *Three Centuries of American Sacred and Secular Music*, Martha Furman Schleifer and Sam Dennison, eds. ([Boston], 1989), 271–76.

10. The sheet music is reproduced by Robert A. Fremont in *Favorite Songs of the Nineties* (New York, 1973), 170–73.

tion, blackface figures represented the perfect inhabitants of a more "natural" landscape.

Realism and the Folkloric:
Jubilee Songs after the Civil War

If blackface characters remained appropriate symbols of rural longing in the postbellum United States, for a variety of reasons they ceased increasingly to function as figures of populist protest in songs. Some people must have considered emancipation the only remedy needed to right the situation of African-Americans: once accomplished, blacks became just like any other ethnic group, and black masks could no longer automatically represent the powerless. The "black scare" further complicated the situation; songwriters could hardly present blacks as rustic heroes to those who actually feared integration with the newly created citizens.[11] The excesses of the powerful and rich had formed the primary concern of early minstrelsy, which hid behind a disguise for protection. But postwar performers often focused on the disguises themselves (or, in the case of black minstrels, on their own ethnicity) and sometimes abandoned protest altogether. Where prewar maskers had claimed authenticity in their presentations as a kind of diversionary ruse (which they often took pains to subvert for comic effect), later minstrels evoked a measure of authenticity as the very point of the exercise. For this reason, fiddle music, which represented the folkloric so successfully in early blackface, did not suffice after the Civil War. When songwriters addressed blacks merely for the sake of doing so, they turned to a "realistic" art, that is, an identifiable imitation of an African-American music familiar to the audience.

The music that first presented itself as a model for "realistic" minstrel songs came from the black religious genre known as the "spiritual," and to understand the steady progression toward "authenticity" after the war, it is helpful to view distant precursors written by antebellum minstrels. A song like Dan Emmett's "Jordan Is a Hard Road to Trabel" (1853)[12] seems at first glance to reflect a casual acquaintance with the African-American sacred music that had drawn some limited attention before the Civil War.[13] But closer examination reveals minstrel style from the old tradition, with predictably flat melodic shape and declamation of text. The general poetic conceit may vaguely resemble the spiritual: it involves the suggestion of a better life in the hereafter and the work

11. The public reception of emancipation in the North is traced in Forrest G. Wood's *Black Scare: The Racist Response to Emancipation and Reconstruction* (Berkeley and Los Angeles, 1968).
12. Reprinted in Nicholas Tawa, *American Solo Songs,* I, 98-101.
13. Deana Epstein gives a detailed account of early publications in *Sinful Tunes and Spirituals: Black Folk Music to the Civil War* (Urbana, Chicago, London, 1977), 241–302.

it takes to get there, summarized in the syncopated refrain which serves as title. But a good deal of social inversion mixes with biblical references in the verse:

> David and Goliath both had a fight,
> A cullud man come up behind 'em,
> He hit Goliath on de head, wid a bar of soft soap,
> And it sounded to de oder side ob Jordan.
> So take off your coat boys, And roll up your sleeves,
> For Jordan is a hard road to trabel I believe.

The "cullud man" is none other than the blackface sage, who gives political advice after he has helped David dispatch Goliath. From here the lyrics digress to purely political matters. One issue in verse four also appears in "Pop Goes the Weasel" (see Chapter 5):

> If I was de legislator ob dese United States,
> I'd settle de fish question accordin,
> I'd give de British all de bones and de Yankees all de meat,
> And stretch de boundary line to de oder side ob Jordan.

The remaining verses go on to praise the election of "Frank Pierce" and warn Louis Napoleon against interference in the Western Hemisphere. All of this is the stuff of populism, and aside from the refrain and Old Testament story, little in the text and nothing in the music suggests a true spiritual.

A decade later in the midst of the war, Henry Clay Work used this same kind of casual allusion to black sacred music in "Kingdom Coming" (1862).[14] As we have seen earlier, Work descended from an abolitionist family and crusaded for many other social issues. He addresses slavery directly in his lyrics:

> Say darkeys, have you seen de massa,
> Wid de muffstash on his face,
> Go long de road some time dis mornin',
> Like he gwine to leab de place?
> He seen a smoke, way up de ribber,
> Whar de Linkum gum-boats lay;
> He took his hat, an lef berry sudden,
> An I spec he's run away!

He then plays very cleverly on the traditional reflex of minstrel inversion by applying it to a real situation. The slave makes fun of the master's obesity, he describes moving into the manor house, and takes revenge on the plantation's

---

14. Reprinted in Jackson, *Popular Songs*, 106–9.

Second Verse.

He six foot one way, two foot tud-der, An' he weigh tree hun-dred pound, His

coat so big, he couldn't pay de tail-or, An' it won't go half way round.

EXAMPLE 6.5   Henry Clay Work, " Kingdom Coming" (Chicago: Root & Cady, 1862)

overseer by locking him up (an extreme variation on the theme of "Jim Crack Corn," Ex. 5.8). He rejoices at this reversal in the chorus:

> De massa run? ha, ha!
> De' darkey stay? ho, ho!
> It mus' be now de kingdom comin',
> An' de year ob Jubilo!

"Jubilo" (Jubilee) is a reference to the Old Testament practice of freeing bondsmen every fifty years; to subjugated blacks it symbolized the end of their servitude. Work combines this notion with the second coming to serve as a symbol of freedom, but he goes no further than hinting briefly. His famous tune for this song (Ex. 6.5) comes right out of the prewar minstrel synthesis of hammered declamation and arched melodic shape. The music is attractive but devoid of any connection to black sacred style.

Blackface songs after the war, however, came to have much closer links with African-American sacred practice through the music of an all-black chorus, the Fisk Jubilee Singers, from the newly created university for freemen in Nashville, Tennessee. Beginning in 1871 and continuing throughout the decade, the small band of vocalists toured most of the middle western and northeastern United States as well as England and parts of the continent.[15] Those who did not hear their music in person could buy it in published arrangements by George White or Thomas F. Seward. No matter whether the Jubilee Singers' music originated in white southern hymnody, or whether the arrangements substantially altered authentic performance,[16] almost all audiences took the spiritu-

15. The best complete narrative about the chorus is J. B. T. Marsh's *The Story of the Jubilee Singers; with Their Songs,* rev. ed. (Boston, n.d.).

16. Questions about the origins of spirituals arise as early as Theodore Seward's commentary in ibid., 122, "It is a coincidence worthy of note that more than half the melodies in this connection are in the same scale as that in which Scottish music is written; that is, with the fourth and seventh tones omitted." George Pullen Jackson gives the most extensive treatment of this "coincidence" in *White and Negro Spirituals, Their Life Span and Kinship* (New York, 1943). But not all authors accept the notion. See Dena J. Epstein, "A White Origin for the Black Spiri-

EXAMPLE 6.6   Thomas Seward, arr. "Sing Low Sweet Chariot"

als for the spontaneous product of African-American folk culture. Thomas Seward introduced his transcriptions, "[The songs] are never 'composed' after the manner of ordinary music, but spring into life, ready-made, from the white heat of religious fervor during some protracted meeting in church or camp."[17] And a British preacher, Dr. Allon, wrote the Reverend Henry Ward Beecher, "Their songs produce a strange, weird effect. Notwithstanding the occasional dash of Negro familiarity and quaintness of expression, they are full of religious earnestness and pathos, and one loses all sense of oddity in the feeling of real and natural piety."[18]

The "oddities" that usually drew most attention from contemporary listeners appear in arrangements like the Jubilee Singers' rendition of "Swing Low, Sweet Chariot" (Ex. 6.6). The text concerns Jesus' heavenly kingdom (found literally after death or metaphorically after emancipation) and relies on imagery of the promised land (Israel's release from bondage) as well as the ascent of Elijah in a chariot. The music presents this story of salvation/emancipation in the distinctive pattern of a solo "call" which unfolds the narrative and a choral "response" featuring the textual refrain, "coming for to carry me home" sung in four-part harmony. The melody is lyrical and not at all monotone, but the melodic scale in "Swing Low" is confined to five pitches (the "pentatonic" selection, here F, G, A, and C, and D, i.e., "with the fourth and seventh degrees omitted"), an arrangement found in many African-American spirituals.

Composers of popular song in the generation after Emmett and Work first

---

tual? An Invalid Theory and How It Grew," *American Music* 1 (1983), 53–59. Charles Hamm observes that White's harmonizations came out of the European tradition (*Yesterdays,* 271–72).

17. Marsh, *Jubilee Singers,* 121.
18. Ibid., 58.

seized on the symbolic imagery of the spiritual and on its responsorial structure to produce more realistic imitations, which began appearing about four years after the first Jubilee tour in 1871. Charles Hamm credits Will S. Hays with the first hit in this genre, ''Angels Meet Me at the Cross Roads'' (1875). The lyrics refer to the usual subject matter, and the verse hints strongly of a call and response:

> Come down, Gabriel, blow your horn,
> Call me home in de early morn;
> Send de chariot down dis way,
> Come and haul me home to stay, O!

But Hamm observes that the true alternation of solo-chorus phrases is missing from ''Angels'' and that the music falls in the rhythmic patterns and harmonic style of the polka.[19]

James Bland comes just slightly closer than Hays to authenticity in his most famous Jubilee song, ''Oh, Dem Golden Slippers!'' (1879).[20] The text, organized in verse and chorus, strongly implies call and response in its discussion of a journey to the promised land:

> Oh, my golden slippers am laid away
> Kase I don't 'spect to wear 'em till my weddin' day,
> And my long-tail'd coat, dat I loved so well,
> I will wear up in de chariot, in de morn;
> And my long, white robe dat I bought last June,
> I'm gwine to git changed Kase it fits too soon,
> And de ole grey hoss dat I used to drive,
> I will hitch him to de chariot in de morn.

But Bland does not set off the line at the end of each quatrain with four-part writing; this he reserves for the well-known chorus that lends its first line to the title of the piece. The melodic writing has parlando qualities, which Bland, like Hays, pairs with harmonic language and rhythmic motion that might easily fit into the mold of a polka (Ex. 6.7; the title may be a reference to dancing). We can still detect hints of earlier minstrelsy in this music, and the tradition of blackface lurks behind some of the images as well: the ''long-tail'd coat,'' the ''ole grey hoss,'' and the obvious non sequitur of changing a robe that ''fits too soon.'' The second verse indulges more traditional tags:

> Oh, my ole banjo hangs on de wall,
> Kase it aint been tuned since way last fall,

19. *Yesterdays*, 272–73.
20. Facsimile in Jackson, *Popular Songs*, 144–47.

EXAMPLE 6.7   James Bland, ''Oh, Dem Golden Slippers'' (Boston: John F. Perry, 1879)

But de darks all say we will have a good time,
When we ride up in de chariot in de morn;
Dar's ole Brudder Ben and Sister Luce,
Dey will telegraph de news to Uncle Bacco Juice,
What a great camp meetin' der will be dat day,
When we ride up in de chariot in de morn.

This mixture of old minstrel symbolism with the barest allusions to sacred vocal music casts the camp or revival meeting in a comic light: these are eccen-

214

tric religious practices. But in spite of the non sequiturs, no symbolic inversion is present here. Bland's other well-known pseudo-spiritual, "In the Morning by the Bright Light" (1879), runs along exactly the same lines.

A revival meeting also forms the backdrop for Sam Lucas's "Every Day'l Be Sunday By and By" (1881). Lucas (1848–1916), born of former slaves in Fayette County, Virginia, enjoyed one of the most distinguished careers on stage of any nineteenth-century entertainer, at first as a member of the Original Georgia Minstrels (an all-black troupe which also included Bland) and later in reviews, plays, and vaudeville. It was Lucas, for instance, who popularized Henry Clay Work's "Grandfather's Clock" (see Ex. 4.4 above).

Lucas comes just that much closer than Bland to authentic practice: "Every Day" displays the call-and-response structure of the classic Jubilee song, with a solo line answered by a choral refrain which becomes the title of the song (Ex. 6.8). The harmony and melody still hearken to the popular practice seen in "Oh! Dem Golden Slippers!" For Lucas adopts the same basic perspective as Bland. Lucas appears on the cover as a dignified, handsome, and stylish gentleman deliberately juxtaposed to the uncouth enthusiasm of the service (Illus. 6.2). The congregation, dressed in its Sunday best, receives inspiration from a wildly gesticulating preacher; his strenuous efforts, however, cannot prevent the young couple in the foreground from courting. The woman behind the tree, dressed in practical attire, laughs at the expense of the worshipers, suggesting that we need not take the proceedings any more seriously than she does. The imagery originates in scripture, and though the allusions are not patently ridiculous, they are wry:

> Dar was Isaac, Peter, John, and James,
> > Every day, etc.
> And now I've told you all de names,
> > Every day, etc.

or:

> When I went down the valley to pray
> > Every day, etc.
> I'll tell you want I say that day,
> > Every day, etc.
> I saw ole Eli on de fence,
> > Every day, etc.
> And God knows I aint seen him since.

Lucas condescends subtly to religion, a stance he adopts in his many other "Jubilee" imitations, including "Dem Silver Slippers" (after Bland's song, 1879), "When We Meet in the Sweet Bye and Bye" (1879), "I'se Gwine in

EXAMPLE 6.8 Sam Lucas, "Every Day'l Be Sunday By and By" (Boston and Chicago: White, Smith, & Co., 1881)

de Valley'' (1879), "Oh, I'll Meet You Dar" (1880), "I Done Got Rid of My Burden" (1881), and "Ring Dem Heavenly Bells" (1883). In this he merely follows the dictates of the genre, and countless songs about revival meetings assume this same posture, like "Down on de Camp Ground" (1880) by Fred Lyons, "Camp Meetin' Fire Bell" (1880) by M. Louis, "De Golden Sunrise" (1881) by Ned Straight, and "Come Jine de Whitewashed Army" ("The Great Salvation Army Song," 1886) by Harry B. Smith and George Schleiffarth.

The pseudo-spiritual's focus on ethnicity for its own sake eventually led to some explicitly negative numbers like Frank Howard's "Pass Down de Centre" (1879). The composer begins his Jubilee song appropriately enough:

> Trab'ling t'wards de balmy skies,
>   Pass down de centre,
> Keep de path before your eyes,
>   Pass, etc.
> Tramp a long de grabble road,
>   Pass, etc.
> Don't get weary wid your load,
>   Pass, etc.

But the search for the promised land gives way to other subjects in a series of long verses:

> Send us a turkey,
> Don't send it C.O.D.,
> Oh yes, "dey come high but we just hab 'em,"
> Times are hard for de darkie,
> Way down in Tennessee;
> Mister Ku-klux cant you let me be.

There are jibes at Reconstruction:

> I'm gwine back to Alabam,
>   Pass, etc.
> Dar I'll be a color'd lamb,
>   Pass, etc.
> For an office I will run,
>   Pass, etc.
> Back to Congress I will come,
>   Pass, etc.

And efforts to help former slaves in the South also come in for attack:

> Greenbacks am plenty,
> Dey weigh de same as gold,
> "Trim your lamps and keep dem brightly burnin'"
> If your pockets are empty,
> Don't stand out in de cold,
> Press a "Freedman's bank" into de fold.

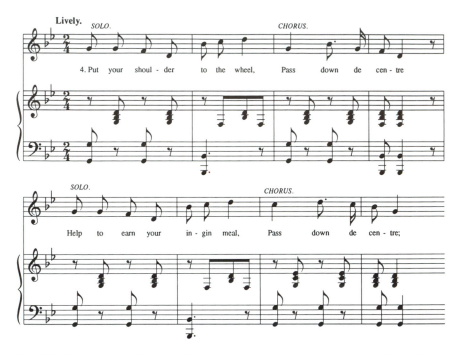

EXAMPLE 6.9   Frank Howard, "Pass Down de Centre" (New York: Willis Woodward & Co., 1879)

The obvious resentment here of the institutions meant to aid ex-slaves would
be worthy of a redemptionist.[21] The lyrics are all the more pointed for their
ironic juxtaposition of biblical images to depictions of what the composer views
as black venality and corruption. Howard has reversed the traditional relationships of minstrel satire by using humor to deride the poor and any pretensions
they might have to power, rather than to criticize the excesses of the wealthy
and powerful. The music reinforces this irony by a parallel combination: the
call and refrain of the verse features the pentatonic scale associated with spirituals (Ex. 6.9), but the concluding solo ("Send us a turkey. . . ") reverts to the
diatonic vocabulary of European music, albeit in minor mode. This musical
incongruity lends the derisive lyrics more than just a hint of sarcasm. "Pass
Down de Centre" cannot be characterized as obscure: Howard (whose real
name was Frank Martindale) had a long and distinguished career as a tenor in
various blackface troupes, the most famous of which was Wilson, Primrose
and West's.[22] "End or Plantation" songs like "Pass Down" occupied a promi-

21. See Eric Foner for a thorough account of all the issues surrounding African-Americans
during this period (*Reconstruction: America's Unfinished Revolution, 1863–1877* (New York,
1988)).
22. Edward Le Roy Rice, *Monarchs of Minstrelsy from "Daddy" Rice to Date* (New York,
1911), 180.

EXAMPLE 6.10   Jacob J. Sawyer, "Blow, Gabriel, Blow" (Boston: W. A. Evans, 1882)

nent place in minstrel shows as opening or concluding numbers with large casts and extravagant production.

The heightened realism in the music of pseudo-spirituals and the increased attention to "Negro oddities" for their own sake led to even more derogatory songs, as criticism of blacks gave way to deliberate malice. Jacob J. Sawyer admonishes the faithful in "Blow, Gabriel, Blow" (1882):

> Darkies pray fo' de time draws nigh,
>   Blow, Gabriel, Blow,
> We'll soon be mountin' up on high,
>   Blow, etc.
> Chicken coops you mus' leave alone,
>   Blow, etc.
> Or Satan 'll cotch you shu's you's bo'n,
>   Blow, etc.

This advice is accompanied by a strictly pentatonic and highly syncopated tune (Ex. 6.10), which bears a distant resemblance to "Gabriel's Trumpet's Going to Blow" as sung by Jennie Jackson of the Jubilee Singers.[23] Presumably Saw-

23. Marsh, *Jubilee Singers*, 195.

219

yer employed his song in a major production number for the very famous and widely traveled Haverly's Colored Minstrels, whom he served as musical director. Other songs in this vein include Edward F. Kelly's "Meet Me at de Cross Roads Hannah!" (1887) and Fred Sperry and Annie Lichter's "Come and Meet Us Dar" (1888), which gives a catalogue of stereotypes about cuisine (pig's feet and possum), music (banjo, of course), and behavior (dancing the cakewalk and stealing chickens). Monroe H. Rosenfeld's "Come Along Sinners" (1881) may represent the absolute nadir of this genre: it admonishes blacks to leave their razors (weapons usually associated with blacks in "coon" songs) at home if they want to reach the promised land.

The Jubilee song declined in frequency after the eighties, in part because large troupes began to disband under the pressure of vaudeville. Realism in such songs depended on choral singing; without a large ensemble the most spectacular effects disappeared. But small minstrel acts, often formed by veterans of the old companies, persisted and even flourished in vaudeville. For these specialty performers Tin Pan Alley composers continued to fashion a few isolated pseudo-spirituals. Monroe H. Rosenfeld, this time using his pseudonym, F. Belasco, contributed the very popular "Johnny Get Your Gun" (1886)[24] for the comedy act of Charles "Buck" Sheffer and Harry Blakely, noted imitators of "plantation darkies."[25] This song features a completely pentatonic melody throughout and the usual call-and-response verse (but without four-part writing; Ex. 6.11). Rosenfeld's lyrics for "Johnny" begins with a conventional image:

> One evenin' in de month of May,
> Johnny get your gun, get your gun,
> I met old Peter on de way,
> Johnny, etc.
> Moses wept and Abram cried,
> Johnny, etc.
> Satan's coming don't you hide,
> Johnny, etc.

And the mention of a gun (to shoot the devil in the third verse) does not assume the overtones that the razor does in the composer's "Come Along Sinners." In fact, "Johnny" reverts just a bit in its last verse to an older style of humor:

> I looked old Satan in the eye,
> Johnny, etc.
> Said he, "I'll want you by and by,"
> Johnny, etc.
> Fetch me up an Alderman,

24. A copy of the original sheet music appears in Jackson, *Popular Songs,* 97–101.
25. Rice, *Monarchs,* 279.

EXAMPLE 6.11   Monroe H. Rosenfeld, "Johnny Get Your Gun" (New York: T. B. Harms, 1886)

> Johnny, etc.
> Put him in my frying pan,
> Johnny, etc.

Jim Crow would certainly damn politicians under similar circumstances, and as if to celebrate this traditional barb, Rosenfeld caps the song with a fiddle-like postlude.

Examples of the Jubilee song appeared into the last decade of the century. Charles Hoyt's *A Trip to Chinatown* interpolated a pseudo-spiritual, "Push Dem Clouds Away" by Percy Gaunt, into the first act. Subtitled "An African Cantata" (1892),[26] its musical vocabulary uses the European common practice, though its text follows the formula of call and response:

> If you want to git to Heaven on de nickelplated road,
> Just push dem clouds away!
> Bring along all yer baggage and check it to de Lord,
> When you push dem clouds away!

26. A reprint of the sheet music appears in Stanley Appelbaum's collection *Show Songs from "The Black Crook" to "The Red Mill"* (New York, 1974), 68–71.

If de train am aspeedin' an' you can't catch on,
When, etc.
You're a coon dat's gone, and wuss dan none,
When, etc.

It was not uncommon to see technological imagery used in connection with paradise in some pseudo-spirituals (in fact, Charles Hoyt contributed an example, see above Ex. 4.12). "Come Aboard de Golden Steamboat" (1886) by Herb G. Chase, "If You Want to Get Aboard Dis Train" (1887) by J. F. Mitchell, "A Gwine to de Promised Land" (steamboat, 1893) by Edward B. Marks and Charles Ohl, and "Climb on My Golden Wheel" (bicycle, 1895) by Harry J. Ballou all modernized the imagery of songs like "Come and Row on de Golden Stream" (1887) by J. O'Halloran and Sam Lucas. "Push Dem Clouds" was more significant because its stage setting was not a revival meeting, nor was it sung in blackface. Instead, it was sung on stage by a group of white people entertaining themselves around a piano in the parlor. Blackface songs were not only manifestations of specialty entertainment, they appeared in sheet music largely for performance in the home. And because they generally demanded piano accompaniment, songs like "Push Dem Clouds Away" must have been purchased by middle-class consumers, no matter how uncouth some people may have considered them.[27]

The tones of the pseudo-spiritual died away, but they left such a vivid image of religiosity that the echoes lingered in songs like "A Hot Time in the Old Town" (1896)[28] by Joe Hayden and Theodore A. Metz. Both the dialect and the narrative intimate an African-American revival meeting:

Come along get you ready wear your bran, bran new gown,
For dere's gwine to be a meeting in that good, good old town,
Where you knowded ev'ry body, and dey all knowded you,
And you've got a rabbit's foot to keep away de hoodo;
When you hear that the preaching does begin,
Bend down low for to drive away your sin,
and when you gets religion,
You want to shout and sing,
there'll be a hot time in the old town tonight, my baby.

27. Nicholas Tawa garners a fair number of citations suggesting that genteel amateurs avoided earlier minstrel songs (*Sweet Songs for Gentle Americans: The Parlor Song in America, 1790–1860* (Bowling Green, OH, 1980), 94–98). But the stridency of the objections to minstrelsy in the cultured musical press indicates that a good many middle class musicians did indulge this rude entertainment (why else would there be so much complaint?), and the large amount of surviving sheet music leads to the same conclusion.
28. Reprinted in Fremont, *Favorite Songs,* 117–21.

The remaining verse in "Hot Time" concerns courtship, a topic usually excluded from pseudo-spirituals. And the style of Metz's music has nothing to do with Jubilee songs; it derives instead from a secular instrumental tradition:

> [Metz] wrote that back in '86 when he was band-leader with the McIntryre & Heath Minstrels. . . . The troupe's train was held up somewhere in Louisiana because a house near the railroad station was afire. The townsfolk were frenziedly rushing water to put it out. The name of the village, posted on the railroad station, was Old Town. McIntyre spotted the sign and remarked: "They're certainly having a hot time in the Old Town to-night." "Yes," replied Heath, "and that's a good song title"—he was quick at such things. He told Metz about the idea and Metz set to work and wrote the music. He had it done in time for the band to play it for the street parade in New Orleans.[29]

Hayden simply provided a text for a march composed a decade earlier.

As late as 1897 Kerry Mills repeated this combination of "characteristic march" and description of an African-American revival in "At a Georgia Campmeeting":[30]

> A campmeeting took place,
> By the colored race,
> Way down in Georgia;
> There were coons large and small,
> lanky, lean, fat, and tall,
> At this great coon campmeeting.
> When church was out,
> How the "Sisters" did shout,
> They were so happy,
> But the young folks were tired,
> And wished to be inspired,
> And hired a big brass band.

The absence of pseudo-sacred style in both "Hot Time" and "Georgia Campmeeting" did not denote a complete abandonment of ethnic realism in blackface songs. Rather, the frame of reference altered with the introduction of the new, demonstrably African-American style found in the music of both Metz and Mills: ragtime. Its arrival was preceded by a change in focus from rural to urban blacks, the last significant development in the history of minstrel song.

---

29. Sigmund Spaeth delivers this anecdote, quoted in Goldberg's *Tin Pan Alley*, 166.
30. Reprinted in Tawa, *Solo Songs* II, 258–61.

The "Coon Song" and the Urban Demon

Just about the same time that Jubilee songs began to offer "realistic" pictures of primitive black religion, composers also fashioned a new image of African-Americans as a racial minority in the city. At the beginning writers treated black people within the same framework as the other notable subgroups, the Irish and the Germans, in part because all ethnic humor traditionally lay in the province of minstrels. Edward Harrigan and Tony Hart, for example, began their act as part of Arlington, Cotton and Kemble's Minstrels before creating a long run of musical comedies about ethnic interaction in New York City. Harrigan's fictional Irish "target company," a kind of uniformed shooting club called the Mulligan Guard (see Ex. 8.13 below), has a black counterpart, "The Skidmore Guard" (1874), which marches to music by David Braham. Each minority takes pride in itself, and the "Skids" are no exception:

> We represent de members
> Of de noble colored troops,
> Who march about de streets of York,
> In French imperial suits,
> Black pantaloons and yaller stripes,
> And helmets trimmed with blue,
> De wenches shout when we turn out
> On South Fifth Avenue.

Harrigan means to make fun of the Skid's pretensions to military grandeur, but no more than he does of their Irish counterparts, whose captain "carried his sword like a Russian duke, whenever he took command." Harrigan generally considers target companies a public nuisance, but he has a great deal of good will toward the solid working folk who join them:

> Dar's Mister Brown, de waiter man
> To de Astor House hotel,
> He's sargent in de second Brigade,
> Division Company L,
> He's six foot high,
> He carried de flag,
> So noble, proud, and gay,
> He took de prize for marching out
> On 'Mancipation day.

Harrigan regards African-Americans as one minority among many, and at the time they did not occupy the lowest rung on New York's social ladder by any means. A commander of the Skidmore Guard, Brother Palestine Puter, leads a society "to prevent the Irish from riding on the horse cars," and favors control

CHORUS.

Nob - by, air - y, light as a fai - ry, Mu - sic play - ing sweet and gay,

Hats a- wav - ing we're pa- rad - ing, March - ing down Broad - way.

EXAMPLE 6.12 David Braham, ''The Skidmore Guard'' (New York: Wm. A. Pond, 1874)

of the Irish, ''Dutch'' (Germans), and Italians by ''stricter quarantine or stronger fumigation.''[31] Braham's music for the song (Ex. 6.12) makes no attempt at ethnic reference, featuring instead a rollicking compound meter more like something from Arthur Sullivan's pen. Though Braham knew ''authentic'' style from his own pseudo-spirituals, it simply did not apply in this context.

Harrigan and Braham's target company spawned countless imitations, including ''The Black Hussars'' (1877), which Fred Kenyon wrote ''expressly for the inimitable character artists, Harrigan & Hart,'' ''Colored Recruits'' (1877) by A. K. Larue, ''The Colored Grenadier'' (1879) by Johnny Carroll, and ''The Colored Regimental Guards'' (1880) by Harry Davies. Skits featuring black target companies enjoyed a vogue in many minstrel companies, and for one of the largest, Haverly's Colored Minstrels, Jacob J. Sawyer wrote ''I'm de Sargent ob de Coonville Guards'' (1881), ''Coonville Guards'' (1881), and ''I'm de Captain ob de Black Cadets'' (1881). Even James Bland followed the fashion in ''The Dandy Black Brigade'' (1881), also written for Haverly's Colored Minstrels in which he performed. The first verse describes

31. Richard Moody, *Ned Harrigan: From Corlear's Hook to Herald Square* (Chicago, 1980), 87–89.

the basic scene of marching down Broadway, while the second draws invidious comparisons with Harrigan's group:

> Our uniforms are very rich,
> How lovely they do look,
> While drilling with the Skidmore Guards
> The golden prize we took;
> Our guns they outshine diamonds,
> And our collars white as snow;
> We break the colored ladies' hearts,
> As down the street we go.

Bland's group, like Harrigan's, exists basically as a fraternal and social organization:

> Our balls are held at Tam'ny Hall,
> Such crowds are always there,
> The finest of the finest,
> And the fairest of the fair;
> The music of the orchestra
> Is so superb and grand;
> You bet we have no equals,
> We're the finest in the land.

Bland supplies a 6/8 march for his non-dialect verse and common time for the chorus. And the cover, like that for "The Skidmore Guard," shows a dignified group of African-Americans in fancy uniforms marching down a city street, without hint of caricature. For the most part, African-Americans in these songs seem to occupy a secure place in the urban landscape.

The focus on African-Americans as part of the northern urban scene, however, eventually aroused fear and derision. Even before the end of the Civil War northerners had harbored apprehensions about the possibility of black migration to the cities in the event of emancipation.[32] In fact a large number of freed slaves did move north, but the overwhelming influx of immigrants from Europe so dwarfed their numbers that African-Americans in most cities of the Northeast and the Midwest had actually declined as a percentage of the population by the close of the century.[33] It may be true, as Forrest Wood suggests, that "as an object of . . . racist scorn, the Negro grew progressively less popular in books, pamphlets, newspapers, periodicals, and speeches" after 1872, but only in the explicitly political arena.[34] Minstrel songs threw fuel on

32. Wood, *Black Scare,* 17–29.
33. See Robert C. Weaver, *The Negro Ghetto* (New York, 1948), 8–20.
34. *Black Scare,* 157.

the fire of an urban "black scare" so intense it prompted James Weldon Johnson to write:

> The status of the Negro as a citizen had been steadily declining for twenty-five years; and at the opening of the twentieth century his civil state was, in some respects, worse than at the close of the Civil War. . . . The outlook was dark and discouraging. The Negro himself had in a large measure lost heart. The movement that Frederick Douglass had so valiantly carried forward had all but subsided.[35]

Songwriters selected the urban dandy as the vehicle for engendering fear. In antebellum minstrelsy Zip Coon was a "larned" western "skoller," transvested to make fun of urban habits and to deride an effete eastern establishment. In the eighties he was converted from a primitive natural philosopher into a primitive brute. James S. Putnam usually receives credit for the first example of this mutation in his "New Coon in Town" (1883), featuring a professional gambler who "dresses like a prince," wears ostentatious jewels, and cheats at dice.[36] Only minor changes in shading transformed this new black dandy into the demon who appears in Sam Lucas's "De Coon Dat Had de Razor" (1885). Lucas probably wrote the lyrics credited to "Professor Wm. F. Quown" (pronounced "coon"); the dedicatee "Harry Woodsum" was likely the white performer Harry Woodson (the stage name of John Archer Shields, 1852–98), a member at various times of Carncross, Thatcher and Ryman's, Woodson and Allen's, and finally Cleveland's Minstrels.[37] Certainly Lucas, as a black composer, would avoid taking credit for the content. The first verse describes a dance:

> I went to a ball de other night,
> At Susie Simpkins hut,
> Where dem coons all carry razors;
> And how dem niggers cut.
> Ole Horace Jinks got in a row
> With slew foot Johny Frazier.
> "Take care," squealed out ole Sally Gum,
> "Dat coon has got a razor."

The second verse leaves an explicit description of the fight:

> He carved poor Johny's coattail off,
> Den cut him to de fat;
> He cut his ear clear off his head,

---

35. *Black Manhattan*, 127–28.
36. See Hamm, *Yesterdays*, 321 and Dennison, *Scandalize*, 287.
37. Rice, *Monarchs*, 238.

EXAMPLE 6.13   Sam Lucas, "De Coon Dat Had de Razor" (Boston and Chicago: White, Smith & Company, 1885)

> Den cut his beaver hat.
> Aunt Hannah said, "for gracious sake
> You'll kill poor Johny Frazier."
> But de coon he didn't notice her,
> But slashed on wid de razor.

Even the police are unwilling to deal with this violent urban dandy, depicted on the cover of the sheet music (Illus. 6.3) wielding a straight razor, dressed in the watch-chain, tail-coat, top hat, and other accessories of "Zip Coon" (the chickens symbolize thievery here, as they do in some pseudo-spirituals). Ironically, this drama also unfolds over the cheerful and spirited march (Ex. 6.13) that seems to have become endemic to songs about urban blacks by this time. Other examples from the genre include "A Bullfrog Am No Nightingale" (1884) by Harry B. Smith and George Schleiffarth, "Dar's a Lock on de Chicken Coop Door" (1885) by Sam Lucas, "Did You Ever Hear a Nigger Say 'Wow' " (1890) by Paul Dresser, and "His Parents Haven't Seen Him Since" (1893) by William DeVere.

It took ragtime to elevate the violent urban "coon" from the status of just one stock part among many in the minstrel shows of the eighties and early nineties to the best-known character in all of popular song at the end of the nineties. The standard history of ragtime tends to be filtered through the revival of the 1970s, which focused on piano rags by "classic" artists such as Scott Joplin. And many accounts place the first appearance of the instrumental form in mainstream American culture at the Columbian Exposition of 1893.[38] But contemporary reports of ragtime accord no such precedence to the purely instrumental genre. They suggest, rather, that ragtime emerged during the eighties and early nineties in cities along the Mississippi (Memphis, Louisville, St. Louis) from the improvisations of African-American pianists, often accompanying songs like Lucas's "De Coon Dat Had de Razor." "Ragtime . . . came north with the rhythm of the coonjiners striding down gangplanks from Mississippi steamers, and of wenches in black-and-tan houses humming plaintive homicidal legends during the boredom of hot afternoons," Edward Marks suggests.[39]

Many of the "homicidal" coon songs of the eighties, as well as many other songs about urban blacks from the period, take their rhythmic cue significantly from the march. Mild syncopation and uneven rhythms had been part of minstrel music since the 1840s, but the new style played a more persistent "ragging" against an "alternating bass" (with a double pattern of alternation: a bass root followed by its block chord, then a different root and its chord, producing a series of leaps from root to triad) taken from the march or "two-step." Ragtime precursors included numbers like "Hot Time" (if we take Theodore Metz's word that he wrote it in 1886 as a song and circus march), "Patrol Comique" (1886), a black "guard" piece, and many other examples.[40] But the earliest *explicit* use of the word "rag" in sheet music occurred in songs (not piano pieces) printed during 1896. (Joplin's classic "Maple Leaf Rag" would not appear until 1899. The first ragtime instructors for pianists were not published until 1897, and even then they contained exclusively transcribed songs.)[41]

The piece that made "ragtime song" synonymous for the general public with "coon song" was Ernest Hogan's "All Coons Look Alike to Me" (1896).[42] Hogan seems to have been born a freeman in 1859 under the name of Ernest Reuben Crowders, and he turned early in life to minstrelsy. After touring with various troupes, he became prominent on the variety circuit and a regular feature of theater in New York, dying in 1909.[43] "All Coons" tells a story of courtship:

38. See Edward F. Berlin's *Ragtime: A Musical and Cultural History* (Berkeley, Los Angeles, London, 1980), 25–29.

39. *They All Sang,* 72.

40. See Berlin, *Ragtime,* chap. 6.

41. Edward Berlin, "Ragtime Songs," *Ragtime: Its History, Composers, and Music,* John Edward Hasse, ed. (New York, 1985), 70–71.

42. Reprinted in Tawa, *Solo Songs,* II, 253–57.

43. Henry T. Sampson, *Blacks in Blackface: A Source Book on Early Black Musical Shows* (Metuchen, NJ, 1980), 375–77. Isidore Witmark claims to have had a substantial hand in some of the lyrics and melody of "All Coons" (*From Ragtime,* 195–96).

Talk about a coon a having trouble,
I think I have enough of ma own,
It's all about ma Lucy Janey Stubbles,
And she has caused my heart to mourn,
Thar's another coon barber from Virginia,
In soci'ty he's the leader of the day,
And now my honey gal is gwine to quit me,
Yes she's gone and drove this coon away,
She'd no excuse,
To turn me loose,
I've been abused,
I'm all confused,
Cause these words she did say. . . .

The chorus then gives Lucy's objections to the various dandy suitors who appear on the cover of the sheet music. The constantly syncopated melody of the refrain shows one kind of ragging against an alternating bass; the music for the more declamatory verse features dotted notes, generally considered another kind. Max Hoffmann, an arranger and early white proponent of ragtime, provides an alternate "Negro 'Rag' Accompaniment" on the next page (Ex. 6.14) which gives the alternating bass pattern to the left hand alone, while reproducing the melody's syncopation in a series of chords for the right hand. Instrumental styles around the turn of the century tended toward motivic economy (the waltz song had taught the lesson at the beginning of the nineties), and this propensity in a "ragged" march fit well with Tin Pan Alley's discovery of the musical "hook" based on sequential repetition. The melody for the words "All coons" essentially repeats a step down for "I've got," then for "And he's just." Vocal ragtime caught on quickly as a musical style because it met one of the essential requirements of Tin Pan Alley publishers.

The combination of melody and accompaniment in "All Coons" proved too attractive for its composer's own good:

The verse of "All Coons Look Alike to Me" was forgotten. The refrain became a fighting phrase all over New York. Whistled by a white man it was construed as a personal insult. Rosamond Johnson relates that he once saw two men thrown off a ferry boat in a row over the tune. Hogan became an object of censure among all the Civil Service intelligentsia, and he died haunted by the awful crime he had unwittingly committed against the race.[44]

Perhaps Edward Marks was being deliberately naïve in his last remark. Hogan, like Lucas and Bland before him, knew that "coon songs" or pseudo-spirituals, even at their most complimentary, existed primarily to display "Ne-

44. Marks, *They All Sang*, 91.

EXAMPLE 6.14   Ernest Hogan, "All Coons Look Alike to Me" (New York: M. Witmark & Sons, 1896)

gro oddities." And Marks wrote later, ". . . men like Williams and Walker were outwardly resigned to all sorts of discrimination. They would sing "coon," they would joke about "niggers," they accepted their success with wide-mouthed grins as the gift of the gods."[45] African-American songwriters and performers were largely governed by the market created by white audiences.

In the hands of white songwriters and performers, negative portraits of African-Americans were usually more extreme. May Irwin, the famous "coon shouter" (a white female singer who specialized in ragtime songs), made one such song, "Mister Johnson" (1896),[46] into a famous number in the New York show *Courted into Court*. Its composer, Ben Harney (1871–1938), was one of the white men prominently associated with ragtime, and he contributed materially to its success by publishing a famous *Ragtime Instructor* in 1897. He wrote "Mister Johnson" in 1895 for a minstrel performance[47] using all the realistic hallmarks: an intricate and active piano part with syncopation in the right hand and alternating bass in the left accompany sporadic syncopation in the voice.

45. Ibid., 96.
46. The sheet music for "Mister Johnson" is reprinted in Appelbaum, *Show Songs*, 98–102.
47. Ibid., xxx.

The two opening melodic phrases in a pentatonic minor mode also feature a call and response reminiscent of a pseudo-spiritual. Each verse tells the tale of a white policeman arresting lawless blacks, first for gambling:

> I went down into a nigger crap game,
> Where de coons were a gambling wid a might and main,
> T'ought I'd be a sport and be dead game,
> I gambled my money and I wasn't to blame,
> One nigger's point was a little, a Joe,
> Bettin' six bits t'a quarter he could make de four,
> He made dat point but he made no more,
> Just den Johnson jump'd thro' de door. . . . .

The ragtime chorus supplies the next line, "Oh! Mr. Johnson turn me loose, don't take me to de calaboose." The last verse turns to stereotypical thievery:

> A big black coon was a lookin' fer chickens,
> When a great big bulldog got to raisin' the dickens,
> De coon got higher, de chicken got nigher,
> Just den Johnson opened up fire.

At least Harney avoided the razor-wielding dandy in this hit, and his other songs like "You've Been a Good Old Wagon, But You Done Broke Down" were less virulent but also less popular (by his publisher's estimate).[48]

"May Irwin's 'Bully Song' " by Charles E. Trevathan (1896)[49] goes a step beyond "Mister Johnson" by renewing the image of the violent African-American demon. Where Jim Crow arrives in town to instruct the President, the Congress, and financiers, "dat bully dat's come to town" intends nothing more than mayhem with a razor, just he is depicted on the cover (Illus. 6.4). The speaker seeks him out in a dance hall to even the score:

> I was sandin' down the Mobile Buck just to cut a shine
> Some coon across my smeller swiped a watermelon rin'
> I drawed my steel dat gemmen for to fin'
> I riz up like a black cloud and took a look aroun'
> There was dat new bully standin' on the ground. . . .
> When I got through with bully, a doctor and nurse
> Wa'nt no good to dat nigger, so they put him in a hearse,
> A cyclone couldn't have tore him up much worse.
> You don't hear 'bout dat nigger dat treated folks so free

48. Witmark, *From Ragtime,* 152–53.
49. Reprinted in Appelbaum, *Show Songs,* 77–81.

When I____ walk dat lev-ee round,____ I'm a

look-in' for dat bul-ly an' he must be found.____

EXAMPLE 6.15 Charles Trevathan, "May Irwin's 'Bully Song' " (Boston, New York, Chicago: White-Smith Music Publishing, 1896)

Go down upon the levee, and his face you'll never see.
Dere's only one boss bully, and dat one is me.

Both James Weldon Johnson and W. C. Handy claimed that "The Bully Song" derived from an African-American folk tune heard along the Mississippi. Trevathan maintained that he had heard it in a St. Louis bordello, and that he merely supplied the lyrics at Irwin's request.[50] In any event, ragtime provided the means by which the song became popular: the verse features a goodly amount of syncopation to the beat of an extroverted march. The chorus has a particularly attractive melody with just a hint of a "blue" note (a chromatic ornament found in the blues), all supported by an alternating bass (Ex. 6.15). "The Bully Song" is a prime example of "realistic" art, where ethnic music (or at least elements of it) has been used to support a stereotype.

Popular art possesses extraordinary diversity at any one time: the violent picture of African-Americans in late-nineteenth-century music was not entirely unalloyed. Songs like Joe Howard's "Hello! Ma Baby" (1899; see Ex. 4.13 above) or John Stromberg's "Ma Blushin' Rosie" (1900) related sympathetic

50. Berlin, *Ragtime*, 56, n. 6; a similar version of the origin appears in Goldberg, *Tin Pan Alley*, 150.

and universal stories of courtship. At the same time Witmark advertised "All Coons Look Alike to Me," he also published Barney Fagan's "My Gal Is a High Born Lady" (1896),[51] a song with ragtime chorus. Fagan (1850–1937),[52] an extremely popular white dancer in both minstrel theater and vaudeville, takes pains to cast African-Americans in a positive light:

> Thar' is gwine to be a festival this evenin',
> And a gatherin' of color mighty rare,
> Thar'll be noted individuals of prominent distinctiveness,
> To permeate the colored atmosphere,
> Sunny Africa's Four Hundred's gwine to be thar,
> To do honor to my lovely fiancee,
> Thar' will be a grand ovation of especial ostentation,
> When the parson gives the dusky bride away!

These lyrics present an extremely polite version of the ethnic "celebration song," which usually involves an extravagant party displaying behavioral peccadillos. These begin as early as 1848 with "De Color'd Fancy Ball," but they become most popular in later blackface with numbers like "Dat Citron Wedding Cake" (1880) by Harrigan and Braham, "Aunt Dinah's Birthday Party" (1884) by Harry C. Talbert, "Rasper's Birthday Party" (1886) by Sam Lucas, "Come to Baltimore" (1892) by Harry Budworth, "Enjoy Yourselves" (1897) by Dave Reed and Charles B. Ward, and "No Cake Comes Too High for Me" (1899) by Dave Reed and Ferdinand Singhi, to mention just a few. Sometimes these gatherings dissolved into pandemonium, just as their Irish counterparts, like "Down Went McGinty" (1889) by Joseph Flynn or "Who Threw the Overalls in Mistress Murphy's Chowder" (1898) by George L. Geifer, end in brouhahas. Lyricists created stereotypes of all ethnic groups in this period, and each had predictable vices. The Irish and the Germans drank and brawled with the best of them, and when African-Americans became the center of attention ". . . the 'possum replaced Widow Nolan's goat in the popular song writer's lexicon," Edward Marks pointed out. "The razor replaced the shillelagh, Mandy became more commonplace than Kathleen, and gin supplanted the cruiskeen lawn."[53] But blacks received by far the worst treatment of any minority at the hands of songwriters, a situation expressed literally in the song "Every Race Has a Flag but the Coon" (1900) by Will A. Heelan and J. Fred Help.

The image of the dandified black demon, more than any other, seems to have lodged in public perception and may have had a serious and immediate influence on subsequent events. The year 1900 marked a turning point in New

---

51. Reprinted in Tawa, *Solo Songs*, II, 281–84.
52. See Rice, *Monarchs*, 216–18; "Barney Fagan," *New York Times* (Jan. 13, 1937), 23.
53. Marks, *They All Sang*, 91–92.

York's race relations. On the evening of August 12 Arthur Harris, a black man, stepped into a shop at Eighth Avenue and 41st Street for a cigar, leaving his wife outside. In his absence she was assaulted by a white man who clubbed Harris when he intervened. Harris defended himself with a pocket-knife, fatally wounding his assailant. The white population exploded in revenge.[54] It does not seem a coincidence that this incident—in which the African-American resembled the stereotype white citizens had been conditioned by popular song to expect—ignited one of the worst race riots in this history of the city. "Realistic" music must have been in the minds of the mob that cried "get Ernest Hogan and Williams and Walker and Cole and Johnson."

This event, as much as any other, prompted African-American songwriters to reject the urban dandy altogether:

> Rosamond Johnson, benevolent, mellow-voiced, industrious, and his brother, who was to become a national leader of his race, were of a different stamp. They wrote songs sometimes romantic, sometimes whimsical, but they eschewed the squalor and the squabbles, the razors, wenches, and chickens of the first ragtime. The word "coon" they banished from their rhyming dictionary, despite its tempting affinity with moon. The coon song died, the coon shouter vanished from the scene during the years of their ascendancy. "We wanted to clean up the caricature," says Rosamond Johnson.
>
> Yet they were human. There is, for instance, the story of "Under the Bamboo Tree," one of the world's hardest songs to forget.[55]

Cole and Johnson's charming song (1902),[56] for all its graceful rhythms and lyricism, marks a retreat from the urban scene to an idyllic land inhabited by noble savages:

> Down in the jungles lived a maid,
> Of royal blood though dusky shade,
> A marked impression once she made,
> Upon a Zulu from Matabooloo;
> And ev'ry morning he would be
> Down underneath a bamboo tree,
> Awaiting there his love to see,
> And then to her he'd sing. . . .

The accompaniment then offers a bit of "primitive" drone before the syncopated chorus (Ex. 6.16). Cole's basic frame of reference is ragtime, but he also finds a way of inverting the melody from the spiritual "Nobody Knows the Trouble I See" (Ex. 6.17) to create an "authentic" picture of ethnicity. He

---

54. I have taken this and my subsequent account from Johnson, *Black Manhattan,* 126–27.
55. Marks, *They All Sang,* 96.
56. Facsimile in Fremont, *Favorite Songs,* 330–33.

EXAMPLE 6.16   Bob Cole, "Under the Bamboo Tree" (New York: Jos. W. Stern & Co., 1902)

and Johnson became famous not only as songwriters but also as producers of black musical reviews in New York like *Shoo Fly Regiment* and *Red Moon* that did much to popularize African-American music in the first decade of the twentieth century.[57]

"Under the Bamboo Tree" may have spelled the end of the violent "coon," but songwriters replaced him with something unfortunate in its way, even if milder. This was the irresponsible, ineffectual black male in songs like "Bill Bailey, Won't You Please Come Home?" by Hughie Cannon (1902), " 'What You Goin' to Do When the Rent Comes 'Round?' (Rufus Rastas Johnson Brown)" by Andrew Sterling and Harry Von Tilzer (1905), and "That's Why They Call Me Shine" (1910) by Cecil Mack and Ford Dabney. Many of these songs feature truly compelling music, even as they revert to the stereotype of the rhythmic darkey, a kind of Jim Crow without political or social sagacity:

> Oh, ma honey, Oh, ma honey,
> There's a fiddle with notes that screeches,

57. A good account of African-Americans on the musical stage during this period appears in Thomas L. Riis, *More Than Just Minstrel Shows: The Rise of Black Musical Theatre at the Turn of the Century* (Brooklyn, 1992).

EXAMPLE 6.17   "Nobody Knows the Trouble I See" (familiar version)

> Like a chicken, Like a chicken,
> And the clarinet is a colored pet,
> Come and listen, Come and listen,
> To a classical band what's peaches,
> Come now, somehow,
> Better hurry along.
>
> [Chorus:]
> Come on and hear, Come on and hear
> Alexander's ragtime band,
> Come on and hear, Come on and hear,
> It's the best band in the land,
> They can play a bugle call like you never heard before,
> So natural that you want to go to war;
> That's just the bestest band what am, honey lamb. . . .

Irving Berlin ended his chorus with a musical quotation from Foster's "Old Folks at Home," and an ecstatic phrase about "Swanee River played in ragtime," bringing us almost full circle to the beginnings of minstrelsy.[58] There can be no doubt that Berlin sincerely admired the African-American musical style that established his early reputation as a songwriter, but this closing citation also reminds us that this more gentle blackface figure retains more than a hint of "Negro oddity."

Blackface song wore its Janus face to the end of the nineteenth century and well into the twentieth. Its content sometimes provoked contempt for African-Americans and sustained a fear and hatred every bit as virulent in northern urban surroundings as it was in the South during this same period. Yet the music betrayed an undeniable fascination with race. The association between ragtime, low-life dives (where most contemporary writers place the origins of the style), and violence exerted all the prurient allure of the forbidden. The waltz in its time had contained a sublimated sexuality that publishers used to interest customers. Ragtime offered a spicier brand of innuendo, as one of its earliest proponents in the publishing business, Isidore Witmark, explains:

58. New York: Ted Snyder, 1911; reprinted in David A. Jasen, *"Alexander's Ragtime Band" and Other Favorite Song Hits, 1901–1911* (New York, 1987), 5–9. Edward Berlin explores the possibility that Irving Berlin may have copied parts of "Ragtime Band" from Joplin in "Scott Joplin's *Treemonisha* Years," *American Music* 9 (1991), 260–76.

If the Nineties were really gay . . . one of the essential reasons is the growing insistence of the new, lively Negroid rhythms that were pushing their
way up from the South. Only a couple of years separated the slow, lachry-
mose, anecdotic measures of *After the Ball* from such early symptoms of
ragtime as *The Bully Song, All Coons Look Alike to Me,* or *A Hot Time in
the Old Town Tonight.* It would be years before the waltz, as a vehicle for
popular song, would be definitely conquered by the jagged two-four rhythms
of the rag. . . .[59]

"Ragging" the white man's stiff and proper march was, after all, a subtle kind
of populist protest. The garish, tawdry, and violent life sometimes portrayed in
"coon songs" held the same attraction for the purchasers of sheet music that
the chronicles of outlaws exerted from time to time on a mostly law-abiding
citizenry. In both cases, exotic characters' ability to deal out swift retribution
or to act instantly upon primitive urges elicited sneaking admiration, even as it
aroused revulsion.

Blackface after the Civil War bestowed a kind of mixed blessing on African-
American performers, as James Weldon Johnson relates:

Minstrelsy was, on the whole, a caricature of Negro life, and it fixed a stage
tradition which has not yet been entirely broken. It fixed the tradition of
the Negro as only an irresponsible, happy-go-lucky, wide-grinning, loud-
laughing, shuffling, banjo-playing, singing, dancing sort of being. Nevertheless, these companies did provide stage training and theatrical experience for
a large number of colored men. They provided an essential training and theatrical experience which, at the time, could not have been acquired from any
other source.[60]

Men like Sam Lucas, James Bland, Billy Kersands, the Bohee Brothers, later
Williams and Walker, and Ernest Hogan played roles that held a personal dis-
taste for them, but the public preoccupation with blackface song provided their
outlet. The turn of the century also proved a high point for African-American
composers of mainstream popular songs, which were sung by many leading
white as well as black vaudevillians. Not until the 1950s would so many black
creative artists hold center stage in the field of popular song.

Blackface song also served as one of the primary vehicles for infusing American popular music with fresh style, elements of which derive from African-
American practice. Just as antebellum minstrel songs had combined strands of
disparate "scientific" and "folkish" styles to form a uniquely American synthesis, later blackface incorporated many new elements into the "mainstream"
musical vocabulary. We can see this graphically in songs from the first several
decades of the twentieth century, where syncopated settings of text against
something very much resembling an alternating bass appeared in a large num-

59. Witmark, *From Ragtime,* 112.
60. *Black Manhattan,* 93.

ber of pieces. These included the obvious examples like "Good Bye, My Lady Love" (1904), or the verse from "Wait 'til the Sun Shines Nelly" (1905), where vocal ragtime loses its racial overtones. And even in later songs like Gershwin's "Someone to Watch Over Me" (1926) or "How Long Has This Been Going On" (1927) or even "Nice Work If You Can Get It" (1937) we can still hear the basic framework of an alternating bass (moving now at an extremely deliberate tempo) serving as a foil for syncopated melody. *Pace* Charles Hamm, much of the music generated by Tin Pan Alley after the First World War is unthinkable without the introduction of ragtime before the turn of the century.[61] However diluted these elements of African-American music may have been by the admixture of other traditions, in the last quarter of the nineteenth century they created a foundation for later popular style, supplying more than external decoration. Blackface, then, enriched the vocabulary of song even as it injured racial progress after the Civil War, writing another significant and ambivalent chapter in America's cultural history.

61. Hamm takes the position that Tin Pan Alley derives its style mainly from Western European sources, and he makes a good case for harmonic language and motivic usage, but not for texture, rhythm or some forms of ornamentation (see *Yesterdays,* 357–75). Though Hamm casts doubt on Alec Wilder's basic view that Tin Pan Alley style derives from African-American sources in the twentieth century (*American Popular Song: The Great Innovators, 1900–1950* (New York and Oxford, 1972), 3–28), Wilder's musical insights are perceptive.

7

The Romantic Savage

American Indians in
the Parlor [1]

Near the beginning of *The Last of the Mohicans* Alice Munro and Duncan Heyward regard "... the upright, flexible figure of [Uncas], graceful and unrestrained in the attitudes and movements of nature." And after noting the "bold outlines of his high, haughty features, pure in their native red" and the "dignified elevation of his receding forehead, together with all the finest proportions of a noble head," they conclude, "it might be a being partially benighted in the vale of ignorance, but it could not be one who would willingly devote his rich natural gifts to the purposes of wanton treachery." [2] This is James Fenimore Cooper's classic nineteenth-century rendering of the noble savage, which revolves at its very heart around a notion Roy Harvey Pearce calls the "historical anteriority" of the American Indian. [3] As the title of the novel suggests, Uncas's death in a mythical and somewhat distant time (1757) ends his noble line, providing both the outcome and the point of the story. For in this romance the idealized past contains an eternal truth for the edification of the present beholder: the Mohicans' nobility, being of the "savage" variety, must yield inevitably to the coming of white civilization. Cooper means to elicit our regret and pity, but also our resignation to inexorable progress.

Any one example of American popular song from the nineteenth century will naturally yield a picture simpler than Cooper's, but taken as a whole the genre presents a vision of the Indian no less complex or romantic. Lyricists either expose contemporary situations in which noble but primitive savages cannot adapt to civilization, or they place Native Americans in a fabled, vanished

1. An abbreviated version of this chapter appeared first under the same title in the *Journal of Musicological Research* 13 (1993).
2. James Fenimore Cooper, *The Last of the Mohicans, a Narrative of 1757* (New York and Scarborough, Ontario, 1980), 61.
3. *Savagism and Civilization: A Study of the Indian and the American Mind* (Baltimore and London, 1965), 200.

land. Indians become examples of civilization's injustice, the objects of nostalgia, and the symbols of idealized love. But an intensely unreal aura surrounds these songs, often manifesting itself in an exalted musical style that accompanies the strangely elevated rhetoric of their texts. The adoption and persistence of this peculiar language, both verbal and musical, reveals with great clarity the distance between the popular American image of Indians and their situation during the 1800s.

The Basic Nature of Native Americans

Curious though it may seem, popular song did not pay a great deal of attention to Indians in the time when their memory must have been freshest in the minds of audiences along the eastern seaboard, where the industry of music publishing originated in the United States. The romantic savage did have precursors who appeared in songs like Sarah Wentworth Morton and Hans Gram's "The Death Song of an Indian Chief" (1791) and Ann Julia Hatton and James Hewitt's "Alknomook, the Death Song of the Cherokee Indian from *Tammany*" (1794).[4] These two descriptions of stoic warriors seem to have enjoyed only limited circulation. Hewitt's "The Wampum Belt" (1797)[5] was more widely known, but tells us little about attitudes toward Native Americans:

> The wampum belt no more can charm,
> The beads from off my arm
> I frantic thrown into the stream.
> No more the mead I rove,
> Or in dances move,
> But pensive water the moon's pale beam.

We find in this text only the proto-romantic version of the Indians' depressive malaise. And even in the beginning of the the nineteenth century, arias like "When the Midnight of Absence," given to Pocahontas in James Nelson Barker and John Bray's "operatic melo-drame" *The Indian Princess*, made surprisingly little mention in their lyrics of anything, real or imagined, that was peculiar to Native Americans.[6]

Indians seem not to have registered much in popular song, and this lack of

4. Both of these appear in W. Thomas Marrocco and Harold Gleason, eds., *Music in America: An Anthology from the Landing of the Pilgrims to the Close of the Civil War* (New York, 1964), 213 and 225–26, respectively.

5. John W. Wagner finds it in three editions, see James Hewitt, *Selected Compositions,* John W. Wagner, ed., vol. 12 of Recent Researches in American Music (Madison, WI, 1980), xiii, 43.

6. For a copy of the piece see *The Indian Princess, or La Belle Sauvage,* vol. 11 of Earlier American Music (New York, 1972), 33–35.

a pervasive, coherent view of their culture (either positive or negative) paralleled the lack of a consistent government policy toward them. In the North they were pushed westward and destroyed when they sided with the British in the War of 1812. In the South they were alternately harried and marked for a process of conversion and civilization conducted by missionaries supported by federal funds.[7] Eventually in the mid-1820s Washington settled on a policy of forced migration made law in the Indian Removal Act of 1830 and prosecuted actively by Andrew Jackson.[8] The subject of Native Americans came much more into vogue during the 1820s with the first of Cooper's Leather-Stocking Tales and with the rise of Andrew Jackson's popularity. Cooper's romanticized view of Indians suggested that they possessed a fundamentally immutable nature that could not be reconciled to Western customs. And this conveniently supported the removal of tribes to the lands west of the Mississippi, rather than preservation of their ancestral territory in conjunction with forced indoctrination into Western culture. Part of Jackson's fame, after all, rested on his exploits as an Indian fighter, and as a planter from a western state he naturally desired the complete domination of European civilization in this part of the country.

Nineteenth-century popular song began to engage Indian topics much more frequently at the end of Jackson's administration, and the initial forays moved swiftly to place aboriginal people in the proper relationship to civilized culture. No better example can be found than "The American Indian Girl" (1835) by J. M. Smith and Charles Edward Horn. This "favorite ballad" begins with what would become a minor cliché in songs about Native Americans: a brief paragraph at the top of the first page setting the scene:

> An American Indian Girl residing in one of the early settlements, upon being asked, in the course of her education, whether she did not think her present situation and prospects more happy, than when wandering in ignorance among the woods—replied in the following strain of feeling and pathos—.

The lyrics, sung appropriately "with simplicity," enunciate her feelings:

> O give me back my forest shade,
> Where once I roam'd so blithe and gay,
> Where with my dusky mates I stray'd,
> In childhood's blest and happy day.
> They told me in the white man's home,
> I'd soon forget my woodlands wild;

7. An account of post-revolutionary and early nineteenth-century attitudes toward Native Americans appears in Bernard W. Sheehan's *Seeds of Extinction: Jeffersonian Philanthropy and the American Indian* (Chapel Hill, 1973).

8. A good summary appears in Leonard Dinnerstein, Roger L. Nichols, and David M. Reimers, *Natives and Strangers: Blacks, Indians, and Immigrants in America*, 2d ed. (New York and Oxford, 1990), 36–43, 64–68.

And never wish again to roam,
The simple native forest child.

In Smith's mind the Indian maiden is an arboreal creature roaming a paradisia-cal landscape. She is homesick:

Each rustling of the forest tree,
That's wak'd by gentle zephyrs bland,
Bears in it murm'ring sound to me
Some vision of my native land!

But even more important, we discover in the second stanza that she takes no solace from the teachings of Western civilization. In European society she suf-fers rather like a wild animal in captivity. Though she may be "benighted in the vale of ignorance," she still retains a certain nobility. Smith characterizes her lofty dignity by his elevated choice of language: the Indian maiden is not merely happy, she is "blithe and gay," she does not play in the forests, she "strays" with "dusky mates," she does not hear the wind, but "gentle zephyrs bland." And she does all this not in some stylized pidgin, but in fully formed, grammatically correct utterances.

Lest we fail to recognize Smith's portrayal of polite, noble savagery, Charles Horn insists on reinforcing it musically with a lovely melody and a delicate accompaniment in the genteel tradition he commanded effortlessly (see Ex. 7.1). In his use of triple meter and dotted rhythms he hints at a courtly dance akin to the minuet. The melody features Italianate touches in profusion, includ-ing enchained appoggiaturas in the prelude and in certain parts of his setting ("They *told* me in the *white* man's home, I'd *soon* forget . . ."). He also specifies a fermata (or "hold") with written cadenza, ironically on the words "simple, native." Just as Smith coins no phrases of stage dialect, Horn does not indulge folkish writing, though he had the tools for a different language at his disposal. His most famous song, "On the Lake Where Droop'd the Wil-low," adapted a folklike minstrel tune. Horn and Smith apparently perceived no contradiction in the combination of "wild" subject matter and Anglo-Italian style simplified for the polite amateur. They proceeded in a idyllic reverie far removed from their subject.

A number of songs during the subsequent years took up the theme of Indians made unhappy by removing them from their natural surroundings and placing them in the midst of Western civilization. To this end Frank Howard and James T. Field constructed a European scene for "The Children in Exile" (1848), in which two Native American children are transplanted to London where they die of the bad city air. And the same thoughts reverberated in Isaac B. Wood-bury's "The Indian's Prayer" (1846), which begins revealingly, "Let me go to my home in the far distant west," another "wild forest land" where "the tall, cedar's wave" and "wild fawns leap."

EXAMPLE 7.1 Charles E. Horn, "The American Indian Girl" (New York: Dubois and Bacon, 1835)

The most explicit portrayal of the unadaptable Native American appears in "The Indian Student" (dedicated to Mrs. Mary Gentry, 1851) by "Mrs. L.L.D.J." This anonymous composer uses minor mode to symbolize both her unusual subject and the pathos of a lament (see Ex. 7.2). Her rhythmic vocabulary suggests a Scottish flavor in its pronounced "snaps," figures combining accented short notes with longer dotted ones on words like "cap," "feather," and "give." Invocation of "Scottish" style in these times constitutes an allusion to the folkish, for alone among her contemporaries this composer thinks to pair a "wild" subject with an exotic musical vocabulary. Her textual imagery might be lifted from a song like "My Heart's in the Highlands" (see be-

244

EXAMPLE 7.2   Mrs. L. L. D. J., "The Indian Student" (New Orleans: Wm. T. Mayo, 1851)

low, Ex. 8.6): the Indian reveals himself in the first verse as a hunter of the "mountain roe," of the "hart" in verse five, as a dweller in an arboreal Eden in verse eight. But most significantly, he has no taste for Western erudition (verse 3):

> Long have I dwelt within these walls,
> And poured o'er ancient pages long,
> I hate the antiquated halls;
> I hate the Grecian poet's song. . . .

His basic nature lies at the root of this aversion (verse 4):

> My soul was formed for nobler deeds,
> This form o'er Indian plains to roam,
> Your bell of call no more I heed,
> I long to see my native home.

The European way of life, then, diminishes his inherently active qualities and represents a captivity he longs to escape in the sixth stanza:

Tis there my brother bounds as free
As the wild eagles soaring wing,
And there my sister thinks of me
At eve as their bow chant they sing.

"Mrs. L.L.D.J." suggests that Native Americans cannot adapt to Western civilization and will not. Wild by disposition and choice, the Indian student's nobility exists only in a savage state.[9] This point of view justified the removal of Indians from contact with European-Americans by calling it both natural and mutually agreeable.

A Fading People

As Native Americans departed for the western wilderness, popular song began to contemplate the vanishing race, usually in the form of laments written as if from an aboriginal point of view. The well-known duo of Eliza Cook and Henry Russell provided one of the best early examples of this type in "The Indian Hunter" (ca. 1837).[10] The title figure appears in the cover engraving (Illus. 7.1, from a slightly later edition that copies the original) as a noble savage with tomahawk in hand, bow and quiver at the ready, overlooking the panoramic view of a wild, Romantic landscape (an iconic cliché).[11] And speaking through him, Cook offers a commentary on the injustice of ejecting American Indians from their ancestral lands:

Why does the white man follow my path,
Like the hound on the tiger's track,
Does the flush on my dark cheek waken his wrath,
Does he covet the bow at my back.
He has rivers and seas where the billows and breeze,
Rear riches for him alone;
And the sons of the wood never plunge in the flood,
Which the white man calls his own.
Yha—then why should he come to the streams where none,
But the red skin dare to swim;

9. Ellwood Parry traces this same idea through paintings by Benjamin West and Edward Hicks in *The Image of the Indian and the Black Man in American Art, 1590–1900* (New York, 1974), 5–41.

10. This dating from Harry Dichter and Elliot Shapiro, *Handbook of Early American Sheet Music* (New York, 1977), 75.

11. Indians often appear in the foreground of landscapes from this period as part of a "truly affective view" of great natural wonders. See Parry, *The Image*, 53–58.

EXAMPLE 7.3   Henry Russell, "The Indian Hunter" (New York: Jas. L. Hewitt, [1837])

> Why should he wrong the hunter one,
> Who never did harm to him. Yha—

Russell casts the music for this plaint, both melody and accompaniment, in his very distinctive style (see Ex. 7.3). He writes ornately for the piano, with a certain amount of florid passage work during interludes. The meter shows kinship to the *romanza,* that genre in Italian opera reserved for characters telling fanciful, often nostalgic tales, and accordingly the vocal melody is a prime example of *bel canto.* Of all the popular composers from this period, Russell seems the most adept at operatic style, which extends particularly to his treatment of the nonsense syllables in the last quatrain of the verse. The first receives a chromatic trill, while the last extends over a series of wide leaps with the usual opportunity at the last for a cadenza "ad lib." Russell's insistence on Italianate ornamentation for these "calls of the wild" betrays again the curious incongruity between subject and style seen earlier in Horn's "American Indian Girl." And like Horn, Russell made this choice deliberately, rejecting the more direct and unadorned idiom he employs in songs like the sentimental "Old Arm Chair" (1840) or the rollicking "Life on the Ocean Wave" (1838).

Ultimately the text of "The Indian Hunter" also begins to reveal a disparity between the persona's and the lyricist's perspective. For though the second verse also expresses outrage about the hunter's plight, it shows Indian culture as essentially different from and developmentally anterior to Western civilization:

> The Father above thought fit to give
> The white man corn and wine;
> There are golden fields where they may live,
> But the Forest shades are mine.
> The Eagle hath its place of rest,
> The wild horse where to dwell;
> And the spirit that gave the bird its nest,
> Made me a home as well.
> Then go back from the red man's track,
> For the hunter's eyes grow dim.
> To find the white man wrongs the one
> Who never did harm to him.

The central misconception here reveals just how low on the progressive scale Native Americans lie in Cook's estimation. Unlike white men, Indians do not participate in husbandry (though the fruits of their agriculture—tobacco, corn, the potato, cocoa, if we range over the whole of the New World—ironically loom large in Western life) but must hunt for sustenance. The red man may sing in lofty tones ("The Eagle *hath* its place of rest . . .") supported by ennobled melody, but he remains undeveloped. Despite their sympathy, Cook and Russell held essentially the same point of view as their fellow artists about Native Americans' fundamentally "savage" nature.

Inevitably the Indian hunter's developmental arrest resulted explicitly in his displacement by civilization. This direct approach appears in John Wallace Hutchinson's "The Indian's Lament" (1846), with "symphonies and accompaniment" by E. L. White. Hutchinson (1821–1908) was one of the leading members of the famous musical family, which often performed numbers by Henry Russell. In fact, the cover engraving for "The Indian's Lament" bears more than a passing resemblance to that for "The Indian Hunter," and it may be that Hutchinson intended to expand on Cook's and Russell's thought. He proceeds methodically by showing first the natural, forested habitat that "the steel of the white man has swept . . . away." Just as the forest and game succumb to the depredations of European technology, Indian tribes fall before superior military force. In the second and third verses the speaker describes the progressive death of his family, in the fourth of his comrades in arms, until he draws the inevitable conclusion:

> And I, and I stand alone as the last of my race,
> Upon this earth I feel I no more have a place,

> Since my home, friends, and kindred are driven away,
> For the steel of the white man, has swept them away.

This race already lives an outdated cultural existence and so must vanish into a fabled land:

> And I, and I must soon follow, the Great Spirit calls
> Me away to the land where the brave never falls,—
> To the bright blissful shores, and the fair forest shade,
> Where the steel of the white man, will never invade.

The Hutchinson family championed social justice,[12] but brother John really advocates no solution to the predicament of Native Americans here. He elicits our sympathy but also our resignation, in part because he writes in tones distant from his subject: the elevated language of the poetry elicits a companion musical style (Ex. 7.4). Hutchinson, perhaps imitating Russell, casts his song in the rhythm of the *romanza,* and if his melody lacks the fluidity of "The Indian Hunter," it nevertheless entertains modest pretensions to operatic grandeur at the end of the verse by leaving an opportunity for an improvised cadenza. E. L. White's arrangement reinforces this soupçon of genteel Italian seasoning with pianistic flourishes in the "symphonies" and just a hint of chromaticism. Here is a tragic tale told in the safety of the parlor by those civilized enough to know why the Indians' cultural backwardness, noble though it might be, spells doom. If outlined in less than scientific terms, the refrain nonetheless informs us that the iron age must replace the stone age, however sad the process.[13] Hutchinson and White repeated this moral and tone in a companion piece, "Glide on My Light Canoe," published during the same year.

A very moving and sympathetic lament for the vanishing race comes in the form of James G. Clark's "The Indian Mother's Lullaby" (1855), which records yet another version of the progress toward extinction. In the first verse Clark sets the scene in a wilderness where the mother comforts her child. We hear the stages of the tribe's defeat in the remaining verses:

> Sleep, while gleams the council fire
> Kindled by thy hunted sire;
> Guarded by thy God above,
> Sleep and dream of peace and love.

---

12. The singing troupe's history appears in John's *Story of the Hutchinsons,* 2 vols. (Boston, 1896 (photofacsimile, New York, 1977)). Hutchinson makes no mention of his songs about Indians in the book, perhaps because he became directly involved in combating the Minnesota Sioux uprising of 1862. Though he attributes much of the trouble to the venality of government agents, he evinces no sympathy for Native Americans in his account, I (347–53).

13. This notion runs surprisingly close to the scientific image of Native Americans during the nineteenth century. See Robert F. Berkhofer, Jr., *The White Man's Indian* (New York, 1978), 33–61.

EXAMPLE 7.4   John W. Hutchinson, "The Indian's Lament" (Boston: Stephen W. Marsh, 1846)

> Dream not of the band that perished
> From the sacred soil they cherished,
> Or the ruthless race that roams
> O'er our ancient shrines and homes.

The singer knows the unalterable course of the future:

> Could thy tender fancy feel
> All that manhood will reveal,
> Couldst thou dream thy soul would share
> All the ills thy father bears. . . .

EXAMPLE 7.5   Marshall S. Pike, "The Indian Warrior's Grave"(Boston: A. & J. P. Ordway, 1850)

Because of the special situation, Clark does not respond to the lofty tone of the lyrics with elevated music. He adopts a triple meter and dotted rhythm to create the impression of gentle rocking that seems to be generic in lullabies (both appear much later, for instance, in Effie I. Canning's much more famous "Rock-a-Bye Baby" (1886)).[14] Clark's may be the most sincere of all the Indian laments.

As we might expect in a culture familiar with death, some nineteenth-century songs considered only the final stages in the steady process of extinction. Marshall S. Pike, who contributed many songs to the repertory of minstrelsy, takes up this theme in "The Indian Warrior's Grave" (1850), written for the Harmoneons, a troupe of itinerant singers. Though the marking "Dolce e Legato" heads the music (Ex. 7.5), Pike does not choose an operatic style, but rather a less lofty synthesis with occasional appoggiaturas (on "river" and "quiver") syncopated in the manner typical of American sentimental style during this period. The accompaniment, supplied by J. P. Ordway, is also much simpler than Russell's or White's. But the poetic imagery is still somewhat elevated:

14. The dotted rhythm occurs only in the chorus; see the facsimile in Robert A. Fremont's *Favorite Songs of the Nineties* (New York, 1973), 235–38.

> In the lone dell,
> While his wigwam defending,
> Nobly he fell
> 'Neath the Hazel boughs bending;
> Where the pale foe and him
> Struggled together,
> Who from his bow
> Tore his swift arrow'd feather.

The Indian's grave endures, ironically marked by a European memorial:

> Ere the next noon,
> The bold warrior was buried;
> And ere a moon,
> His tribe westward had hurried;
> But a rude cross,
> With its rough chisel'd numbers,
> Half hid with moss,
> Tells, "the red warrior slumbers."

The appearance of Cooper's *Mohicans* in a revised edition (1850) [15] led to a more august version of Pike's conceit in George Martin's "The Grave of Uncas" (1850), and the theme lived on in songs like the graphically titled "They Are Gone, They Are Gone" by T. Wood (1855). The publication in 1855 of Longfellow's *Song of Hiawatha* also prompted songs in this tradition, including Charles C. Converse's "The Death of Minnehaha" (ca. 1856) and its companion piece "Onaway!"

It remained for Henry Clay Work, that indefatigable social critic, to pen the final chapter in the story of the Indians' banishment. After the end of the Civil War, the nation turned its attention to settling the remainder of the western lands, and resettling the Native Americans west of the Mississippi on reservations. The conflicts of the sixties and seventies often resulted initially from incursions of the railroads into Indian territories, and the cover of Work's "The Song of the Red Man" (1868) [16] literally encapsulates these events. The engraving depicts a group of feathered Indian braves, perched on a forested outcropping, peering across the plains to a steam train issuing from a large, industrialized port city in the East. As the sun figuratively dawns on Western dominance, the train drives a herd of buffalo in front of it. Work's lyrics present an even more vast historical narrative that begins with the arrival of Europeans:

15. In his introduction to this second edition Cooper discusses his view of Indians, *Mohicans*, v–viii.

16. Republished in Henry Clay Work, *Songs*, Bertram G. Work, ed., vol. 19 of Earlier American Music (New York, 1974), 21–25.

> When the palefaces came in their white-wing'd canoes,
> Long ago, from the sunrising sea,
> When they ask'd for a lodge, and we did not refuse,
> Happy then was the red man, and free.
> He could then choose a spot for his wigwam to stand,
> Where the forest was crowded with game;
> For the blue rolling lake and the ever smiling land
> Were his own till the palefaces came,
> For the broad grassy plains and forests deep and grand
> Were his own till the palefaces came.

The second verse concerns the Indians' betrayal by traders, the introduction of alcohol, and ensuing war (in the spirit of temperance, demon rum receives credit for inciting braves to battle).[17] The last installment of the story moves to more recent history:

> When the oaks, pines and cedars were fell'd to the ground,
> 'Twas a sight that with sorrow we saw;
> For the game fled affrighted, and no food was found
> For the old chief, the papoose and squaw.
> Driven westward we came, but the paleface was here,
> With his sharp axe and death-flashing gun;
> And his great iron horse now is rumbling in the rear,
> *O, my brave men!* your journey is done.
> Like the beaver and elk, like the buffalo and deer,
> *O, my brave men!* your journey is done.

Work's last metaphor for the removal of Native Americans is most revealing: they resemble animals losing their habitat to encroaching development. Like writers before him, Work does not choose to see the conflict in terms of a battle between two civilizations (however unequal) in which the invaders conquer the original inhabitants of a region and then colonize their land. Instead, Indians are like an inferior species unable to defend against rapid changes in their environment. The pronounced march Work employs to set his "Song of the Red Man" (Ex. 7.6) has less to do with battle than with progress. The logical outcome of its tread will be extinction, in either event:

> They came! they came! like the fierce prairie flame
> Sweeping on to the sun-setting shore:
> Gazing now on its waves, but a handful of braves,
> We shall join in the chase nevermore

17. See Work's "Come Home, Father!," ex. 2.6 above.

EXAMPLE 7.6 Henry Clay Work, "Song of the Redman" (Chicago: Root & Cady, 1868)

> Till we camp on the plains where the Great Spirit reigns,
> We shall join in the chase nevermore.

Native Americans lingered on only as spirits in Fordyce H. Benedict and Charles A. Fuller's "Manitoba Bells" (1879). A legendary chieftain lends his name to the title, and the first two verses prepare the story of mysterious bell-like sounds issuing from his former haunts. The tones serve as a remembrance:

> Once were his, so many people;
> Over all the prairie swells,

> Came his warriors at the chiming
> Of these wondrous island bells.
> Now his voice but faintly echoes
> Round the wigwams of the west;
> Few the braves that hear him calling;
> In the spirit land they rest.

They also sound the funeral knell:

> Manitoba wave your sceptre
> To the far Pacific swell,
> Ever with your music calling,
> Where your scatter'd people dwell;
> Let them catch the distant murmur,
> 'Till around your island throne,
> Swells the requiem of your people;
> "Manitoba reigns alone."

For this lost people Fuller selects a musical conceit—operatic style—long since discarded in the rest of popular song. To be sure he has updated his point of reference: where Russell employs a simplified version of Bellini, Fuller uses dramatic melodic leaps, a rich harmonic vocabulary, and chromaticism to intimate something more like simplified Verdi (see Ex. 7.7). The composer even goes so far as to modulate briefly to A-flat minor in this elevated music for a noble, vanished tribe. The discrepancy between lofty European style and aboriginal subject reveals again the songwriters' distance from their material. They published "Manitoba Bells" during the last campaigns against the Plains Indians and Apaches, pretending that the western Indians had already gone to a fabled reward rather than disappearing into the squalid obscurity of government reservations.

The Symbolic Indian

The aura of the mythical surrounding Native Americans led to their most prominent role in nineteenth-century popular song, as symbols in courtship of legendary beauty and fidelity, and also of nostalgic loss. Very often such pieces unfold as stories or fables set in a romanticized past. The tale of Pocahontas, a favorite in literature, made its way early into ballad opera (as we have seen above) and also into isolated popular songs. George Pope Morris takes it up in his lyrics for a song by Henry Russell entitled "The Chieftain's Daughter" (1841). Morris adopts the stereotypical gesture of quoting the legend as a pref-

EXAMPLE 7.7   Charles A. Fuller, "Manitoba Bells" (New York: Spear & Dehnoff, 1879)

ace to the song from a version in *"Sketches of Virginia."*[18] After Pocahontas saves Smith from the anger of her father, Powhatan, the account runs:

> Whether the regard of this glorious girl for Smith ever reached the feeling of love is not known. No favor was ever expected in return. "I ask nothing of Captain Smith," said she of an interview she afterwards had with him in England, "in recompence for what I have done, but the boon of living in his memory."

Morris uses his first verse to give the details of Smith's impending fate and the second to relate Pocahontas's intercession, while the third records the outcome and moral:

> "Unbind him!" gasped the chief,
> "It is your king's decree!"
> He kissed away her tears of grief,
> And set the captive free.
> 'Tis ever thus, when, in life's storm
> Hope's star to man grows dim,
> An angel kneels in woman's form,
> And breathes a prayer for him.

Though Russell sets this text strophically, he marks various sections of each verse with a separate tempo indications, reflecting the emotional pitch he deems appropriate to the situation (his own performances apparently epitomized the melodrama so loved by audiences of his time).[19] He designates the first verse "Quasi andante ma con molto espressione," while he assigns the impending *mort* an "Animato quasi" and the moral a considered "Andante." But the writing is more than just superficially Italianate: here we have the arched melodic rise and fall of *bel canto* (see Ex. 7.8). The lovely, ornate piano prelude completes this picture of a legendary noble savage as the acme of feminine virtue.

"Wenona of the Wave" (1855) by T. Ellwood Garrett and Francis Woolcott offers another tale of an Indian maiden's heroic resolve with a more tragic outcome. The "Legend" on the first page of this sheet music runs:

> The daughter of a Dacota or Soux [sic] Chief named Wenona was betrothed to a young warrior of her tribe whom she did not love, but whom her parents would force her to marry. She fled from her home—followed by her lover, and reached [the precipice called "Wenona's Bluff"]—telling him, that if

18. For a discussion of Smith's story and its retelling as legend in American literature see Jay B. Hubbell, "The Smith-Pochohantas Literary Legend" in his *South and Southwest* (Durham, NC, 1965), 175–204.

19. For a firsthand account of Russell's performances and their effect, see George Frederick Root, *The Story of a Musical Life* (Cincinnati, 1891), 18.

EXAMPLE 7.8 Henry Russell, "The Chieftain's Daughter" (New York: Firth & Hall, 1841)

he did not cease his pursuit she would leap over, which she accordingly did—he not being willing to relinquish his bride—and met her death. The young brave wept, and as the Legend goes, the tears he shed on that occasion, made Lake Pepin.

The three verses without chorus repeat the story literally in an dramatized and elevated language that appears quite clearly, for instance, in the second verse describing the rejected lover's approach:

> Dark he stood beside the maiden,
> Breathing fond desire;

> With his sighs the air was laden—
> Warmer glowed his Indian fire.
> "Fair Wenona I have sought thee,
> Woo'd thee night and day;
> At the Chieftain's price have bought thee,
> To my wigwam haste away."

Woolcott tries to match this high form of address with an equally high musical style. Before the last section of each verse he writes out a scalar cadenza, preceded by a "rallentando" and followed by "Tempo con Espressione." But he cannot quite reconcile these strivings toward art music with his basically popular melos, with its uneven rhythms and flat contours (see Ex. 7.9). The strange combination is awkward and self-conscious, but the composer's intent to ennoble is clear.

Aspirations to elevated style are equally evident in a happier story of courtship, "The Indian Lover" (1863)[20] by A. T. Emery and O. C. Jillson. No preface spells out the situation in this song, but it appears that the Indian speaker is courting a white maiden:

> Wilt thou come to my home, lily brow,
> Wilt thou come to my faithful breast?
> My wigwam is low, and my couch is of straw,
> Though gentle and soft is my rest. . . .

He compares himself favorably to a white lover:

> Then come from thy beautiful home,
> Come away from the smoking feast;
> Our fare will be plain, our table the ground,
> But the paleface has loved thee least;
> He smiles on thee now—he is courting thy favor,
> But he of the dark brow will leave thee, oh! never.

He wins the maiden in the end, and the happy couple repair appropriately to their "beautiful Eden." Jillson's music does not attain the elevated style of the text (it bears some resemblance to the tune of "Red River Valley"). But the music gives evidence of an attempt at heightened display, especially in the concluding phrase (Ex. 7.10) with its octaves, wide range, and appoggiaturas on "quiver" and "ever." The composer wants an emphatic and demonstrative finale.

The favorite symbolic use of Native Americans from mid-century on played on their status as a vanished race to invoke nostalgia for an idealized lost be-

---

20. The copyright is assigned to H. M. Higgins of Chicago.

EXAMPLE 7.9 Francis Woolcott, "Wenona of the Waves" (St. Louis: Balmer &
Weber, 1855)

loved. The tale did not always appear in tragic tones, however: Marion Dix
Sullivan's "The Blue Juniata" (1844)[21] paints a sprightly portrait of the love
between the Indian maiden, Alfarata, and an unnamed brave. As the first verse
intimates (see Ex. 7.11), she inhabits arboreal climes of great natural beauty.
Accordingly the cover engraving (Illus. 7.2) repeats the iconic cliché used for
"The Indian Hunter" by adapting it to represent a lovely young woman. In the
third verse Sullivan describes her lover:

21. This edition lists Edward L. White as arranger, that is to say, he probably provided the
"symphonies" and accompaniments for piano. Little is known of Sullivan, save that she married

EXAMPLE 7.10   O. C. Jillson, "The Indian Lover" (New York: J. L. Peters, 1863)

> Bold is my warrior good,
> The love of Alfarata,
> Proud waves his snowy plume
> Along the Juniata.
> Soft and low he speaks to me,
> And then his war-cry sounding,
> Rings his voice in thunder loud
> From height to height resounding.

Ultimately the theme turns to loss in the last verse:

> So sang the Indian girl,
> Bright Alfarata,
> Where sweep the waters
> Of the blue Juniata.
> Fleeting years have borne away
> The voice of Alfarata,

J. W. Sullivan in Boston during 1825; see Judith Tick's *American Women Composers Before 1870* (Ann Arbor, MI, 1983), 146–47.

EXAMPLE 7.11   Marion Dix Sullivan, "The Blue Juniata" (Boston: Oliver Ditson, 1844)

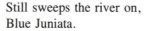

Still sweeps the river on,
Blue Juniata.

Mark Twain recalled this title from minstrel shows, "In the beginning the songs were rudely comic, such as 'Buffalo Gals,' 'Camptown Races,' 'Old Dan Tucker,' and so on; but a little later on sentimental songs were introduced, such as 'The Blue Juniata,' 'Sweet Ellen Bayne,' 'Nelly Bly,' 'A Life on the Ocean Wave,' 'The Larboard Watch,' etc." [22] The catchy quality of Sullivan's dance-like rhythms and occasional melodic syncopations make "Juniata" a good candidate for minstrel performance. Twain must have perceived it as sentimental because it evokes a standard imagery. The beloved's "jetty locks," and "gay songs" have been "borne away" by the "fleeting years," for which the running waters of the river provide a metaphor. And in addition there are the sentimental, though not really Italianate, appoggiaturas on "Juni*a*ta" and "*flow*ing." The Indian garb in Sullivan's version intensifies nostalgia precisely because the departed beauty belongs to a lost people. Judith Tick points out that "Juniata" became one of the most popular parlor songs of the nineteenth

22. *The Autobiography of Mark Twain,* Charles Neider, ed. (New York, 1959), 61.

century, appearing in widely published anthologies as late as the beginning of the twentieth century.[23]

Songs about the lost beloved typically adopted a more melancholy tone, and the nineteenth-century does not lack Indian examples in this mode. In Edward L. White and J. E. A. Smith's "The Sachem's Daughter" (1850) an Indian maiden disappears forever into the clutches of white strangers, a event that also raises the issue of injustice. More typically, the maiden dies of natural causes, like the half-bred "Bell Brandon" (Francis Woolcott and T. E. Garrett, 1854), who lies "'neath a tree by the margin of the woodland" and expires in the perplexing way of nineteenth-century women because of the unearthly beauty imparted by "the life-current of the Red Man" in her veins. "Zimenia," by C. E. Rowley and H. Thayer (1869), drowns and, most romantic of all, meets her lover in the afterlife.

One of the most sentimental tales of a departed Indian beauty appears in "Hee-Lah-Dee!" by Katie Belle Wichmann and N. P. Tivolie (1873), which returns long after the Civil War to the beautiful, limpid rhythms of the *romanza* (Ex. 7.12). Wichmann provides background on tribal custom first:

> Among the superstitions of the Seneca Indians, was one remarkable for its singular beauty. When a maiden died, they imprisoned a young bird until it first began to try its powers of song, and then, loading it with messages and caresses, they loosed its bonds over her grave, in the belief that it would not fold its wing, nor close its eyes, until it had flown to the spirit-land and delivered its precious burden of affection to the loved and lost.

Only then does she repeat the legend:

> Hee-lah-dee—(which signifies—"pure fountain," or, "a spring of bright, clear water"), was an Indian maiden born in the far West, where the tribe, the Seneca Indians, dwelt. The brave young chieftain, Stan-an-pat, or "Bloody Hand," loved Hee-lah-dee. . . . According to the bond of their betrothal, three moons were to pass away, ere Stan-an-pat could claim his bride; but ere the third moon had risen, the Great Spirit spoke to the spirit of Hee-lah-dee and called it to the happy hunting ground.

The lyrics rearrange the several elements of a long and prominent elegiac tradition in American popular song. Reduced to their basics, they generally include a mourner, a grave situated in some place of great natural beauty, and birds who come as representatives of nature to commiserate about the "loved and lost." The best-known member of the genre must be Septimus Winner's "Listen to the Mocking Bird" (1855; see Ex. 3.12 above), which "Hee-Lah-Dee!" presents in a variation. As a result of things Indian from the mythical past, Wichmann has assumed a higher tone than Winner: in place of his mock-

23. See, for instance, Helen Kendrick Johnson et al., eds. *The World's Best Music: Famous Songs and Those Who Made Them* (New York, 1902), I, 184.

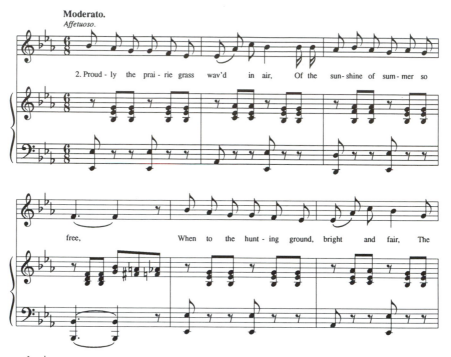

EXAMPLE 7.12   N. P. Tivolie, "Hee-Lah-Dee!" (Philadelphia: Lee & Walker, 1873)

ing bird she gives us a "tiny songster" to sing of the chieftain's sorrow. His melancholy leads him away from war-like inclinations in the second verse to a life of constant mourning in the third verse (a distraction that also befalls the character in Winner's song):

> Weary and lonely the mournful chief,
> As he grieves for his lov'd Hee-lah-dee—
> Birdling go sing of his sorrow and grief,
> Sing sweetly to lost Hee-lah-dee;
> Over her grave, the Indian brave,

Kneeling, bids thee to flee;
Close not thy wing, till thou dost sing—
Sing sadly to lov'd Hee-lah-dee.

The music for "Hee-Lah-Dee!" also takes the high road. The short phrases and continual syncopations that had become generic in popular style after the Civil War find no resonance in Tivolie's Italianate melodic curves, which must have seemed quaint even in their own time. And they were probably intended in just this way, an archaic style for the charming practices of a vanished race. The engraving by Th. Sinclair & Son on the front of this sheet music (Illus. 7.3) reinforces its air of retrospection, for it uses essentially the same image—Indian title figure, her dishabille modestly cloaked, standing by a riverbank of unspoiled beauty—seen some thirty years before on the cover of "The Blue Juniata."

At the end of this period songwriters reduced the symbolism entailed in the Indian beloved to the connotations engendered by the mention of an exotic name. In "Oclemena" (1888) by Charles A. White the title figure plays an object of desire in a story of failed courtship without any other reference whatever to Native American custom or way of life. In this case the lost beloved is no paragon of virtue, for she breaks her vow of marriage in the first verse for reasons supplied in the second:

Woo'd and lost like knights of old
With all the manhood of my soul,
Bow thee to wealth's sordid shrine,
And this is why you'll not be mine.
O that we had never met,
No remorse or keen regret,
Like a dream this change has fell,
Oclemena oh farewell.

White does not mean to suggest that Native Americans are venal in this song, nor that they are unfaithful. The lyrics do not really concern Indians, but merely borrow an ostensibly aboriginal name (the cover depicts the main character incongruously adorned by the headdress of a full chief) to produce a distinctive title. In this spirit, American culture has retained many Indian names, a practice so widespread in the nineteenth century that Mark Twain and Charles Dudley Warner could quip in *The Gilded Age:*

It is the fashion in New England to give Indian names to the public houses, not that the late lamented savage knew how to keep a hotel, but that his warlike name may impress the traveler who humbly craves shelter there, and make him grateful to the noble and gentlemanly clerk if he is allowed to depart with his scalp safe.[24]

Despite the shallowness of his reference, White does retain one vestigial family trait from the genre of nineteenth-century popular songs on Indians: he indulges in an overwrought musical style much like that in "Manitoba Bells" (Ex. 7.7 above). Even the slightest of references to Native Americans seems to elicit an elevated musical language. Otherwise, "Oclemena" resembles the many other nostalgic numbers White penned about the death of children or the longing of slaves for their plantation homes.

The use of Native American women as symbols of beauty persisted into the twentieth century, when overt racism finally began to overtake songs in this vein. "Navajo" (1903),[25] by Harry H. Williams and Egbert Van Alystyne, presents the story of an Indian woman courted by an African-American. Because she plays the object of desire, the Native American beloved receives somewhat better treatment than her black suitor:

> Down on the sand hills of New Mexico,
> There lives an Indian maid,
> She's of the tribe they call Navajo,
> Face of a copper shade,
> And ev'ry evening there was a coon,
> Who came his love to plead,
> There by the silv'ry light of the moon,
> He'd help her string her beads,
> And when they were all alone,
> To her he would softly crone *[sic]*.

Van Alystyne sets this verse in minor mode, a common gesture in ragtime songs around this time (see, for instance, Ex. 8.17 below), and indeed, the chorus reveals a "coon song," with a gently syncopated melody placed against an "alternating" bass:

> Nava, Nava, my Navajo,
> I have a love for you that will grow,
> If you'll have a coon for a beau,
> I'll have a Navajo.

Nineteenth-century songwriters rarely condoned phrases about Indians that explicitly equated them with a group traditionally held to be ignoble (though this

24. *The Gilded Age: A Tale of To-day* (Seattle and London, 1968), 153.
25. Facsimile in Nicholas Tawa, *American Solo Songs 1866 Through 1910,* vol. 2 of *Three Centuries of American Sacred and Secular Music,* Martha Furman Schleifer and Sam Dennison, eds. ([Boston], 1989), 228–31.

song may show the cumulative effects of the previous century's implicit ranking of Native Americans low on the scale of civilized development). In any event, the lyricist does not portray Indians as evil or violent, and he invokes the stereotype of the exotic beloved mainly to create an aura of fabled romance.

A more pointed but at the same time shallower symbolism runs through Vincent Bryan and Gus Edwards's "Tammany" (1905),[26] which plays on the name of the legendary Indian chief in its connection to the New York Democratic machine. Interpolated into the Broadway musical *Fantana,* the lyrics maintain ironically that the political organization appropriating the Indian as symbol enjoys a history exactly opposite from the one featured in *Hiawatha* and "Navajo" (the lyrics almost certainly refer to the song just discussed):

> Hiawatha was an Indian, so was Navajo,
> Pale-face organ grinders killed them many moons ago.
> But there is a band of Indians, that will never die,
> When they're at the Indian club, this is their battle cry:
>
> *[Chorus:]*
> Tammany, Tammany,
> Big Chief sits in his tepee, cheering braves to victory.
> Tammany, Tammany,
> Swamp 'em, Swamp 'em, get the "wampum," Tammany.

The series of ethnic tags continues in verses three and four: organ grinders (i.e., Italians) also appear in the guise of "Chris Columbo" whose vote the machine enlists, just as it martials the Irish electorate through patronage in the police department. These Indians, unlike their namesakes, conquer each new wave of invading Europeans. The remaining verses address the activities of various contemporary political figures, ending with the opposition of William Randolph Hearst to the Tammany machine.

The ultimate irony in this song lies in Edwards's music: he selects a stereotypical "tom-tom" motif for his minor-mode verse (see Ex. 7.13). Just when songwriters no longer take Native Americans at all seriously in their lyrics, they invoke a musical archetype of Indian ethnicity. In this song the irony may be unintentional, though: it appears that interest in the music of Native Americans on the part of classical composers toward the end of the nineteenth century simply migrates into popular culture during the twentieth.[27] Nowhere does this become so clear as in the song "From the Land of the Sky-Blue Water" by Nelle Richmond Eberhart and Charles Wakefield Cadman (1909). Listed by

26. Stanley Appelbaum reprints the sheet music in *Show Songs from "The Black Crook" to "The Red Mill"* (New York, 1974), 238–42; his commentary appears on p. xlvii.

27. For a discussion of sources for Native American music and its use by classical composers see Francis Brancaleone, "Edward MacDowell and Indian Motives," *American Music* 7 (1989), 359–81.

EXAMPLE 7.13   Gus Edwards, "Tammany" (New York: M. Witmark & Sons, 1905)

Cadman as Op. 45, no. 1 (out of a collection of *Four American Indian Songs*), the piece lies somewhere between the classical and the popular. It lays claim to both ethnological and scholarly authenticity because it is "founded" upon "Omaha Tribal Melodies collected by Alice C. Fletcher," but at the same time its beginning line has gained a kind of immortality in the popular (and commercial) imagination.

Nineteenth-century popular song addressed Native Americans in a substantially different way from popular literature, if we accept Robert J. Berkhofer's characterization of the dime novel:

> No matter how important the Indian might be to the Western plot and genre,
> he usually served in the end as a backdrop rather than the center of attention,

for to do otherwise would have discarded simplicity for complexity and violated the premises of popular culture production. If the Indian was to be taken seriously, his motives and his culture would have to be presented as alternative values and lifestyles to White civilization, thereby introducing ambiguity into the genre. . . . Thus, the Indian either posed an immediate threat to the hero who then wiped him out or he vanished shortly before the advance of civilization when it finally came in all its fullness to the West.[28]

In sheet music Indians rarely appeared as any kind of threat,[29] and their treatment is more subtle in its implications than Berkhofer finds in popular literature. By and large, nineteenth-century songwriters tended to sympathize with the plight of Native Americans. Lyricists endowed them with the virtues of beauty, courage, steadfastness, and fidelity, and many authors disapproved the injustice done them by the rapacity of European civilization. But the manner in which songwriters portrayed Native Americans undermined, perhaps even contradicted, their sympathy and admiration. Just as he was among the first to deal with Indians in song, Henry Russell also summarized, fittingly enough, the attitudes of his colleagues at the end of the century in his autobiography:

> The noble red man that ones reads of in my friend Fenimore Cooper's delightful books, is fast becoming a thing of the past, and soon will be but a mere memory and a name. Even in my day the baleful influences of civilisation were beginning to tell upon these wild children of the forest and prairie. . . . Thus it is that, in the present year of grace, the *noble* red man has ceased to exist. In his stead, there still lives the degenerated, half-civilised Indian, whose days, like those of his erstwhile companion of the prairies, the buffalo, are numbered.[30]

Lyricists and composers during the nineteenth century turned Indians into progressively distant abstractions of an exotic but developmentally arrested nobility. And by means of this well-intended romanticization, accomplished through elevated music and exalted speech, they gently consigned the aboriginal peoples of North America to oblivion.

28. Berkhofer, *White Man's Indian*, 98.

29. Only one song in my survey, an alternate texting of John Hill Hewitt's "Mary Blane" (Baltimore: F. Benteen, 1848), actually attributes a violent act to Native Americans. Robert C. Toll writes of anti-Indian skits in minstrelsy, but the songs seem not have been sufficiently appealing to enter the general repertory of music for the parlor. See *Blacking Up: The Minstrel Show in Nineteenth-Century America* (New York, 1974), 164–68.

30. Henry Russell, *Cheer! Boys, Cheer! Memories of Men and Music* (London, 1895), 164–66.

8

Out of Many, One?

Western European Ethnicity

One of the most acute issues facing Americans throughout their history has been the conduct of a multi-ethnic society, which has always entailed an act of balancing contradictory impulses to satisfy competing interests. In the United States after World War II "the myth of the melting pot"[1] has gradually yielded to "the new particularism," a move that constitutes nothing more than a repositioning between two, very old extremes:

> The essential dilemma, of course, is the opposition between a strategy of integration and one of pluralism. Although the contrast has many dimensions, it can be summed up as a question of boundaries. The integrationist looks toward the elimination of ethnic boundaries. The pluralist believes in maintaining them. . . . Integration is pledged to the great community which is yet to be realized: the brotherhood of mankind. Pluralism holds fast to the little community: the concrete local brotherhood which is rooted in the past. Integration in its modern form expresses the universalism of the Enlightenment. Pluralism rests on the diversitarian premises of romantic thought.[2]

The representation of Western European ethnicity in nineteenth-century popular song not only sets the stage for our current situation, it also presents an alternate point of view. For songwriters in the during the 1800s charted a course almost, but not quite, opposite to the one pursued in the twentieth century. They began with a pluralistic, romantic view, treasuring the "characteristic" in the context of rural, foreign climes and ended by extolling assimilation amidst the turbulence of America's cities, where large numbers of immigrants settled (by 1890 some 62 percent of all foreign-born lived in urban surround-

---

1. I borrow this phrase from Roger Daniels, *Coming to America: A History of Immigration and Ethnicity in American Life* (New York, 1990), 17–18.

2. The phrase "new particularism" as well as this passage come from John Higham's *Send These to Me: Immigrants in Urban America*, rev. ed. (Baltimore and London, 1984), 230–31, 234.

ings as opposed to 26 percent of native white Americans).[3] Lyrics and music trace changing ideas about how disparate European groups arriving on these shores might relate to one another.

Manifestations of the "Characteristic"

American popular song prized the "characteristic" in its approach to ethnicity during the first half of the nineteenth century mostly because it fell strongly under the influence of Western European culture. Speaking of German Romantic Opera and *opéra comique,* Carl Dahlhaus suggests, ". . . to the early-nineteenth-century mentality, 'characteristic' meant idiosyncratic rather than general or typical, the exception rather than the rule, 'interesting' and 'striking' rather than 'nobly simple,' coloristic rather than statuesque."[4] By its very nature, this aesthetic had particularly close ties to the love of folk music and the folkish in general. And the inhabitants of the British Isles, where most direct influences on early nineteenth-century American culture originated, cultivated these passions every bit as much as the Continentals did. In fact, the British instigated the vogue for collecting folk songs in the eighteenth century, so much so that one classic history of German *Volkslieder* bears the title "From Percy to the Wunderhorn."[5] Beginning with the publication of William Thompson's *Orpheus Caledonius* in 1726, collections of Scottish folk song also had an increasingly important influence on British composers, and interest in Irish song followed at a distance with Edward Bunting's *A General Collection of the Ancient Irish Music* in 1796.[6] Bunting gathered his traditional airs at a convocation of Irish harpers in 1792, and British immigrant James Hewitt cited this same gathering as the source for his own foray into Irish ethnicity, *The Music of Erin* (1807).[7]

It is tempting to think that Hewitt's concern for Irish music responded to the presence in the United States of Irish immigrants.[8] But his preface to the collec-

3. Ibid., 22.

4. *Nineteenth-Century Music* (Berkeley and Los Angeles, 1989), 69–70.

5. Heinrich Lohre, *Von Percy zum Wunderhorn,* vol. 22 of Palaestra (Berlin, 1902).

6. For a discussion of Bunting in relationship to Thomas Moore's *Irish Melodies,* see Charles Hamm, *Yesterdays: Popular Song in America* (New York, 1979), 46–47.

7. Hewitt's preface seems to allude to the convocation:"Notwithstanding the celebrity which the bards of Ireland had obtained for their musical compositions from the remotest antiquity, we have the strongest reason to believe that no general collection of their works had ever been made previous to the year 1792, when a meeting was convened in the north of Ireland of the few lingering members of that once sacred order, which had spread 'the light of song' over the gloom of unillumined ignorance, or softened the ferocity of uncivilized heroism." *Music of Erin* (New York, [1807]), 1.

8. Hamm implies just this in *Yesterdays,* 42–43. The number of Irish in the United States during the early years of the Republic can be overestimated. The census of 1790 lists only 3.6 percent of the population as hailing from southern Ireland; 5.9 percent were Scotch-Irish, quite a different group. See Daniels, *Coming to America,* 77–87.

tion makes it clear that he was attracted to the "characteristic" quality of the tunes:

> To the ear, which is alone made up to the delicacies of Italian music, or the refinements of scientific composition, the following melodies will probably sound wildly inelegant, or barbarously simple; but they are not offered as the correct effusions of musical talent, schooled into science, corrected by experience, and sanctioned by the reigning modes; but as "the native wood notes wild" of those, whose genius, unimproved by art, unrestrained by rule, only vibrated, like the far famed statue of Memnon, to the genial beam of heaven's own light,—as specimens of national music, strongly characterized by those idiomatic features, which to musical philosophy afford so wild a field for reflection.[9]

Because Hewitt sought idiosyncrasies of the "folk" in his material, he lay great store by authenticity. The title page of his collection speaks of "Original Hibernian Melodies" and translation or imitation of poetry by the "Ancient Irish Bards." The antiquity of the actual sources is open to question: Hamm observes that less than a century had passed since the death of the bard Carolan, who figures prominently in Hewitt's assemblage.[10] But there can be no doubt that the music meets the criteria of the "characteristic" from the very first song, "Ah Who Is That, *or Emunh a Cnuic, or Ned of the Hill*" (Ex. 8.1). The melody, minus its graces and a few itinerant passing tones, is pentatonic (the five notes are F, G, A, C, and D), it has a peculiarly irregular phrase structure (three measures plus four) by the standards of "scientific" music, and it exhibits the very large leap of a seventh between the first and second phrase often found in Irish melodies. The lyrics present us with a serenade, but one that ends more explicitly than the genteel model adopted by Italianate songs of courtship later in the century:

> Like a soft gloomy cloud thine hair
> Tinged with the setting sun's warm rays,
> And lightly o'er thy forehead fair,
> In many a spiry ringlet plays,
> Oh! come then rich in all thy charms;
> For Eva I'm as rich in love,
> And panting in my circling arms;
> I'll bear thee to old Thuars grove.

The imagery is rural and the language slightly elevated, much as Hewitt's accompaniment refines and elaborate the tune. The setting has been crafted to

9. *Music of Erin*, 2.
10. *Yesterdays*, 55.

EXAMPLE 8.1   James Hewitt, arr., "Ah Who Is That, *or Emunh a Cnuic, or Ned of the Hill*" (New York: James Hewitt, [1807])

display a beautiful if irregular gem; it does not detract from the melody's Irish authenticity but places it in the best light.

With these demonstrably Irish melodies also come texts of explicitly Irish reference, as in *"Oh! Farewell Dear Erin or Drimemduath."* Its tune falls in a minor mode (the scale usually associated with sadness and bereavement) which fits its nostalgic lyrics:

> Oh! farewell dear Erin my Country adieu,
> And farewell my soul's dearer Idol to you.
> Tho' forc'd from my love and my Country to part,
> Yet Eveline and Erin still hold my sad heart.

In spite of its longing for the old country, Hewitt probably did not select this text because he has in mind some prospective audience of Irish expatriots susceptible to the sentiment. He chose it, rather, for its "authentic" conceit: it looks back to the fabled land of origin because the "characteristic" resides in that rural, folkloric realm. In this instance Hewitt was a collector of curiosities intrigued by ethnicity per se.

Where Hewitt publicized authenticity by asserting it in the title of his collection and explaining it in his preface, other songs relied on musical types to

EXAMPLE 8.2 Anonymous, "My Deary" (Baltimore: Carr's Music Store, [ca. 1814])

suggest such connections. One such piece is "My Deary!" (ca. 1814), which employs a jig (Ex. 8.2) to impart the proper tone for a tale nowhere near so elevated as those in Hewitt's *Music of Erin*. The lack of any attribution on this sheet music suggests that the piece may originate in the store of folk ballads ubiquitous in late colonial song and still popular in the early years of the Republic. The narrative is comic, about a spinster whose suitors court her for money, with an explicitly ethnic result. In the last verse, one suitor relates:

> She consented that I for the license should go,
> When across her, mean time, came a tall Irish beau,
>   Who, like me, in pocket was peery;
> Out of his calf's head such sheep's eyes threw he,
> That a queer little hop o' my thumb she call'd me,
>   So he diddled me out of my deary!
>   Pretty deary! Tiddy di fol dol lol de rol de de.

Comic songs often dealt with the peculiarities of human behavior and therefore fall naturally into considerations of ethnic color (a manifestation of the "interesting" and "striking" rather than the "nobly simple"). The sheet music does not claim that the tune is authentically Irish, but it seems folkloric enough to fit this rural tale with an Irish outcome. During this period songs of the ethnic had to display openly the curiosities meant to attract the public, and these features appeared in the music as much as in the text.

A third, more removed approach to ethnic subjects—failing authenticity or the appearance of authenticity—drew on a series of stock devices established as symbolic in the minds of the audience. This tactic produced pieces that invoked the "characteristic" in their lyrics by constructing catalogues of sup-

EXAMPLE 8.3   Peter K. Moran, "Barney Brallaghan" (New York: Bourne, 1830)

posed ethnic peculiarities. Dublin-born immigrant Peter K. Moran relates the Irish love of whisky in his "Crooskeen Lawn" (ca. 1823), which speaks of the brew as it is distilled and consumed in the old country and features a refrain in Gaelic. The composer did not mean to indite his countrymen for their drinking, but regarded their enthusiasm instead as a distinctive trait. Another song arranged by Moran, "Barney Brallaghan" (1830), displays the catalogue of musical traits appropriate in such songs. To set the basic folkish scene Moran employs a sustained bass note, or "pedal" for the first nine measures, an allusion to the frequent use of drones in folk music (Ex. 8.3). Melodic eccentricity is manifested in its three-measure phrases intermixed with occasional two-measure units ("and weather scorning"). Though the tune turns out to be diatonic eventually, it begins as if it were pentatonic and avoids the smooth, arched shape of Italianate gentility. It also indulges a "snap," the uneven rhythm which accents the short note on words like "scorning" and "morning." This rhythmic tick appears in real Irish melodies (we will see that it occurs in Scottish music as well), and it is another sign of the irregular. But here it is only a token; the tune for "Barney" seems not to originate in the folk repertory but in the stage presentation of an actor, given on the cover as "Mr. Todd."

The serenade depicted in the lyrics of "Barney Brallaghan" imitates a type of futile courtship that appears frequently in folk songs: either the woman leans out the window and tells her suitor to leave, or she refuses to awaken. Barney has the latter problem of drawing Judy Callaghan's attention over her snoring. But in the course of trying to rouse her, he conveys a good deal about his situation. He lives in the Irish countryside, working as a farmer:

> I've got an acre of ground, I've got it with potatoes,
>   I've got tobacco a pound, I've got some tea for the Ladies;
> I've got the ring to wed, some whisky to make us gaily,
>   A mattress feather bed, and a handsome new shillelah. . . .

Not only is he associated with typical food and drink, he is also a fiddler. These standard signs, together with the accompaniment, the odd phrase structure, rhythms, and melodic shape, are enough to lend an impression of folkishness that satisfies a Romantic desire for the piquant. And many other songs, plaintive, festive, and patriotic, followed a similar course, like "Ellen Aureen" (ca. 1825) by John Monro, or the anonymous "Hurrah for the Emerald Isle" (1830), or "Kate Kearney" (ca. 1835), which relates a tale of an Irish Lorelei who (for the sake of rhyme) "lives on the banks of Killarny."

"Folkish" style like that found in "Barney Brallaghan" coexisted with folkloric authenticity, and the latter did not die away by any means. As late as the fifth decade of the century James G. Maeder produced arrangements like "Elleen Asthore, No. 2 of a Series of Original Irish Melodies" (1841) with words by John Inman. In one of those helpful explanations which sometimes preface sheet music on exotic subjects during this period, Inman notes:

> It may not be inexpedient to mention, for the benefit of such as have not read many of the "Irish novels," that Asthore is one of the numerous synonims [sic] for darling that slip so smoothly and expressively, from the tongues of susceptible Irishmen, and belongs to the same class as Vourneen, Acushla, &c.

The lyrics present a standard narrative of courtship, beginning with praise of the beloved's beauty, a description of a first meeting at "Donnybrook Fair," the first dance, and a pledge of eternal fidelity:

> My love it was honest and faithful and true,
> And better than that, 'twas a winning love too;
> Soon the day will come round with the Priest to the fore,
> And for life she is mine this dear Ellen Asthore.

The fleeting use of Gaelic, the rural setting, and the mention of a priest are all token references to ethnicity. Authenticity, as the title informs us, resides in

276

EXAMPLE 8.4   James Maeder, arr., "Elleen Asthore" (Boston: E. H. Wade, 1841)

the melody, which is entirely pentatonic (Ex. 8.4) and has much in common with many other Irish folk melodies, though Maeder does not list his source for this particular tune (it may derive from his own experience, since he was born in Dublin). His accompaniment has the same droning bass as Moran's "Barney Brallaghan," another clue to the coloristic nature of the music.

As late as 1865 American-born lyricists and composers like Mrs. M. A. Kidder and Henry Tucker still engaged in folkish serenades like "Open the Door, Dear Arrah, for Me" (1865). Tucker, composer of widely popular numbers like "Weeping, Sad and Lonely, or When This Cruel War Is Over" (1862) and "Sweet Genevieve" (1869), writes in a distinctly American idiom for "Open the Door." But Kidder's lyrics intimate the rustic Irish serenade depicted on the cover (Illus. 8.1). The song hails from an early production of Dion Boucicault's *Arrah-Na-Pogue,* set in County Wicklow. Mrs. Kidder meant her song as an interpolation for Act I, Scene 2, when Sean comes to his fiancée's "dure" just before his wedding and "sings through the keyhole":[11]

> So ope the door softly, dear Arrah, for me,
>   For without it is dreary and cold;

11. The cues comes from Dion Boucicault, *Arrah-Na-Pogue, or The Wicklow Wedding,* Seamus De Burca, ed. (Dublin, n.d.), 10. Kidder and Tucker's song replaces Boucicault's less elaborate number.

> And I miss the bright warmth in my disolate heart,
> That reflicts from your tresses of gold.

Unlike suitors in contemporary Italianate serenades, this young man is ultimately successful: Arrah remonstrates after this song, "I'll strike back, ye vil-
lian! *(He kisses her; she pushes him away).* Isn't this putry treatment for a
lone woman?" [12]

Kidder's lyrics for "Open the Door," Moran's accompaniment for "Barney
Brallaghan," and Maeder's arrangement for "Elleen Asthore" all looked in
their different ways to the rural environs of the old country and sought the
"characteristic" quality of ethnicity in folkloric authenticity or in the folklike.
Sporadic examples of this genre continued to appear in later decades, and famous composers occasionally tried their hands at the genre, as did Frank Howard in "O'Googerty's Wedding" (1869) and later Henry Clay Work in "Mac
O'Macorkity" (1877).

While Irish exoticism was the most piquant, Scottish exoticism was the most
widely imitated in the first decades of the nineteenth century, if the sheer bulk
of surviving sheet music is any indication. [13] From the eighteenth century onward Scottish folk songs had been well represented in collections and in ballad
opera. This tradition is reflected in nineteenth-century songs like "The Ill
Wife" (ca. 1816), in which a husband complains in pentatonic melody and
Scottish brogue of his mate's cooking and nagging. A second tradition, pseudo-
Scottish songs, had been all the rage in the British commercial parks called
pleasure gardens during the eighteenth century, and according to Hamm some
of these pieces by James Hook enjoyed immense popularity in the United States
around the turn of the nineteenth. [14] Pieces like Mary Ann Pownall's "Jemmy
of the Glen" (ca. 1796), the plaint of an abandoned country girl, [15] or Benjamin
Carr's "My Jockey" (1820), a song of courtship sung supposedly from a
woman's point of view, were mined from this vein. Interest in the Highlands
as an exotic wilderness also received a great boost around the turn of the century from the poetry of Robert Burns and later from Sir Walter Scott's writings.

Songs like "Balquither" (ca. 1820), arranged by Fredrick Fest, usually intimate folkloric authenticity on the title page with phrases like "A Popular
Scotch Air." Many of these pieces are only folkish, but they succeed well
enough in their masquerade. Fest begins with a symphony featuring stereotypi-

---

12. Ibid., 11.

13. I do not mean to contradict Hamm's assertion that Moore's *Irish Melodies* were more
popular in the United States than Burns's *Scots Musical Museum.* But in my survey of sheet-music
collections, American songs on Scottish ethnicity outnumber by far those involving Irish ethnicity
during the first four decades of the century. Perhaps the widespread availability of Moore's collection made additions to the Irish repertory by other composers superfluous. See Hamm, *Yesterdays,* 59–61.

14. Ibid.

15. A copy appears in Judith Tick, *American Women Composers Before 1870* (Ann Arbor, MI,
1983), 60–61.

EXAMPLE 8.5 Fredrick Fest, arr., "Balquither" (Philadelphia: G. E. Blake, [ca. 1820])

cal "bagpipe" accompaniment—open fifths droning in the bass for the first two measures. And the second phrase (Ex. 8.5) also includes an obligatory snap (now Scottish in this context) for the word "bonnie." Aside from these features, there is nothing particularly unusual about the musical language of "Balquither," but the lyrics take up this slack by using a few words of dialect and combining them with a description of an idyllic, wild land:

> While the lads o' the South
>   Toil for bare war'ly treasure,
> To the lads o' the North
>   Ev'ry day brings its pleasure:
> Though simple are the joys
>   The brave Highlander possesses,
> Yet he feels no annoys,
>   For he fears no distresses.

The lyrics do not embrace reality but seek to escape it—

> To our dear native scenes,
>   Let us journey together,

279

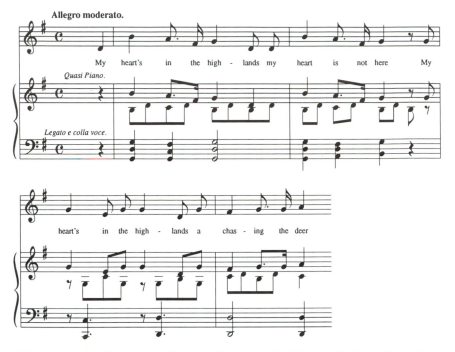

EXAMPLE 8.6   Henry Russell, "My Heart's in the Highlands" (New York: J. L. Hewitt, 1837)

> Where glad innocence reigns
> 'Mang the braes o' Balquither.

—because they appeal not to the patriotic sentiments or homesickness of Scottish immigrants in the United States, but because they engage a larger audience partaking in the Romantic fantasy of a rural paradise. Thomas Van Dyke Wiesenthal sketched a similar portrait in "The Ingle Side" (ca. 1825), as did Charles Feist in "The Scotch Harper" (ca. 1830), an anonymous composer in "My Ain Fire Side" (ca. 1830), and many others, including those in Great Britain who set the fashion.

Henry Russell contributed a well-known example of this genre in his version of Robert Burns's "My Heart's in the Highlands" (1837). The background of this song is instructive, for Russell appropriated its tune from a setting (imported in 1837 by the firm of John F. Nunns, Philadelphia) of the same poem by Henry Phillips, a British singer and composer. Russell extends and recasts the melody, polishing vocal ornaments and adding a highly elaborate accompaniment that exhibits no folkish elements at all (see Ex. 8.6). In this case "authenticity" resides entirely with the use of Burns's idealized vision, rendered in part from Russell's sheet music:

EXAMPLE 8.7   Charles Edward Horn, "Let Us Haste to Kelvin Grove" (New York: Dubois & Stodart, 1827)

> Oh! farewell to the highlands, farewell to the north,
> The birth place of valor, the country of worth;
> Wherever I wander wherever I rove,
> The hills of the highlands forever I love.

Ethnic identity dwells in the native land, and its expression depends here on lyrics by a native Scotsman. Russell (under the influence of Phillips) invokes the subject for its exotic appeal; to him it is both a beautiful fantasy and a curiosity.

Idealized climes also formed the perfect surroundings for idealized romance, as in Fredrick Fest's "Dearest Lassie" (ca. 1824), in Richard L. Williams's "Kind Robin Looes Me," or in Charles Edward Horn's "Let Us Haste to Kelvin Grove" (1827), based on an earlier song (1824) by the British composer John Sims. Horn, a recent British immigrant when "Kelvin Grove" appeared, indulges mock-Scottish tones that manifest themselves most obviously at cadences on the words "bonnie lassie, O" (see Ex. 8.7). The peculiar slowing of rhythmic motion is meant to emphasize the one Scottish phrase amidst a text that is otherwise quite ordinarily genteel:

But I soon must bid adieu, bonnie lassie, O,
To this fairy scene and you, bonnie lassie, O,
   To the streamlet winding clear,
   To the fragrant scented brier,
E'en to thee, of all most dear, bonnie lassie, O,
And when on a distant shore, bonnie lassie, O,
Should I fall mid'st battle's roar, bonnie lassie, O,
   Wilt thou Ellen, when you hear
   Of thy lover on his bier,
To his mem'ry shed a tear, bonnie lassie, O.

Lovers often leave the fabled land to fight for king and country in these mildly folkish songs. They follow the tradition of the extraordinarily popular "Blue Bells of Scotland" ("Oh! where and oh where is your Highland Laddie gone? He's gone to fight the French for King George upon the throne"), often attributed in sheet music to an English actress, Dorothea Bland Jordan.[16] Most of the songs rely on mock-Scottish qualities—a few words of dialect, a Scottish phrase, a snap here or there—to invoke the "characteristic," but they invoke it all the same.

In addition to mock-Scottish songs, authentic folk songs on the topic of courtship continued to appear in arrangements, as well. T. T. Craven provided an accompaniment for "Jock O' Hazeldean" (ca. 1830), a traditional song to which Walter Scott added three stanzas; there were similar settings of "Comin' Thro' the Rye" and "The Highlander's Bride" (ca. 1830). And even though the Scottish craze died down in the 1840s, as late as 1859 the fashion of folk-loric authenticity persisted in George Frederick Root's arrangement of "Oh Are Ye Sleeping Maggie" (1859). The tune for the chorus of "Maggie" (Ex. 8.8) much resembles a familiar folk song, "What Do You Do with a Drunken Sailor," and must surely originate in the oral repertory. It has no raised leading tone (no C sharp moving to the tonic D), and it features "Scottish snaps" in profusion. The text, laced with dialect throughout, relates the episodes in a serenade:

Abune my breath I dinna speak,
For fear I'll rouse your wankrife daddie,
Could's the blast upon my cheek.
Rise, O rise, my bonnie laddie!

As this last line (spoken by the woman) suggests, the suitor gains entrance and exults in the final chorus:

16. The text greatly resembles one by Annie McVicar Grant. For a history of the song see Helen Kendrick Johnson et al., eds., *The World's Best Music: Famous Songs and Those Who Made Them* (New York, 1902), II, 426.

EXAMPLE 8.8   George Frederick Root, arr., "Oh Are Ye Sleeping Maggie" (Chicago: Root & Cady, 1859)

Now since you're waking Maggie
Now since your waking Maggie
What care I for howlet's cry,
For boortrie bank or warlock craigie?

The outcome of Scottish serenades, like Irish ones, tends to reverse the result of genteel serenades, where lover and beloved remain at a chaste, chivalric distance. Set unambiguously in the Scottish highlands, this piece possesses both folk melody and brogue. It is a triumph of the coloristic and idiosyncratic, tied to a rustic, foreign locale.

It seems incredible that there should be so little popular sheet music concerning German ethnicity in early-nineteenth-century America. Speakers of the language (from the areas of present-day Germany, Austria, Switzerland, Czechoslovakia, Poland, and the Baltic states) came in very large numbers to the colonies, especially to Pennsylvania where they nearly formed a plurality of settlers (33 percent in the 1790 census as opposed to 35 percent British).[17] People of German stock were the largest minority in the United States around

17. Daniels, *Coming to America*, 67.

1800. But then, songs on ethnicity did not reflect societal reality; they resulted from a Romantic vision dictated by a predominantly British culture obsessed with the exoticism of Scotland and Ireland. The rare lyrics involving the German "characteristic" were usually set in Switzerland or the Tyrol, locations comparably picturesque to the Scottish Highlands.

None of these idealized songs addressed the issue of ethnic relations in the United States directly, but their coloristic nature had definite implications for the American view of ethnicity. Culture in these pieces was rooted in foreign climes and ingrained in basic nature. Though the songs were not intended xenophobically and though they rarely condemned foreign ways (even when comic), they implied a kind of immiscibility among people who constantly looked back to the lands of their origins. In the early nineteenth century this may not have been as destructive as it might first appear, even in a country populated by different ethnic groups. The United States during this period has been called "a society without a core."[18] As late as 1831 the density of population was extremely low (13 million people occupying a territory of 1,750,000 square miles). The central government had little influence on everyday life: only 666 government workers resided in Washington, D.C., and the remaining 10,825 federal employees mainly operated the postal service (along with a few customs houses and embassies).[19] Power was localized, and decentralization "enabled local ethnic clusters to keep a certain distance from one another, particularly where economic competition could be acute."[20] The romanticized notion in popular song of an exotic ethnicity tied inextricably to the old country seems to have caused little conflict under these circumstances.

The "Second Immigration" and Transition

This relatively placid ethnic scene changed with the "second immigration," starting in the 1820s and increasing exponentially through the 1840s. The tide began in the Northeast with the Irish: between 1820 and 1830 only 54,338 arrived on American shores, but 207,381 came between 1831 and 1840, and the flood in the next decade saw the immigration of 780,719 Irish men and women, mostly to the cities.[21] The rural Midwest was the major recipient of a similarly large group of German immigrants, growing from 7,729 between 1820 and 1830 to 152,454 from 1831 to 1840 and reaching its prewar peak at 951,667 between 1851 and 1860.[22] This heavy influx of mainly Catholic foreigners so alarmed the largely Protestant native population that it gave rise to

---

18. Robert H. Wiebe, *The Search for Order, 1877–1920* (New York, 1967), 12.
19. Higham, *Send These to Me,* 182.
20. Ibid., 185.
21. Daniels, *Coming to America,* 129–30.
22. Ibid., 146.

a powerful and extensive revolt against immigration and played no small role in reconfiguring American politics. Secret fraternal organizations formed, like the Order of United Americans and the Order of the Star Spangled Banner, with members pledged to vote for native-born, Protestant candidates and enjoined to respond to non-members, "I know nothing." The Know Nothings elected many representatives to state legislatures during the height of xenophobic frenzy in the early 1850s and ultimately destabilized the Whig party. While disavowing nativism, the newly formed Republicans picked up some of the pieces and formed discreet alliances with the Know Nothings.[23]

Songwriters could not ignore the new waves of foreign-born Americans. The long history of interest in the "characteristic" may have contributed to nativist fear by focusing on the immiscibility of ethnicity.[24] And though few signs of Know Nothing sentiments appeared directly in popular song, composers and lyricists seemed loathe to set the rural and piquant aside. The combination of old aesthetic and new circumstance resulted in a species of transitional songs that actually mentioned immigrants but still saw them tied irrevocably to their native lands.

Since the major houses of music publishing resided mainly in the East at the time, these pieces focused on the Irish who settled predominantly in that region. In Eliza Cook and Charles Horn's "Norah McShane" (1841) the male immigrant has sailed over "the big sea" to make his fortune, but he sighs for his homeland and vows to return to the beloved named in the title. Mrs. Price Blackwood and William R. Dempster contribute the "Lament of the Irish Emigrant" (1843), "Portraying," their helpful preface explains, "the feelings of an Irish peasant previous to his leaving home, calling up the scenes of his youth under the painful reflection of having buried his wife and child, and what his feelings will be in America." Dempster (b. 1808), a British immigrant, played an active role in the musical life of New York as a singer of Scottish and English "ballads" (popular songs).[25] Though his music contains a few "Scottish" snaps (used here for their generally folkish connotations), he does not adopt an "authentic" style for this piece, choosing an American declamatory argot with a few Italianate touches (like an extensive cadenza at the end of each verse; see Ex. 8.9). Blackwood's lyrics make no concessions to dialect and adopt a rather high tone:

> I'm sitting on the stile, Mary
> Where we sat side by side,

---

23. A very good summary of this period in American history appears as part of James McPherson's chapter "Slavery, Rum, and Romanism" in *Battle Cry of Freedom: The Civil War Era* (New York, 1988), 117–44.

24. John Higham sees Romantic concepts of ethnicity at the root of nativism, in *Strangers in the Land: Patterns of American Nativism, 1860–1925*, 2d ed. (New York, 1975), 131–35.

25. Grace D. Yerbury, *Song in America from Early Times to About 1850* (Metuchen, NJ, 1971), 259–60.

EXAMPLE 8.9   William R. Dempster, "Lament of the Irish Emigrant" (Boston: Wm. H. Oakes, 1843)

> On a bright May morning long ago,
> When first you were my bride.
> The corn was springing fresh and green,
> And the lark sang loud and high,
> And the red was on thy lip, Mary
> And the love light in your eye.

In successive verses the speaker tells of the spot where he buried his wife and child, and concludes that there is nothing left for him in his native land. Though the song still looks back with nostalgia, it directly addresses the immigrant's reasons for leaving and discards the musical "characteristic" in favor of an amalgamated style.

Blackwood and Demptser's "Lament" must have struck a chord, for it elicited "The Answer to the Lament of the Irish Emigrant" (1844) from John S. Murphy and T. Bissel, in which Mary promises to watch over her husband's peregrinations. "The Irish Maiden's Lament" (1847) by Miss. S. C. Cobb and F. W. Paisely provided another variation, giving a combination of oppression and misfortune as reasons for emigration. L. V. H. Crosby's "The Emigrant's

Farewell'' (1852) also recounted the effects of overcrowding in the old country. First disease overcame the young;

> Then the famine came stalking with gaunt bony finger;
> And our landlord was ruthless and pitiless sure;
> And sweet Kathleen, our blue-eyed—but why should we linger,
> Recounting our sorrows—who cares for the poor?
> Yes, God careth for us. Then no more repining.
> Though we fly from this desolate country away
> To the free happy West; as each day is declining
> For the land of our fathers we'll fervently pray.

Crosby (ca. 1824–84) organized the Boston Harmoneons in 1845 and probably wrote this number for the minstrel stage.[26] Its musical vocabulary comes from the normal stock of mid-century, as does "Kathleen Mavourneen" (in many versions during the 1850s), attributed to Mrs. Crawford and Nicholas F. Crouch. This song shows a man leaving his beloved in the rural climes of Ireland, a theme Mrs. Crawford used again in "Kathleen Aroon" (ca. 1855). Even George Cooper and Stephen Foster indulged this conceit in "Sweet Emerald Isle That I Love So Well" (1864). Most of these songs combine a depiction of a rustic countryside, the grief of parting, and a longing for the old country. But they speak with the voice of those who have already become disillusioned with their old lives: this genre begins to idealize the promise of the New World as much as it does the beauty of the old.

The transitional view of Irish immigrants reached the height of fashion in the period around the Civil War. One of the best examples is "Pat Malloy" (1865) from the pen of Dion Boucicault (1820–90), with music by Dan Bryant (1833–75) of minstrel fame. Boucicault (or Bourcicault as he appears in this sheet music) immigrated to the United States via France around 1856 and wrote a series of plays on Irish themes with a distinctly patriotic bent (he set *Arrah-Na-Pogue,* mentioned earlier, amidst the rebellion of 1798).[27] Bryant, leader of the troupe that premiered "Dixie's Land," was Irish-American (born Daniel Webster O'Brien), and made quite a reputation playing in Irish dramas. According to Edward LeRoy Rice, "in May 1865, [Bryant] sailed for Europe, and in Dublin, Ireland, and Liverpool, England, he gave several performances of Celtic characters."[28] Boucicault's lyrics tell the three stages of Pat Malloy's story, beginning with his reasons for emigrating, spoken by his mother:

26. Edward Le Roy Rice, *Monarchs of Minstrelsy, from "Daddy" Rice to Date* (New York, 1911), 50.

27. See Joyce Anne Flynn, "Ethnicity After Sea-Change: The Irish Dramatic Tradition in Nineteenth-Century American Drama," (Ph.D. dissertation, Harvard University, 1985), 20–30. Boucicault collaborated with E. H. House in providing the play with a famous patriotic song, "Wearing of the Green" (New York: H. B. Dodworth, 1865), a variation on a traditional Irish folk song.

28. *Monarchs of Minstrelsy,* 88.

"I've fourteen children Pat" says she "which heav'n to me has sent,
But childer ain't like pigs you know, they can't pay the rent!"
She gave me ev'ry shilling there was in the till,
And kiss'd me fifty times or more, as if she'd never get her fill. . . .

As in other transitional songs, we find a modicum of realism here: the Irish
leave because of expanding population (residents of the island doubled in number between 1791 and 1841).[29] Pat (depicted on the cover in appropriate rags,
Illus. 8.2) moves to Britain in the second verse but finds the economic climate
there unrewarding. The third verse relates his ultimate solution:

From Ireland to America across the seas I roam,
And every shilling that I got, ah sure I sent it home;
Me mother couldn't write but oh there came from Father Boyce:
"Oh, heaven bless you" Pat she says—I hear me mother's voice!
But now I'm going home again, as poor as I began,
To make a happy girl of Moll and sure I think I can;
Me pockets they are empty but me heart is fill'd wid joy:
For ould Ireland is me country, and me name is Pat Malloy.

Boucicault addresses the plight of Irish immigrants squarely enough, but still
portrays them as longing for the magical country of their birth (though ironically, the Irish were among the least likely to re-emigrate, and this included
Boucicault himself, who could not return for political reasons). Bryant, an
Irish-American, feels no inclincation to use authenticity in support of Boucicault's nostalgia. The melody (with accompaniment by John P. Cooke, Ex.
8.10) divides the long lines of poetry into the standard, short, two-bar phrases
of American minstrelsy. Bryant avoids the syncopations of blackface but also
the stereotypical "snaps" and uneven rhythms of "ethnic" style. And his melody does not even hint at an unusual scale. The "characteristic" has disappeared from the music in this song, but its lyrics still end in the old notion of
immiscibility (marked by Pat's return to "ould Ireland"). Other songs in this
vein include "My Love Nell" (1867) by Wm. Carelton, about a female immigrant, "Katy McFerran" (1867) by Will S. Hays, and "Kathleen Machree"
(1868) by Frank Stanley.

A faint hint of the transitional Irish immigrant appears as late as "I'll Take
You Home Again Kathleen" (1876)[30] by Thomas P. Westendorf. Westendorf
(1848?–1923) apparently wrote the song while teaching in a school for delin-
quent boys in Plainfield, Indiana, and the words come in answer to "Barney,
Take Me Home Again" by George W. Persley, a friend and collaborator.[31]

29. Daniels, *Coming to America,* 128–29.
30. Ibid., 83–86.
31. The complete story of this song and an fairly extenstive biography of Westendorf appears
in Richard S. Hill's "Getting Kathleen Home Again," *Notes* 5 (1948), 338–53.

EXAMPLE 8.10   Dan Bryant, "Pat Malloy" (New York: Wm. A. Pond & Co., 1865)

Westendorf does not give anything in the way of specific location to identify this immigrant's rural origins:

> I'll take you home again, Kathleen,
> Across the ocean wild and wide,
> To where your heart has ever been,
> Since first you were my bonny bride.
> The roses all have left your cheek,
> I've watched them fade away and die;
> Your voice is sad when e'er you speak,
> And tears bedim your loving eyes.

The general mention of the sea voyage and the Irish name "Kathleen" is all the information Westendorf provides as a frame of reference. His music falls in the generic style of the seventies: short phrases, slightly chromatic melody, fuller piano accompaniment than we generally find in the sixties, and just a touch of bathos in some mild dissonances resolved downward (for instance on "across"). The idealized old country has been replaced by nostalgia for "old friends" and a "mother's humble cot," possibly in order to make the song more generally appealing.

Popular songs about German ethnicity during this period appear seldom in

289

sheet music. But one of these rare songs, "Der Deitcher's Dog" (1864)[32] by Septimus Winner, became well known under the title "Oh where, Oh where ish mine little dog gone." Winner's setting still clings to the "characteristic": the melody comes from a well-known German folk song, "Zu Lauterbach hab' ich mein Strumpf verloren." And Richard Jackson suggests that its nonsense chorus (to the syllables "Tra la la . . . ") imitates yodelling.[33] Not only does this "comic ballad" employ dialect, it cites the German love of drinking—

> I loves mine lager 'tish very goot beer,
> Oh where, Oh where can he be . . .
> But mit no money I cannot drink here.
> Oh where, Oh where ish he.

—that formed a constituent part of Know Nothing objections to both the German and Irish (temperance came to form part of their platform). In other verses the German character looks back to the land of his birth with nostalgia, and expresses something of his indiscriminate tastes in cuisine:

> Un sasage ish goot, bolonie of course,
> Oh where, Oh where can he be . . .
> Dey makes um mit dog und dey makes em mit horse,
> I guess de makes em mit he.

Though there had been longstanding resentment of the large German population of Pennsylvania where Winner lived, his song is not in the end deeply derisive. Other songs begin to take note of the Germans around this time, including "Ile, or Vay Down in Bennsylvanny" (1865) by Hans Schmidt, "Keiser's Dog," (1869) written in imitation of Winner by Gus Williams and Eddie Fox, and even an isolated contribution by Will S. Hays, "I Don't Can Tolt You Vy" (1870), about ethnic courtship. All of these songs were comic, and their nativist leanings were mild and indirect.

Explicit mention of mid-century nativism in popular song came, ironically, after its political importance had waned as a result of a temporary drop in the rate of immigration and because sectional conflict increasingly commanded the nation's attention. The Civil War helped to win more tolerance of immigrants in the urban, industrial North, a process about which one song written during the period gives striking and direct testimony. We know little about its author, Kathleen O'Neil, save that the cover of her song, "No Irish Need Apply" (1863), bills her as an "Irish Vocalist." The title of her song originated in an advertisement from the London *Times,* according to a preface reprinted in the

32. Reprinted in Richard Jackson's *Popular Songs of Nineteenth-Century America* (New York, 1976), 57–60.
33. Ibid., 268.

sheet music: "WANTED.—A smart active girl to do the general house work of a large family; one who can cook, clean plate, and get up fine linen preferred. N.B.—No Irish need apply." The phrase was common enough in the United States as well,[34] but O'Neil used the North's anti-British sentiment to suggest that the catch-phrase was un-American. She combined this psychological persuasion with a timely appeal to Irish heroism in combat:

> Now what have they against us, sure the world knows Paddy's brave,
> For he's helped to fight their battles, both on land and on the wave,
> At the storming of Sebastopol, and beneath an Indian sky,
> Pat raised his head, for their General said, "All Irish might apply."
> Do you mind Lieutenant Massy, when he raises the battle-cry?
> Then are they not ashamed to write, "No Irish need Apply"?

Several other verses give details of Irish prowess in war, prominently mentioning the name "Sheridan," among others. In the last verse O'Neil turns her gaze deliberately away from Europe to the present situation in America:

> Ah! but now I'm in the land of the "Glorious" and "Free,"
> And proud I am to own it, a country dear to me,
> I can see by your kind faces, that you will not deny
> A place in your hearts for Kathleen, and All Irish may apply.
> Then long may the Union flourish, and ever may it be
> A pattern to the world, and the "Home of Liberty!"

For this patriotic statement O'Neil adopts the most American of musical languages drawn from the repeated-note patter of the minstrel stage (see Ex. 8.11). This song begins to deal with present realities instead of the romanticized past.

The Irish and Germans often formed whole brigades in the Army of the Republic, giving the impression of solidarity with the northern cause among ethnic groups.[35] When sons from the "varied immigrant North of America" went off to war, "parents spent less time thinking about the far-off land of their fathers, more in thinking about the land of their children," Marcus Lee Hansen observes. "When the war ended, foreign languages and foreign customs had not disappeared, but ideals had changed. All who lived in America, alien-born and native-born, were resolved to become one people."[36] Hansen's

---

34. See Daniels, *Coming to America,* 131.

35. Though in point of fact, the Irish were under-represented among the Union troops as were German Catholics, both of which groups tended to have Democratic allegiances and to oppose emancipation. German Protestants were staunch Republicans. See McPherson, *Battle Cry of Freedom,* 217–23, 606–7.

36. Marcus Lee Hansen, *The Atlantic Migration 1607–1860. A History of the Continuing Settlement of the United States* (Cambridge, MA, 1940), 306.

EXAMPLE 8.11   Kathleen O'Neil, "No Irish Need Apply" (Cleveland: S. Brainard & Co., 1863)

vision of sudden unanimity may seem exaggerated. But placed in an extended temporal framework and qualified by a more precise notion of just what unity means, the generalization finds some resonance in American popular song.

The Realities of the Urban America

Before Americans could "become one people" they needed to recognize the actual situation of the various ethnic groups dwelling in the United States. The seventies, sometimes labeled "the age of confidence,"[37] proved a good time to address ethnic reality in the America. And because the industry of popular music resided almost exclusively in urban climes, songwriters naturally chose to deal with the immigrants dwelling in large cities. Two main groups, the Irish and the Germans, attracted the bulk of attention, though as lyricists and composers carried their work into the more troubled eighties, they began to take cognizance of the Jews and Italians who arrived in growing numbers toward the end of the century.

37. John Higham, *Strangers in the Land*, 12–34.

Chief among the songwriters dealing with European ethnicity was the team of Edward ("Ned") Harrigan and David Braham, who published over the course of the seventies, eighties, and nineties almost 200 pieces dealing with ethnic and racial interaction in New York City. Harrigan (1844–1911) was Irish-American, born on the Lower East Side of New York in the working-class neighborhood of Corlear's Hook (then known as Cork Row).[38] He began his career in blackface, teaming up with Tony Hart in 1871 during a run in Chicago. The duo soon became famous for ethnic impersonations and established itself in New York, where the short skits Harrigan had written for the act developed into full-length plays. For two decades he was an extremely successful actor-manager-playwright, directing his own company and owning a theater during part of the period. Braham (1838–1905) emigrated with his brothers from England in 1856. All of them took jobs as fiddlers in the minstrel theaters of New York. David would become the orchestra director for Harrigan's company, and Harrigan married Braham's daughter, Annie.

Harrigan based his songs about ethnicity on the neighborhood centered in the Sixth Ward (around Five Points at the junction of Baxter, Worth, and Park streets). The area was said to contain in one census of the time "only ten native-born white Americans . . . as compared with eight hundred and twelve Irish, two hundred and eighteen Germans, a hundred and eighty-nine Poles, a hundred and eighty-six Italians, thirty-nine Negroes, and a scattering of unclassifiable persons . . . ."[39] Harrigan's chief affections lay with the Irish, whose life on the Lower East Side he recorded in songs like "The Babies on Our Block" (1879):[40]

> If you want for information,
> Or in need of merriment,
> Come over with me socially
> To Murphy's tenement;
> He owns a row of houses
> In the First ward, near the dock,
> Where Ireland's represented
> By the Babies on our Block.

These Irish men, women, and their American offspring by no means forget their origins, but they think of them only in the context of their new urban life:

> There's the Phalens and the Whalens
> From the sweet Dunochadee,

---

38. Most of this biographical information comes from Richard Moody, *Ned Harrigan: From Corlear's Hook to Herald Square* (Chicago, 1980).

39. E. J. Kahn, Jr., "Profiles," *The New Yorker* (March 26, 1955), 40.

40. Reproduced in Stanley Appelbaum's *Show Songs from "The Black Crook" to "The Red Mill"* (New York, 1974), 17–20.

They are sitting on the railings
With their children on their knee,
All gossiping and talking
With their neighbors in a flock,
Singing "Little Sally Waters,"
With the Babies on our Block.

In fact, the idealized, rustic life of the old country appears rarely in Harrigan's songs. He celebrates the promise of the New World for "the poor, the workers, and the great middle class . . . [whose] trials and troubles, hope and fears, joy and sorrows, are more varied and more numerous than those of the Upper Ten."[41] And that promise is fulfilled, Harrigan suggests in the third verse of "Babies," by upward mobility and natural talent:

It's good-morning to you landlord;
Come, now how are you today?
When Patrick Murphy, Esquire,
Comes down the alley way,
With his shiny silken beaver,
He's as solid as a rock,
The envy of the neighbors' boys
A-living on our Block.
There's the Brannons and the Gannons,
Far-down and Connaught men,
Quite easy with the shovel
And so handy with the Pen. . . .

For this "photograph of life to-day in the Empire City"[42] Braham supplies a patter song that reflects the professional polish of the minstrel theater in which he had over twenty years experience by the time he wrote this music (Ex. 8.12). The repeated notes, graceful use of a few simple chords with a bit of chromaticism at cadences, and natural declamation of text announce that this is a realistic portrait of an American scene from the seventies.

The Irish characters in Harrigan and Braham songs are not interested so much in assimilation into American society as they are in participation or finding a comfortable and secure niche. The first step in this process, as O'Neil's "No Irish" suggested earlier, was serving in the armed forces (in fact, Harrigan's older brother, William, had died in the Civil War). "The Gallant '69th' " (1875) shows, *"Allo Marciale,"* immigrants retaining their ethnic identity, even as they fight for the North:

41. "American Playwrights on the American Drama," *Harper's Weekly* 33 (Feb. 2, 1889), 98.
42. Ibid., 97.

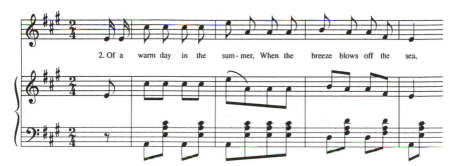

EXAMPLE 8.12   David Braham, "The Babies on Our Block" (New York: Wm. A. Pond, 1879)

> Should America call on her soldier boys,
> To the front we'd boldly go;
> For a righteous cause, our Nation's laws,
> Give battle to the foe.
> We'll ne'er forget old Ireland,
> But keep our powder dry,
> "Faugh a ballagh" our cry, clear the way,
> To conquer or to die.

Participation led to success and rising status. "Paddy Duffy's Cart" (1881)[43] lists the fate of boyhood companions through successive verses:

> Oh, there was Tommy Dobson, now a senator;
> Billy Flyn and Johnny Glyn, oh they were kill'd in war:
>
> Oh, there was Henry Gleason, now a millionaire;
> Curly Rob and White Bob, they're living on the air:
>
> Oh, there was Larry Thomson was a chum of mine,
> Lemmy Freer and Sandy Greer, they died in forty-nine:
> All merry boyish comrades, recollections bring,
> All seated there in Duffy's cart on summer nights to sing.

The gold rush, the Civil War, running for political office, and financial success form the better memories of Harrigan's characters. In response to the sentimental sketch Braham provides a much more lyrical setting than he does for "Babies on Our Block." This Irish-American nostalgia for the urban scene in which the second generation grew up is a frequent feature of Harrigan songs, appearing in numbers like "My Dad's Dinner Pail" (1883) or "Maggie Mur-

43. Appelbaum, *Show Songs*, 28–33.

phy's Home'' (in fashionable waltz-time, 1890). And because these numbers emphasize the life of the immigrant per se rather than fond memories of the old country, they rarely elicit "authentic" or mock-folkish responses from Braham (exceptions may be the minor mode of "The Widow Nolan's Goat"[44] from 1881 or a few brief hints at pentatonicism in "My Dad's Dinner Pail"). Even when a composer of this generation invokes a sentiment like "Remember Boy, You're Irish" (by W. J. Scanlan, 1886),[45] he does not suggest a return to the old country, and his musical style falls squarely in the American idiom.

Because Harrigan espoused and practiced realism in his plays and songs, he did not omit Irish vices from his repertory. The most prominent of these was drinking to excess, which occasioned comments in the last verse of Harrigan and Braham's most famous song, "The Mulligan Guard" (1873).[46] The song ridicules the paramilitary social clubs called "target companies" of which there were "at least three hundred" in New York, according to Harrigan.[47] These groups would don fancy uniforms (see Illus. 8.3), march to a rural area, practice shooting, drink, and return in disorder. Thus Harrigan's last verse in dialect for Braham's spirited march (Ex. 8.13):

> When we got home at night boys,
> The divil a bite we'd ate,
> We'd all set up and drink a sup
> Of whiskey strong and nate.
> Thin we'd all march home together,
> As slippery as lard,
> The solid min would all fall in,
> And march with the Mulligan Guard.

This same proclivity for whisky provided the central conceit for Harrigan and Braham's "John Riley's Always Dry" (1881), "I Never Drink Behind the Bar" (1882), "My Little Side Door" (1884), "Have One with Me" (1887), and "Paddy and His Sweet Poteen" (1889).

The Irish inclination to tipple carried over into songs like Joseph Flynn's "Down Went McGinty" (1889),[48] in which a hapless Irishman undergoes a series of tribulations to a "Tempo di Schottische." After he takes a pratfall to win a five-dollar bet:

> From the hospital Mac went home,
> When they fix'd his broken bones,

44. Ibid., 24–27.
45. Ibid., 34–37.
46. Ibid., 13–16.
47. "American Playwrights," 97.
48. Reprinted in Robert A. Fremont's *Favorite Songs of the Nineties* (New York, 1973), 74–77.

EXAMPLE 8.13   David Braham, "The Mulligan Guard" (New York: Wm. A. Pond & Co., 1873)

> To find he was the father of a child;
> So to celebrate it right,
> His friends he went to invite,
> And he soon was drinking whisky fast and wild;
> Then he waddled down the street
> In his Sunday suit so neat,
> Holding up his head as proud as John the Great,
> But in the sidewalk was a hole,
> To receive a ton of coal,
> That McGinty never saw until just too late.

The further repercussions take McGinty to jail and then land in him in the river, where he drowns. Despite this ending, the song is comic, written by an Irishman, and takes its musical cue from Braham's patter accompaniments for Harrigan's songs. Other songs in this vein included Frank Hayden's "Just Pay Our Respects to Maguiness" (1886) and Charles Horowitz's "McKenny's Silver Wedding" (1886), among many others.

The Irish talent for politics provided Harrigan's other main target. "The Aldermanic Board" (1885) finds a chorus of politicians singing their own praises, while "Old Boss Barry" (1888) specifically mentions the graft of a ward captain. When Harrigan's quintessential Irish-American, Dan Mulligan, runs for office in *The Mulligan Guard Nominee* (1880), he tries to win the vote with promises of patronage for everyone but the German partisans of his eternal rival, the "Dutch" butcher, Gustavus Lochmuller (though they are both "democrats"). In the last verse of "Hang the Mulligan Banner Up" (1880), Mulligan sings:

> Then concentrate each delegate, oh, rally, rally all!
> With might and main, oh, once again, we'll take the City Hall!
> When in the aldermanic chair bold Daniel takes his seat,
> We'll capture all the patronage, and lashings for to eat.
>
> *[Chorus:]*
> Then hang the Mulligan banner up so boldly to the winds,
> Now give it room, the Mulligan boom,
> We'll leave the Dutch behind;
> All Africans, Italians, and Scandinavians,
> Come, rally round your leader, boys, bold Daniel Mulligan.

The patronage Dan has in mind, we discover in another song, will engage supporters to count the sparrows flying in Central Park. Like all politicians in Harrigan's dramas, Dan turns out to be garrulous and prone to malaprops: "Fellow citizens and friends of the Mulligan champagne, there is no power or oratory or forensic debility in any Dutch Hessian like Lochmuller to defeat me."[49]

The corrupt politician, the bibulous Irishman—these, along with the more positive pictures, were all stereotypes for which Harrigan made no apologies. Drama and popular song demanded ethnicity be represented by a group of finite characters. In Harrigan's view the shame would have been personal indictments: "Though I use types and never individuals, I try to be as realistic as possible." An artist had to portray all aspects of human nature:

> In the realism which I endeavor to employ I believe in being truthful to the laws which govern society as well as to the types of which it is composed. A playwright drops to a low level when he tries being a moralist, but to a much lower level when he gilds vice and sin and glorifies immorality. All these are parts of life, and as such are entitled to be represented in the drama. The true realist will depict them as they are. . . . Though [the playwright] discover virtue in criminals and tramps, he will not be blind to the qualities which outweigh and crush it down; and above all he will portray the fact that right-doing, kindness, and good nature are in the majority and "control the machine."
>
> Though there are shams everywhere to be pricked and ridiculed, and hum-

---

49. Moody, *From Corlear's Hook,* 102–3.

bugs to be exposed and laughed out of existence, these are only incidents which, though they appear and disappear incessantly, are not parts of the real humanity beneath. The adage "to hold the mirror up to nature" is as applicable to the swarming myriads of New York as to the Greek warriors before Priam's city, or the lord and nobles who surround the Tudors.[50]

The display of human foibles, leavened by a sense of humor, promoted tolerance and understanding, not only in Harrigan and Braham's view but in the eyes of many songwriters. The use of comic types did not pass entirely without controversy, as an Irish paper, *The Boston Pilot,* noted:

> The attempt of some Irishmen in New York to boycott Harrigan and Hart's Theatre because they "made fun of the Irish" is too ridiculous to be seriously noticed. Mr. Harrigan, an Irish-American, proud of his race, makes fun of certain New York Irish types because the fun really is there to be drawn out. The Irishman who could be offended at *The Mulligans* or *Cordelia's Aspirations* is not sure of himself or his people.[51]

The Irish community must have agreed with the sentiment, for Harrigan's audience came largely from their ranks, if we are to believe Richard Moody.[52]

Germans formed the second prominent European ethnic group found in most American cities and in Harrigan plays. In fact, for sheer numbers of immigrants, the Germans eclipsed the Irish. But only two-fifths of German-speaking people settled in large urban areas, mostly in the Midwest, and they remained less prominent in popular song for this reason.[53] One of Harrigan and Hart's earliest hits on the minstrel stage was a German comic routine called "The Little Frauds," published as sheet music in 1872. In his more elaborate stage productions of later years Harrigan wrote numbers like "The Turn Verein Cadets" (1883), which features a junior version of the target company, *alla tedesca.* Though the German characters in Harrigan's plays usually speak in "stage dialect" (that is, with a heavy German accent), this song contains only a few phrases, perhaps because the singers are second-generation youths:

> When the moon shines bright on a summer's night,
> We go out on a grand parade;
> The Arion Club is a handsome sight
> All dress'd in a masquerade;
> Such pretty German boys,
> Their mothers' little joys,
> Oh! hootey, tootey, Kleiner Deutscher Pets;

50. "American Playwrights," 98.
51. *The Boston Pilot,* Jan. 5, 1884, as cited in Flynn, "The Irish Dramatic Tradition," 36.
52. *Dramas from the American Theatre, 1762–1909* (Cleveland and New York, 1966), 544.
53. See Daniels, *Coming to America,* 149.

In soldier's clothes away we go,
In the Turnverein Cadets.

This is fairly standard representation of minority pride (the word "Aryan" had not yet gained its more unsavory, twentieth-century associations), much like that featured in "The Mulligan Guard" or "The Skidmore Guard." Harrigan never suggested that the sense of ethnic identity had diminished in the diversity of the urban scene. But by the same token, his ethnic representations existed in a strictly American context. Harrigan devoted fewer songs to the Germans because they were less visible than the Irish, and because he had a natural affinity for his own group.

The most prominent writer of songs about German ethnicity was, not unexpectedly, German-American himself, born Gustave Wilhelm Leweck in Yonkers, New York. After serving in the Civil War, Leweck quickly developed a reputation for his impressions of German immigrants under the stage name of Gus Williams (1847–1915). He starred at Tony Pastor's variety house and moved later to roles in full-length plays during the late seventies. Charles K. Harris remembered Williams as "a charming fellow with a fund of humor and a heart of gold," adding he was "one of the finest German comedians that ever appeared upon the stage."[54] At his best, in songs like "Don't Give de Name a Bad Blace" (1871), Williams takes a revealing look at the urban scene:

I keep a zaloon in dis cidy,
I sell weisbeer und oder drinks too,
Und alzo I keep a lunch gounter,
My dables und chairs dey vas new;
But a lod of does loafers gome in dere,
Und dey try for to knock me aboud,
But I tole you dey can't fool dis Dutchman,
For I hit dem rite all of de mout.

The violence never proceeds very far, however, because the character's wife stops the fight by calling out the refrain in the title. Germans usually came to the United States seeking economic opportunity, rather than fleeing political oppression and famine. They often brought some capital with them, and they found urban employment in services like baking, butchering, innkeeping, tailoring, and nursing. Like the Irish, they drank, and in a heavily German city like Cincinnati, there were in 1860 some 2000 establishments selling drinks, one for every hundred residents.[55] Williams painted ,a realistic picture in "Don't Give de Name."

Because Germans, unlike the Irish, were not native speakers of English,

54. *After the Ball: Forty Years of Melody* (New York, 1926), 29–30.
55. Daniels, *Coming to America,* 151.

their problems in America involved language. For this reason Williams deals extensively in malaprops, reversed grammar, and mispronunciations that cause misunderstandings. In the third verse of "Don't Give de Name,"

> Some roosders vat gome in my zaloon,
> Does vat is drinking I mean,
> Venever dey get drough a drinking,
> Vill dell me to "set dem oud again";
> Und dat vey they keep on a dalking,
> I say, pay gentlemens, it vas late!
> But dey look, und dey make dere eye dat vay,
> Und dell me "put dat down on de schlate."

SPOKEN   Und I say, gentlemens ve dont got some schlates, und den vone big fellar dells me to keep id in my head und dat he would gome around in de morning und kick it oud, und den I tole him dat ve dont do business dat vey, he says you dont eh? I zays no sir, not of de gourt-house knows herself und I dink she don't, und of you don't pay me gwick I vill put a head off you, und I would have done it too, only for my wife, who cried oud—

In the second verse the German innkeeper is cheated at cards, simply because he doesn't know the rules of "Poger."

Williams sets this tale to music (if, indeed, the setting is his; he often collaborated with unnamed composers) in 3/8 time, which may indulge just a hint of the ethnic reference to the waltz (although by this time the dance had lost many of its original associations; see Ex. 8.14). This very mild reference does not obscure Williams's exclusive concern with the urban life of ethnic Germans in the New World rather than their nostalgia for the old. Moreover, Williams goes farther than Harrigan in raising the question of assimilation, albeit indirectly. For the problems of his German characters suggest that getting along in their new surroundings depends on learning the predominant language and customs. Williams delivered this message in many of his other songs, including "Vat's de Brice of Beans, Jake?" (1870) about a German merchant, "Seven Oud" (1872) about gambling, "The Belle of the Ball" (1873) about being deceived in courtship, "Gus Williams' German Band" (1873), "Twenty-seven Cends" (1875) about street peddlers, and "The German 5th" (lyrics by Harry Bennett, 1876).

Because Germans often came with training or with capital in hand, Williams did not stress upward mobility as often as Harrigan. But occasional songs reveal such ambitions in his characters, like "Vaiter! Vaiter! Hot Potato" (1880):

> I've always fancied dot I'm sharp,
> Und know my vays aboud;
> Aldough I am a German,

301

EXAMPLE 8.14 Gus Williams, "Don't Give de Name a Bad Blace" (Boston: Louis P. Goulaud, 1871)

> I'm mistaken I find out,
> For every time I get a start,
> I seem to miss my way,
> Und every business I get in
> Is certain not to pay;
> I've been a clerk in a barber shop,
> Vere work is not so slow;
> I've kept all sorts of little sdores,
> But nothing seems to go;
> I run an elevator vonce
> Dot did go up and down;
> Und now I am vaiter
> In a restaurant up town.

In the end the character hates his subordinate position so much that he saves his money to buy a "lager-bier saloon" of his own. This number must have been popular, for it inspired at least one imitation, "The German Waiter" (1884) by Charles A. Loder and Louis F. Boos.

Despite their love of beer, drunkenness usually did not count among stereotypical German vices. Their excess in celebration songs involved eating instead. Williams's most famous contribution to this genre is "Mygel Snyder's Barty" (1872), where he describes the groaning board:

> Ven subber id vas ready und I sat me down to ead,
> Dere vas dripe und gakes und onions, bodadoes und bigs-feed,
> Ve all ead very hard, bud Miss Krouse got very sick,
> Ve called de doctor und he sait she had de colorie.

SPOKEN   Yes, Miss Krouse got de colorie. She vas trying to ead a mincepie mit a tooth-prush in id und id didn't agree vid her. But den dot subber dable vas loaded mit all de indelicacies of de season. . . . Afder subber dere vas such nice singing. Vone man got ub und singed a song vot vent like dis: "He flies drough de air mit his mout full of cheese, he vas a young man vot chewed ub a drapeze," or someding like dot anyhow; den ve all joined in de ghorus.

The melody for this song bears not the slightest trace of anything ethnic in its bumptious compound time and pleasant melody, which comes right out of American theater music. There was as little spite in Gus Williams as there was in Edward Harrigan. His comedy proceeded from an affection for his own ethnic background and an intimate knowledge of the "type," even as it gently criticized those immigrants who did not adapt to their new surroundings or did so imperfectly. The popularity of his songs persisted through the eighties and briefly into the nineties, long enough for T. B. Harms to republish his numbers from Goulaud's or White and Goulaud's plates under its own imprint.

By the eighties one subgroup of German immigrants, those of Jewish descent, had grown large enough in New York to occasion notice from songwriters there. Harrigan and Braham recognized their increasing numbers with a melodrama called *Mordecai Lyons,* which included a song by the same title (1882). This seems to be the first in a long, though not extensive, line of songs establishing the stereotype of Jews as dealers in second-hand merchandise (one of the last would be "Second Hand Rose" (1921) by James F. Hanley and Grant Clarke), and such a portrait can be directed either positively or negatively. Harrigan shows both sides in "Mordecai Lyons," with a title character who is generous and kind, if thrifty:

> On Sunday I goes, I put on my new clothes,
> They cost me a five-dollar note,
> Go by the horse car I ride awfully far,
> It's cheaper than wagon or boat;
> I do what I can, I'm not a mean man,
> I don't let a beggar pass by,
> A penny I give, oh, the poor man must live;
> I can't take it all when I die.

[*Chorus:*]
Old clothes! I buy and sell,
Walk in the store, I'll treat you so well;
Now, old clothes! when it's hard times,
Come buy of Mordecai Lyons.

Mordecai's counterpart, however, is his pawnbroker brother, who feeds on the misfortune of others rather than relieving it:

Mid vatches and diamonds, sealskin overcoats
At six months, at forty percent;
Three balls is the sign, the number is nine,
You can see his Terms Cash on the wall;
He's worth I am told just one million in gold,
He made on the black Friday fall.

Both characterizations use the same sprightly waltz by Braham. John Higham points out in his essays on anti-Semitism during this period that stereotypes are rarely simple: they very often embrace conflicting sentiments (the primitive African-American sage, the extinct noble Indian, the industrious, oafish German, and so forth).[56] Harrigan meant to show all sides of a basically kind human nature, but the characterization of Jews took a sharper tone. Harrigan and Braham revived this theme in "Baxter Avenue" (1886).

Frank Dumont tended toward the more negative side of the Jewish stereotype eight years after "Mordecai Lyons," in another waltz-song, "Jacob and Solomon Rosenstein" (1890). Dumont (b. 1848) spent most of his career playing in several famous minstrel companies, and he formed his own in Philadelphia just as minstrelsy waned in popularity.[57] His delineation of two pawnbrokers living on Baxter Street touches on the root of anti-Semitism:

The merchants are jealous of our bargain store,
But we'll stay in the business until they are poor,
We move thro' the crowd and the both of us cry,
Sleeve buttons, shoe laces, who wants to buy.
As we go peddling in our second-hand suits,
We don't watch the customers, we watch the goods,
For two smarter sheenies you never will find,
Like Jacob and Solomon Rosenstein.

Yet there is also a note of admiration here: in the aggressive marketing of street peddling, the two entrepreneurs are not dishonest, merely better businessmen

56. See *Send These to Me*, 99.
57. Rice, *Monarchs of Minstrelsy*, 198.

than the competition. And interestingly enough they have ceased speaking in dialect. These ethnic types cannot be fooled the way Gus Williams's barkeep was, and they cannot be held back from grasping the principles of American enterprise.

One of Harrigan and Braham's songs last songs, "They Never Tell All What They Know" (1893) shows the rise of Jewish New Yorkers out of the lower middle classes. The clever Jewish narrator (whose refrain provides the title of this number in waltz time) focuses on a specific neighborhood:

> It's Hester street, Essex street, Bow'ry, Canal,
> Oh, dear! what a wonderful show,
> Just go look around the east side of town,
> Where they never tell all what they know.

He holds up the ideal of Christians and Jews living together like brothers, shows some of the dodges used to make a fortune (including a secondhand merchant who collects the fire insurance on his shop and a woman who marries an old man for his money), and finishes:

> They say some of our people are hungry today,
> To me that is awfully funny,
> Find Hebrews a tramp, oh you can't with a lamp,
> They're bankers with plenty of money,
> There's many a case, when some of our race,
> Let dollars like water to flow,
> We're out [of] the dust and riches or bust,
> But I never tell all what I know.

Harrigan obviously disapproves of Jewish parvenus. But at the same time he borrowed his basic plot from the central narrative he applied to all other immigrant groups: those who worked hard rose in wealth and status, and won acceptance, however grudging, in their new country.

Italians, the other ethnic group that grew steadily more prominent in songs of the eighties, appeared even more rarely than Jews. Italians had migrated in small numbers to the United States for much of the nineteenth century, playing prominent roles as artisans and musicians. Between 1820 and 1880 census figures give a total of only 81,277 immigrants from Italy, while from 1881 to 1890 over 307,309 arrived on American shores.[58] A large number of these returned to their native land, perhaps as many as half. But this new surge brought unskilled laborers rather than artisans, and the new influx of low-wage workers caused pointedly negative characterizations in the unstable climate of the eighties. One such song was George Austin Morrison's "The Organ

---

58. See Daniels, *Coming to America*, 188–97.

Grinder Song'' (1882) from the burlesque *William Penn*. This admittedly undistinguished number lists, nonetheless, some of the real occupations pursued
by Italians in the United States, ''To Delmonico as a waiter I go./Street clean-
ing no pleasant I find.'' The immigrant finally arrives at the profession that
supplies the title, but this serves mainly as a ploy invoking ethnic references to
music in the chorus:

> Just so! Do tell! We want to know.
> Playing Sweet Violets, de pennies he gets,
> White Wingas and Pull down the Blindas!
> But Il Trovatore is the great repertoire,
> Of Italian organ grinders.

This stage reference to Italians was widely used: as late as 1905 the song
''Tammany'' (see Ex. 7.13 above) names ''Chris Columbo'' as one of the
''pale-face organ grinders'' who vanquished American Indians.

Frank Dumont refers briefly to the stereotype of Italian street musicians in
''The Dagoe Banana Peddler'' (1888), though his main portrait touches on a
frequent occupation of Italians as greengrocers. Dumont's song has yet another
stylish waltz chorus (Ex. 8.15), and this musical type meshes oddly with Dumont's violent portrayal of Italians. They are the only group besides African-
Americans depicted with weapons (the Irish and Germans threatened fisticuffs
but rarely came to actual blows):

> My brudder he play-a the fiddle,
> Some-a time I play-a de harp.
> On-a Sunday, de boot-a I black-a,
> In-a bisness I getta very sharp,
> My fadder you know was a brigand.
> But he was hung by de neck,
> I always have my good stilletto,
> Where de police can never suspect.

The cities of late-nineteenth-century America were far from benign and pacific
spots, and ethnic violence often erupted in spectacular ways. But when the
gory details appeared in popular song, prejudice and fear were also at hand. At
the same time he paints this very negative picture, however, Dumont also
shows the enterprise and ingenuity in Italian immigrants that was held to produce upward mobility for new residents of urban America.

Even when the result was repellent, the ''realism'' of the seventies and eighties substantially changed the representation of Western European ethnicity in
popular song. Composers moved the scene of ethnicity from fantastic rural
settings to the gritty, bustling climes of America cities. It should not surprise
us that some of these portraits are unpleasant, revealing both suspicion and

EXAMPLE 8.15   Frank Dumont, ''The Dagoe Banana Peddler'' (New York: Willis Woodward, 1888)

hatred. For while songwriters like Harrigan, Williams, and Dumont focused on events closer to home, the very piquancy of their stereotypes revolved around the distinctive ethnic characteristics that separated one group from another. These authors saw little profit in highlighting the central culture, even when they relied on a loosely generic musical style for the accompaniment to their lyrics.

European Ethnicity in Tin Pan Alley

The newly centralized industry of popular song had profound effects on the content of pieces about ethnicity. The pointed stereotypes that seem to grow increasingly negative in the late eighties and early nineties ultimately had little place in art meant to be marketed as widely as possible. Severe alienation of any group would result in the loss of their business (the highly racist material propounded in blackface in the late nineties suggests that publishers did not initially anticipate much financial gain from African-American customers, though they soon learned differently). Stereotypes did not disappear suddenly or entirely, but they were gradually muted, as were purely local portraits of individual ethnic groups. A centralized industry needed to address itself more generally and to assert a set of national values. For all these reasons, Tin Pan Alley song of the nineties (and beyond) invested heavily in the notion of integration and assimilation, at the same time it sought to create a central culture which might claim allegiance superseding both local and ethnic ties.

Charles Lawlor and James Blake's "The Sidewalks of New York" (1894)[59] shows the transition to popular song's new emphasis on integration. Vestiges of the seventies' approach remain in the explicit use of Manhattan as the location for "Casey's old brown wooden stoop" and in the reference to the old stereotypes representing the three traditionally important ethnic groups:

> That's where Johnny Casey,
> And little Jimmy Crowe,
> With Jakey Krause the baker,
> Who always had the dough,
> Pretty Nellie Shannon,
> With a dude as light as cork,
> First picked up the waltz step
> On the sidewalks of New York.

But this is as far as the stereotypes for the Irish, African-Americans, and Germans go. They do not engage in any typically "ethnic" behavior, they do not grow up in poverty, and they do not contend with one another. In fact, the famous waltzing chorus explicitly suggests integration in its last lines:

> East side, West side,
> All around the town,
> The tots sang "ring a rosie,"
> "London Bridge is falling down";
> Boys and girls together,
> Me and Mamie Rorke,
> Tripped the light fantastic,
> On the sidewalks of New York.

The children unite in their enthusiasm for the nationally popular craze of the waltz. The song encourages not only integration but the centrality of the culture it exemplifies.

When the waltz song began to provide the initial foundation for the creation of a nationally marketed popular song, it's use in strong ethnic stereotyping (of the kind found, say, in Dumont's "Dagoe Banana Peddler") became inappro-

---

59. Reprinted in Fremont, *Favorite Songs*, 259–62.

priate. In a song like Maude Nugent's "Sweet Rosie O'Grady" (1896)[60] ethnicity appears solely in the mention of the title character's name. Nugent was a singer at the Abbey, a dance hall on Eighth Avenue between 26th and 27th streets, where the patronage was mainly Irish.[61] But she had a much wider public in mind when she chose a chorus in waltz time, as Edward Marks knew well:

> She sang it for us while Stern picked it out at the piano, and we told her it wouldn't do. You see, there had been a whole cycle of "name" waltz songs, starting with Harry Dacre's "Daisy Bell," imported from England in 1890. We thought this cycle was on the wane.[62]

When Marks and Stern rejected the song, Nugent left the office, headed in the direction of their competition. But after a few seconds of reconsideration, Marks ran to catch her and secure the song for his catalogue. The first verse sets the scene clearly enough:

> Just down around the corner of the street where I reside,
> There lives the cutest little girl that I have ever spied;
> Her name is Rose O'Grady, and I don't mind telling you,
> That she's the sweetest little Rose the garden ever grew.

Aside from her urban background, we learn nothing more about Rosie. Her ethnicity has been immured in national style (see Ex. 8.16) and assimilated by this means into the general popular culture to meet the demands of a far-flung market. This is equally true for songs that make a point of ethnicity, like Chauncey Olcott's "My Wild Irish Rose" (1899). Aside from repeating the word "Irish," this waltz song contains no dialect, no references to "characteristic" behavior, and no mention of a particular neighborhood in a large city. The Irish simply melted into American popular song (the few pieces that speak nostalgically of Ireland, like "Where the River Shannon Flows" (1906), were exceptions that proved the rule).

The Germans disappeared almost completely from Tin Pan Alley. On the rare occasions they did appear, mention of their ethnicity was often ironic. It seems at first that the narrator in Vincent P. Bryan and Harry Von Tilzer's "Down Where the Wurzburger Flows" (1902)[63] has an old-fashioned case of nostalgia:

60. Ibid., 290–93.
61. Edward B. Marks and Abbott J. Liebling, *They All Sang, from Tony Pastor to Rudy Vallée* (New York, 1934), 21.
62. Ibid., 34.
63. Reprinted by Nicholas Tawa in *American Solo Songs 1866 Through 1910*, vol. 2 of *Three Centuries of American Sacred and Secular Music*, Martha Furman Schleifer and Sam Dennison, eds. ([Boston], 1989), 123–26.

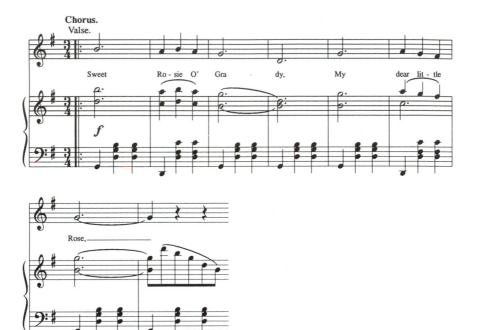

EXAMPLE 8.16   Maude Nugent, "Sweet Rosie O'Grady" (New York: Jos. W. Stern, 1896)

Now poets may sing of the dear Fatherland,
And the soft flowing dreamy old Rhine;
Beside the Blue Danube in fancy they stand,
And they rave of its beauties divine;
But there is a spot where the sun never shines,
Where mirth and good fellowship reign;
For dear old Bohemia my lonely heart pines,
And I long to be there once again.

This verse merely sets up a comic surprise: the real object of longing is not even a place in Bohemia, but a brand of beer:

Take me down, down, down where the Wurzburger flows, flows,
    flows,
It will drown, drown, drown all your troubles and cares and woes;
Just order two seidels of lager, or three,
If I don't want to drink it, please force it on me,
The Rhine may be fine but a cold stein for mine,
Down where the Wurzburger flows.

The humor in this song does not depend on the malaprops and mispronunciations that had formed the stock of earlier songs on German ethnicity. Instead, Bryan has overemphasized the ethnic content of his verse to set the comic hook of the chorus. Seen in retrospect, the first line of the lyrics pokes gentle fun at the cliché of the fabled native land as it used to appear in songs. The outcome of this comic reversal must have appealed immediately to the audiences at saloons like Koster and Bial's in New York, where pieces initially gained popularity with the aid of much lubrication from the "Wurzburger" in question.[64]

Where the Irish and Germans lost their accents and assimilated, the two "newer groups" (that is, "newer" in large numbers) of Italians and Jews remained slightly more separate in popular song. But the central, national style of Tin Pan Alley began to absorb even these. A good example of this process appears in "Sweet Italian Love" (1910)[65] by Irving Berlin and Ted Snyder. Berlin uses dialect in his lyrics clearly enough:

> Ev'ryone talk-a how they make-a da love,
> Call-a da sweet-a name-a like-a da dove,
> It make me sick-a when they start to speak-a,
> 'Bout the moon 'way up above.
> What's-a da use to have-a big-a da moon?
> What's-a da use to call-a da dove?
> If he no like-a she, and she no like-a he,
> The moon can't make them love. . . .

But dialect aside, the lyrics do not mention a specific location for this song, nor does the situation or sentiment contain anything peculiarly Italian. This is a standard love song rendered ethnic mostly by its title. Snyder's use of ragtime music for this setting tends to blunt the ethnic frame of reference and absorb the conceit. The contrast between African-American style and Italian dialect is especially poignant in the chorus:

> But Sweet Italian love, Nice Italian love,
> You don't need the moon-a-light to tell her,
> In da house or on da roof or in da cellar,
> Dat's Italian love, Sweet Italian love;
> When you kiss-a your pet, And it's-a like-a spagette,
> Dat's Italian love!

Even when Italians wrote music for such songs, as Al Piantadosi did for George Ronklyn's lyrics to "My Muriuccia Take a Steamboat" (1906), they used the most identifiably "American" of all musical styles, ragtime.

---

64. See the first chapter of Marks's *They All Sang* for an account of the process for plugging a song.

65. Reproduced in Tawa, *Solo Songs,* II, 321–25.

Berlin collaborating with Edgar Leslie took the same approach to Jewish ethnicity in "Sadie Salome Go Home!" (1909).[66] Berlin and Leslie's story revolves around a situation that is anything but peculiarly Jewish:

> Sadie Cohen left her happy home
> To become an actress lady,
> On the stage she soon became the rage,
> As the only real Salomy baby.

This elicits understandable consternation from her sweetheart:

> From the crowd Moses yelled out loud,
> "Who put in your head such notions?
> You look sweet but jiggle with your feet.
> Who put in your back such funny motions?
> As a singer you was always fine!
> Sing to me, 'Because the world is mine!' "

While the names and a bit of sporadic dialect suggest ethnic associations in this song, the lyrics speak mainly about the new independence of women and the commotion caused by changing mores (the boyfriend "Mose" comically plays the conservative role, both in his objections to Sadie's dishabille on stage and her independent career). Before we interpret the use of minor mode in the verse of this song as a reference to ethnic "exoticism," we should remember a number in this same genre that adopted a similar arrangement, "Good Bye, My Lady Love" (1904). For "Good Bye" Joe Howard cast his verse about a jilted suitor in minor mode to set off the ragtime chorus in major mode. "Sadie Salome" repeats this contrast (Ex. 8.17) and presents a variant on the situation found in "Good Bye" or "Meet Me in St. Louis, Louis," merely adding Jewish names. Despite their ethnic vocabulary, Sadie and Mose participate in a generically American dilemma and music.

Historians of nativism will tend to see Tin Pan Alley's emphasis on integration and assimilation as a symptom of the "nationalist nineties."[67] And others will regard these tendencies as part of the quest, motivated mainly by greed, to create a nationally marketable popular art. Without discounting either influence entirely, we should remember here that the industry of popular music itself was feeling the effects of ethnic change at the turn of the century, for composers, lyricists, and publishers increasingly came from the Jewish population of urban centers, particularly New York City. Charles Harris, Edward Marks, Joseph Stern, Irving Berlin, Isidore Witmark, and many others descended from Jewish

---

66. Ibid., 316–20.
67. I borrow the term from a chapter in Higham's *Strangers in the Land.*

EXAMPLE 8.17   Irving Berlin and Edgar Leslie, "Sadie Salome Go Home!" (New York: Ted Snyder, 1909)

stock, and in the golden era of Tin Pan Alley after World War I almost all composers and many lyricists were Jewish. It is not at all ironic that one of the most excluded groups should be involved in promoting assimilation and integration by creating a self-consciously national art. For a first-generation immigrant like Berlin, acceptance in American society as well as the upward mobility granted by financial success must have seemed of paramount importance. And it might even be said that such composers understood more deeply than other Americans the value of a central, national culture.

The notion of an American "melting pot" may well have been a myth as far as intersocial relations between ethnic groups was concerned, but it formed an ideal. Songwriters at the end of the nineteenth century came to a conscious realization that if ethnic groups still tended to live separately, popular music was able to absorb a variety of ethnic and racial influences, nonetheless. Everybody could listen enthusiastically as Irish women were praised to the strains of the waltz, or Italians and Jews dealt with the trials of American life to the strains of European marches ragged by African-American rhythms. And after the First World War, all would celebrate the sophisticated harmonies of French classical music in combination with motivic manipulation learned from German composers by Jewish-Americans who seasoned the product with ornaments from African-American blues. American popular song in Tin Pan Alley participated on one side of the strategy composers felt essential for all ethnic groups: "to exist and yet not exist, to be needed and yet to be unimportant, to be different and yet to be the same, to be integrated and yet to be separate."[68]

68. Joshua Freeman quoted in Higham, *Send These to Me*, 12.

References

Allen, Robert C. *Horrible Prettiness: Burlesque and American Culture*. Chapel Hill, NC: Univ. of North Carolina Press, 1991.

"American Playwrights on the American Drama," *Harper's Weekly* 33 (Feb. 2, 1889), 97–100.

Appelbaum, Stanley, ed. *"Peg O' My Heart" and Other Favorite Song Hits, 1912 & 1913*. New York: Dover, 1989.

———, ed. *Show Songs from "The Black Crook" to "The Red Mill."* New York: Dover, 1974.

Austin, William W. *"Susanna," "Jeanie," and "The Old Folks at Home": The Songs of Stephen Foster from His Time to Ours*. New York: Macmillan, 1975.

Babcock, Barbara A., ed. *The Reversible World: Symbolic Inversion in Art and Society*. Ithaca, NY, and London: Cornell Univ. Press, 1978.

Bakhtin, Mikhail. *Rabelais and His World*. Trans. Helene Iswolsky. Bloomington, IN: Indiana Univ. Press, 1984.

Barnett, Louise K. *The Ignoble Savage: American Literary Racism, 1790–1890*. Westport, CT, and London: Greenwood Press, 1975.

"Barney Fagan," *New York Times* (Jan. 13, 1937), 23.

Berkhofer, Robert F., Jr. *The White Man's Indian*. New York: Alfred A. Knopf, 1978.

Berlin, Edward A. *Ragtime: A Musical and Cultural History*. Berkeley: Univ. of California Press, 1980.

———. "Scott Joplin's *Treemonisha* Years," *American Music* 9 (1991), 260–75.

Birdseye, George. "America's Song Composers," *Potter's American Monthly* 12 (1879), 28–31, 145–48, 213–15, 284–88, 333–35, 433–36.

Bland, James A. *Album of Outstanding Songs*. Ed. Charles Haywood. New York: Edward B. Marks, 1946.

Bordman, Gerald. *American Musical Theatre: A Chronicle*. 2d edition. New York: Oxford Univ. Press, 1992.

Boucicault, Dion. *Arrah-Na-Pogue, or The Wicklow Wedding*. Ed. Seamus De Burca. (Dublin: P. J. Bourke, n.d.).

Brancaleone, Francis. "Edward MacDowell and Indian Motives," *American Music* 7 (1989), 359–81.

Bray, John, and James Nelson Barker. *The Indian Princess, or La Belle Sauvage.* Earlier American Music, Vol. 11. New York: Da Capo Press, 1972.

Brown, Charles H. *Agents of Manifest Destiny: The Lives and Times of the Filibusters.* Chapel Hill, NC: Univ. of North Carolina Press, 1980.

Brown, Dee. *Hear That Lonesome Whistle Blow: Railroad in the West.* New York: Holt, Rinehart and Winston, 1977.

Carr, Benjamin. *Selected Secular and Sacred Songs.* Ed. Eve R. Meyer. Recent Researches in American Music, Vol. 15. Madison, WI: A-R Editions, 1986.

Cockrell, Dale, ed. *Excelsior: Journals of the Hutchinson Family Singers, 1842–1846.* Sociology of Music Series, Vol. 5. Stuyvesant, NY: Pendragon Press, 1989.

Cooper, James Fenimore. *The Last of the Mohicans, a Narrative of 1757.* New York and Scarborough, Ontario: *New American Library,* 1980.

Crawford, Richard, ed. *The Civil War Song Book.* New York: Dover, 1977.

Curry, Leonard P. *The Free Black in Urban America 1800–1850.* Chicago and London: Univ. of Chicago Press, 1981.

Dahlhaus, Carl. *Nineteenth-Century Music.* Berkeley and Los Angeles: Univ. of California Press, 1989.

Daly, John Jay. *A Song in His Heart.* Philadelphia: Winston, 1951.

Damon, S. Foster. *The Negro in Early American Songsters.* Chicago: Univ. of Chicago Press, 1934.

————, ed. *Series of Old American Songs.* Providence, RI: Brown Univ. Library, 1936.

Daniels, Roger. *Coming to America: A History of Immigration and Ethnicity in American Life.* New York: Harper Collins, 1990.

D'Emilio, John, and Estelle B. Freedman. *Intimate Matters: A History of Sexuality in America.* New York: Harper and Row, 1989.

Dennison, Sam. *Scandalize My Name: Black Imagery in American Popular Music.* New York and London: Garland, 1982.

Dichter, Harry, and Elliot Shapiro. *Handbook of Early American Sheet Music.* New York: Dover, 1977.

Dinnerstein, Leonard, Roger L. Nichols, and David M. Reimers. *Natives and Strangers: Blacks, Indians, and Immigrants in America.* 2d ed. New York and Oxford: Oxford Univ. Press, 1990.

Dormon, James H. "The Strange Career of Jim Crow Rice," *Journal of Social History* 3 (1969–70), 109–22.

Dreiser, Theodore. *Sister Carrie.* New York: Holt, Rinehart and Winston, 1957.

Dreiser, Vera, and Brett Howard. *My Uncle Theodore.* New York: Nash, 1976.

Emerson, Ralph Waldo. *The Conduct of Life.* Boston and New York: Fireside Edition, 1909.

Epstein, Barbara Leslie. *The Politics of Domesticity: Women, Evangelism, and Temperance in Nineteenth-Century America.* Middletown, CT: Wesleyan Univ. Press, 1981.

Epstein, Dena J. "A White Origin for the Black Spiritual? An Invalid Theory and How It Grew," *American Music* 1 (1983), 53–59.

————. *Music Publishing in Chicago Before 1871: The Firm of Root & Cady 1858–1871.* Detroit Studies in Music Bibliography, Vol. 14. Detroit: Information Coordinators, 1969.

————. *Sinful Tunes and Spirituals: Black Folk Music to the Civil War*. Urbana, Chicago, and London: Univ. of Illinois Press, 1977.

————. "The Folk Banjo: A Documentary History," *Ethnomusicology* 19 (1975), 347–71.

Ewen, David. *All the Years of American Popular Music*. Englewood Cliffs, NJ: Prentice-Hall, 1977.

Fairchild, Hoxie Neale. *The Noble Savage: A Study in Romantic Naturalism*. New York: Russell & Russell, 1961.

Flynn, Joyce Anne. "Ethnicity After Sea-Change: The Irish Dramatic Tradition in Nineteenth-Century American Drama." Ph.D. dissertation, Harvard University, 1985.

Foner, Eric. *Reconstruction: America's Unfinished Revolution, 1863–1877*. New York: Harper & Row, 1988.

Foster, Stephen C. *Household Songs*. Earlier American Music, Vol. 12. New York: Da Capo Press, 1973.

————. *Minstrel-Show Songs*. Earlier American Music, Vol. 14. New York: Da Capo Press, 1980.

————. *The Music of Stephen Foster*. Ed. Steven Saunders and Deane L. Root. 2 vols. Washington and London: Smithsonian Institution Press, 1990.

————. *The Social Orchestra for Flute or Violin: A Collection of Popular Melodies Arranged as Solos, Duets, Trios, and Quartets*. Earlier American Music, Vol. 13. New York: Da Capo Press, 1973.

————. *Stephen Foster Song Book*. Ed. Richard Jackson. New York: Dover, 1974.

Fremont, Robert A., ed. *Favorite Songs of the Nineties*. New York: Dover, 1973.

Gibson, Arrell Morgan. *The American Indian, Prehistory to the Present*. Lexington, MA, and Toronto: D. C. Heath, 1980.

Goertzen, Chris, and Alan Jabbour. "George P. Knauff's *Virginia Reels* and Fiddling in the Antebellum South," *American Music* 5 (1987), 121–44.

Goldberg, Isaac. *Tin Pan Alley: A Chronicle of the American Popular Music Racket*. New York: John Day, 1930.

Hamm, Charles. *Yesterdays: Popular Song in America*. New York: W. W. Norton, 1979.

Hansen, Marcus Lee. *The Atlantic Migration 1607–1860. A History of the Continuing Settlement of the United States*. Cambridge, MA: Harvard Univ. Press, 1940.

Harris, Charles K. *After the Ball: Forty Years of Melody*. New York: Frank-Maurice, 1926.

Hasse, John Edward, ed. *Ragtime, Its History, Composers, and Music*. New York: Schirmer Books, 1985.

Haywood, Charles. "Negro Minstrelsy and Shakespearean Burlesque," in *Folklore & Society: Essays in Honor of Benj. A. Botkin*. Ed. Bruce Jackson. Hartboro, PA: Folklore Associates, 1966. Pp. 77–92.

Hewitt, James. *Selected Compositions*. Ed. John W. Wagner. Recent Researches in American Music, Vol. 12. Madison, WI: A-R Editions, 1980.

Hewitt, John H. *Shadows on the Wall, or Glimpses of the Past*. Baltimore: Turnbull Brothers, 1877 (photofacsimile, New York: AMS Press, 1971).

Higham, John. *Send These to Me: Immigrants in Urban America*. Revised ed. Baltimore and London: Johns Hopkins Univ. Press, 1984.

317

————. *Strangers in the Land: Patterns of American Nativism, 1860–1925*. 2d ed. New York: Atheneum, 1975.

Hill, Richard S. "Getting Kathleen Home Again," *Notes* 5 (1948), 338–53.

————. "The Mysterious Chord of Henry Clay Work," *Notes* 10 (1953), 211–25, 367–90.

Hindman, John Joseph. "Concert Life in Ante Bellum Charleston." Ph.D. dissertation, Univ. of North Carolina at Chapel Hill, 1971.

Howard, John Tasker. *Stephen Foster, America's Troubadour*. New York: Thomas Y. Crowell, 1953.

Hubbell, Jay B. *South and Southwest: Literary Essays and Reminiscences*. Durham, NC: Duke Univ. Press, 1965.

Hutchinson, John Wallace. *Story of the Hutchinsons*. Ed. Charles E. Mann. 2 vols. Boston: Lee and Shepard, 1896 (photofacsimile, New York: Da Capo Press, 1977).

Jackson, Charles O., ed. *Passing: The Vision of Death in America*. Contributions in Family Studies, Vol. 2. Westport, CT, and London: Greenwood Press, 1977.

Jackson, George Pullen. *White and Negro Spirituals, Their Life Span and Kinship*. New York: J. J. Augustin, 1943.

Jackson, Richard, ed. *Democratic Souvenirs: An Historical Anthology of 19th-Century American Music*. New York, London, and Frankfurt: C. F. Peters, 1988.

————, ed. *Popular Songs of Nineteenth-Century America*. New York: Dover, 1976.

Jasen, David A., ed. *"Alexander's Ragtime Band" and Other Favorite Song Hits, 1901–1911*. New York: Dover, 1987.

"Joe Howard Dies; Vaudeville Star," *New York Times* (May 21, 1961), 87.

Johnson, Helen Kendrick, Frederick Dean, Reginald DeKoven, and Gerrit Smith, eds. *The World's Best Music: Famous Songs and Those Who Made Them*. 4 vols. New York: University Society, 1902.

Johnson, James Weldon. *Black Manhattan*. New York: Alfred A. Knopf, 1930.

Kahn, E. J., Jr. "Profiles," *The New Yorker* (March 19, 1955), 42–67; (March 26, 1955), 39–72; (April 2, 1955), 45–67; (April 9, 1955), 41–81.

Kasson, John F. *Civilizing the Machine: Technology and Republican Values in America, 1776–1900*. New York: Grossman, 1976.

————. *Rudeness & Civility: Manners in Nineteenth-Century Urban America*. New York: Hill and Wang, 1990.

Kasson, Joy S. *Queens and Captives: Women in Nineteenth-Century American Sculpture*. New Haven and London: Yale Univ. Press, 1990.

Koger, Alicia Kae. "A Critical Analysis of Edward Harrigan's Comedy." Ph.D. dissertation, University of Michigan, 1984.

Levine, Lawrence W. *Highbrow/Lowbrow: The Emergence of Cultural Hierarchy in America*. Cambridge, MA, and London: Harvard Univ. Press, 1988.

Lawrence, Vera Brodsky. "Mr. Hewitt Lays It on the Line," *19th Century Music* 5 (1981–82), 3–15.

Loesser, Arthur. *Men, Women and Pianos*. New York: Simon and Schuster, 1954.

McMurry, Nan Marie. " 'And I? I am in a consumption': The Tuberculosis Patient, 1780–1930." Ph.D. dissertation, Duke University, 1985.

Maeder, Clara Fisher. *Autobiography of Clara Fisher Maeder*. New York: Dunlap Society, 1897.

Mahar, William J. " 'Backside Albany' and Early Blackface Minstrelsy," *American Music* 6 (1988), 1–27.

318

Marks, Edward B., and Abbott J. Liebling. *They All Sang, from Tony Pastor to Rudy Vallée*. New York: Viking Press, 1934.

Marrocco, W. Thomas, and Harold Gleason, eds. *Music in America: An Anthology from the Landing of the Pilgrims to the Close of the Civil War*. New York: W. W. Norton, 1964.

Marsh, J. B. T. *The Story of the Jubilee Singers; with their Songs*. Boston: Houghton, Mifflin, n.d.

McPherson, James M. *Battle Cry of Freedom: The Civil War Era*. New York: Oxford Univ. Press, 1988.

Moody, Richard. *Ned Harrigan: From Corlear's Hook to Herald Square*. Chicago: Nelson-Hall, 1980.

————, ed. *Dramas from the American Theatre, 1762–1909*. Cleveland and New York: World, 1966.

Mumford, Lewis. *The Myth of the Machine: Technics and Human Development*. New York: Harcourt, Brace & World, 1966–67.

"The Myth of Joe Howard Lingers in a Familiar Air," *New York Times* (June 4, 1961), 85.

Nathan, Hans. *Dan Emmett and the Rise of Early Negro Minstrelsy*. Norman: Univ. of Oklahoma Press, 1962.

Nevin, Robert P. "Stephen Foster and Negro Minstrelsy," *Atlantic Monthly* 20 (1867), 609–16.

Odell, George C. D. *Annals of the New York Stage*. 15 vols. New York: Columbia Univ. Press, 1927–49.

"The Origin of Minstrelsy: Dan Emmett's History of the Wanderings of the First Troupe," *New York Clipper* 25, no. 8 (May 19, 1877), 61.

Parry, Ellwood. *The Image of the Indian and the Black Man in American Art, 1590–1900*. New York: George Braziller, 1974.

Paskman, Dailey. *"Gentlemen, Be Seated!": A Parade of the American Minstrels*. Rev. ed. New York: Clarkson N. Potter, 1976.

Pearce, Roy Harvey. *Savagism and Civilization: A Study of the Indian and the American Mind*. Baltimore and London: Johns Hopkins Univ. Press, 1965.

Pelissier, Victor. *Pelissier's Columbian Melodies: Music for the New York and Philadelphia Theaters*. Ed. Karl Kroeger. Recent Researches in American Music, Vols. 13–14. Madison, WI: A-R Editions, 1984.

Pike, G[ustavus] D. *The Jubilee Singers, and Their Campaign for Twenty Thousand Dollars*. Boston: Lee and Shepard, 1873.

Redway, Virginia Larkin. "The Carrs, American Music Publishers," *Musical Quarterly* 18 (1932), 150–77.

Remini, Robert V. *Andrew Jackson and the Course of American Freedom, 1822–1832*. Vol. II. New York: Harper and Row, 1981.

Rice, Edward Le Roy. *Monarchs of Minstrelsy, from "Daddy" Rice to Date*. New York: Kenny, 1911.

Riegel, Robert Edgar. *The Story of the Western Railroads*. New York: Macmillan, 1926.

Riis, Thomas. *More Than Just Minstrel Shows: The Rise of Black Musical Theatre at the Turn of the Century*. Brooklyn: Institute for Studies in American Music, 1992.

Root, Deane L. *American Popular Stage Music, 1860–1880*. Ann Arbor: UMI Research Press, 1981.

Root, George Frederick. *The Story of a Musical Life.* Cincinnati: John Church, 1891.

Russell, Henry. *Cheer! Boys, Cheer! Memories of Men and Music.* London: John Macqueen, 1895.

Sacks, Howard L., and Judith R. Sacks. "Way Up North in Dixie: Black-White Musical Interaction in Knox County, Ohio," *American Music* 6 (1988), 409–27.

Sampson, Henry T. *Blacks in Blackface: A Source Book on Early Black Musical Shows.* Metuchen, NJ, and London: Scarecrow Press, 1980.

Sanjek, Russell. *American Popular Music and Its Business. The First Four Hundred Years.* 3 vols. New York and Oxford: Oxford Univ. Press, 1988.

Saxton, Alexander. "Blackface Minstrelsy and Jacksonian Ideology," *American Quarterly* 27 (1975), 3–28.

Schivelbusch, Wolfgang. *The Railway Journey: The Industrialization of Time and Space in the 19th Century.* Leamington Spa, Hamburg, and New York: Berg, 1986.

Scott, Walter. *The Complete Poetical Works of Sir Walter Scott.* Ed. Horace E. Scudder. Boston and New York: Houghton Mifflin, 1900.

Sheehan, Bernard W. *Seeds of Extinction: Jeffersonian Philanthropy and the American Indian.* Chapel Hill: Univ. of North Carolina Press, 1973.

Sloane, David Charles. *The Last Great Necessity: Cemetaries in American History.* Baltimore and London: Johns Hopkins Univ. Press, 1991.

Sonneck, Oscar George Theodore. *A Bibliography of Early Secular American Music.* Rev. William Treat Upton. Washington: Library of Congress Music Division, 1945.

Southern, Eileen. "In Retrospect: Gussie Lord Davis (1863–1899), Tin Pan Alley Tunesmith," *Black Perspective in Music* 6 (1978), 188–230.

Spaeth, Sigmund. *A History of Popular Music in America.* New York: Random House, 1948.

Stallybrass, Peter, and Allon White. *The Politics and Poetics of Transgression.* Ithaca, NY: Cornell Univ. Press, 1986.

Stein, Charles W., ed. *American Vaudeville as Seen by Its Contemporaries.* New York: Alfred A. Knopf, 1984.

Stowe, Harriet Beecher. *Uncle Tom's Cabin.* New York: Dodd, Mead, 1952.

Tawa, Nicholas E. *Sweet Songs for Gentle Americans: The Parlor Song in America, 1790–1860.* Bowling Green, OH: Bowling Green Univ. Popular Press, 1980.

———. *The Way to Tin Pan Alley: American Popular Song, 1866–1910.* New York: Schirmer Books, 1990.

———, ed. *American Solo Songs Through 1865. Three Centuries of American Sacred and Secular Music,* Vol. 1. Ed. Martha Furman Schleifer and Sam Dennison. [Boston]: G. K. Hall, 1989.

———, ed. *American Solo Songs 1866 Through 1910. Three Centuries of American Sacred and Secular Music,* Vol. 2. Ed. Martha Furman Schleifer and Sam Dennison. [Boston]: G. K. Hall, 1989.

Taylor, Bayard. *Eldorado; or, Adventures in the Path of Empire: Comprising a Voyage to California, via Panama; Life in San Francisco and Monterey; Pictures of the Gold Region, and Experiences of Mexican Travel.* 18th ed. New York: G. P. Putnam, 1864.

Tick, Judith. *American Women Composers Before 1870.* Ann Arbor, MI: UMI Research Press, 1983.

Toll, Robert C. *Blacking Up: The Minstrel Show in Nineteenth-Century America.* New York: Oxford Univ. Press, 1974.

Twain, Mark. *The Autobiography of Mark Twain.* Ed. Charles Neider. New York: Harper & Brothers, 1959.

———— and Charles Dudley Warner. *The Gilded Age: A Tale of To-day. Seattle and London: Univ. of Washington Press, 1968.*

Tyler, Linda L. " 'Commerce and Poetry Hand in Hand': Music in American Department Stores, 1880–1930," *Journal of the American Musicological Society* 45 (1992), 75–120.

Tyrrell, Ian R. *Sobering Up: From Temperance to Prohibition in Antebellum America, 1800–1860.* Westport, CT, and London: Greenwood Press, 1979.

Wagner, John W. "James Hewitt, 1770–1827," *Musical Quarterly* 58 (1972), 259–76.

Ward, David. *Poverty, Ethnicity, and the American City, 1840–1925.* Cambridge Studies in Historical Geography, Vol. 13. Cambridge: Cambridge Univ. Press, 1989.

Ward, John William. *Andrew Jackson, Symbol for an Age.* New York: Oxford Univ. Press, 1962.

Weaver, Robert C. *The Negro Ghetto.* New York: Harcourt, Brace, 1948.

Wiebe, Robert H. *The Opening of American Society, from the Adoption of the Constitution to the Eve of Disunion.* New York: Alfred A. Knopf, 1984.

————. *The Search for Order, 1877–1920.* New York: Hill and Wang, 1967.

Wilder, Alec. *American Popular Song: The Great Innovators, 1900–1950.* New York and Oxford: Oxford Univ. Press, 1972.

"William M. Whitlock. The Origin of Negro Minstrelsy," *New York Clipper* 26, no. 3 (April 13, 1878), 21.

Winans, Robert B. "The Folk, the Stage, and the Five String Banjo in the Nineteenth Century," *Journal of American Folklore* 89 (1976), 407–37.

Witmark, Isidore, and Isaac Goldberg. *From Ragtime to Swingtime.* New York: Lee Furman, 1939.

Wittke, Carl. *Tambo and Bones: A History of the American Minstrel Stage.* Durham, NC: Duke Univ. Press, 1930 (photofacsimile, New York: Greenwood Press, 1968).

Wolfe, Richard J. *Secular Music in America, 1801–1825.* 3 vols. New York: New York Public Library, 1964.

Wood, Forrest G. *Black Scare: The Racist Response to Emancipation and Reconstruction.* Berkeley and Los Angeles: Univ. of California Press, 1968.

Work, Henry Clay. *Songs.* Ed. Bertram G. Work. Earlier American Music, Vol. 19. New York: Da Capo Press, 1974.

Yerbury, Grace D. *Song in America from Early Times to About 1850.* Metuchen, NJ: Scarecrow Press, 1971.

Zanger, Jules. "The Minstrel Show as Theater of Misrule," *Quarterly Journal of Speech* 60 (1974), 33–38.

Index of Song Titles

Index of Names

Abraham, Maurice, 155
Abt, Franz, 108
Adams, Frank, 80
Adams, John Quincy, 170
The Aeolians, 185
Allen, George N., 101
Angelo, H., 111
Arlington, Cotton and Kemble's Minstrels,
  224
Arne, Thomas, 6
Arnold, Samuel, 7
Atkins, Henry, 144
Atwill, 60
Avery, H., 89

Bakhtin, Mikhail, 161
Ball, Ernest R., 52
Ballou, Harry J., 222
Balmer and Weber, 61
Barker, James Nelson
  The Indian Princess, 241
Barton, Major J., 128–30
Bayly, Thomas Haynes, 20
Beazell, J. W., 89
Beecher, Henry Ward, 212
Beers, Ethel Lynn, 18
Belasco, F. *See* Rosenfeld, Monroe H.
Bellini, Vincenzo, 20, 113, 255
  I Puritani, 13
Benedict, Fordyce H., 254
Bennett, Harry, 301
Bennett, S. Fillmore, 118
Benteen, F. D., 181
Berkhofer, Robert J., 268
Berlin, Irving, 155, 311–13
Berlioz, Hector

Overture to *Rob Roy,* 13
Overture to *Waverly,* 13
Berry and Gordon, 192
Bethune, George W., 84
Bicknell, G., 54
Biddle, Nicholas, 166
Bingham, G. Clifton, 67
Birdseye, George, 132
Bischoff, J. W., 141
Bishop, Henry Rowland, 19
  Clari, or the Maid of Milan, 19
Bissel, T., 286
Bissell, T., 115
Blackwood, Mrs. Price, 285–86
Blake, James, 308
Blakely, Harry, 220
Bland, James A., 201–3, 206, 207, 213, 215,
  225–26, 230, 238
The Bohee Brothers, 238
Boieldieu, François-Adrien
  La Dame blanche, 13
Bonbright, Stephen S., 206
Bonnhorst, C. F. von, 93
Boos, Louis F., 302
Boston Harmoneons, 287
Boucicault, Dion, 287–88
  Arrah-Na-Pogue or The Wicklow Wedding,
  277, 287
Bourne, W. H., 48
Boyers, S. H. M., 46
Brackett, Frank H., 69
Bradbury, William B., 52
Bragdon, Loren, 89
Braham, David, 105, 115, 145, 206–7,
  224–25, 234, 293–96, 303–5
Braham, John, 207

330